Thomas S. Braga

Juan Rodríguez Cabrillo

Juan Rodríguez Cabrillo
by Harry Kelsey

Huntington Library • San Marino

Copyright © 1998
The Henry E. Huntington Library and Art Gallery
Designed by Ward Ritchie
Published 1986
First paperback edition 1998

Library of Congress Cataloging in Publication Data
Kelsey, Harry
      Juan Rodríguez Cabrillo

      Biography: p.
      Includes index.
      1. Cabrillo, Juan Rodríguez, d. 1543, 2. Explorers—
America—Biography. 3. Explorers—Spain—Biography.
4. America—Discovery and exploration—Spanish.
5. California—Description and travel—To 1848.
1. Title.
E125.C12K35   1985   970.01'6 [B]   85-8396
ISBN 0-87328-176-4

Huntington Library Press
1151 Oxford Road, San Marino, CA 91108
626.405.2172

For Mary Ann
. . . and all her admirers

Contents

Illustrations

Foreword

ANYONE WHO READS THIS BOOK WILL LEARN that I have not given a fully conclusive answer to one of the most intriguing questions about Juan Rodriguez Cabrillo: Where was he born? More than that, I have questioned the conventional thinking about the place of his death, introducing uncertainty where none existed before.

This is regrettable and for a time I worried about it. Then, a friend—a scientist—set me straight. Two or three years ago Dr. Giles W. Mead, Jr., told me, "It is axiomatic that true heroes like Cabrillo never die." Good enough. The problem of his death was settled. Dr. Mead continued, "A natural corollary must be that such heroes likewise are never born." What could be clearer? The scientific method made a complex question simple. But this need not stop the controversy, and for many people it will not.

Regardless, I owe a debt of gratitude to Dr. Mead for creating an atmosphere conducive to research during his years as director of the Los Angeles County Museum of Natural History. I am grateful for his continuing counsel and aid since that time. In addition, I wish to thank Dr. James Thorpe, former director of the Huntington Library for his many kindnesses and those of the entire staff of the library. I also thank his successor, Dr. Robert Middlekauff, for keeping the Huntington a place whose sole aim seems to be the promotion of research. Dr. Martin Ridge, head of reasearch at the Huntington has aided my work in a number of important ways, not the least of which has been an appointment as a visiting fellow, which entitled me to a large desk and a comfortable chair in a quiet part of the stacks.

Most of the other members of the Huntington Library staff have helped me in one way or another, including Cary Bliss, Valerie Franco, Janet Hawkins, Sue Hull, Noelle Jackson, Joanna Jenkins, Barbara

Quinn, Virginia Renner, Mary Robertson, Virginia Rust, Leona Schonfeld, Mary Alice Shumate, Elsa Sink, Doris Smedes, Daniel Woodward, and Mary Wright. I am also indebted to Henry E. Huntington and the trustees of the Huntington Library for creating and maintaining this incomparable collection of rare books and documents.

The major source of unpublished material for this study was in the Archivo General de Indias in Seville, Spain. During several trips to Seville the archival staff allowed me to work my way through pertinent portions of the several million documents in their custody. My special thanks go to Rosario Parra Cala, director of the archives, María Antonia Colomar, vice director, and to Loli Betrán, Carmen Gálvez, Pedro Rubio Moreno, Gloria Muñiz, and Manuel Romero. Several North Americans living in Seville, including Dr. G. Douglas Inglis, Victoria Johnson, and Wendy Kramer, helped me decipher some of the very difficult paleography of the sixteenth century. In addition Dr. Inglis helped me obtain copies of obscure Spanish imprints. Pilar Redondo López de Inglis opened the rare book collection of the University of Seville Library for my use and gave me general assistance in locating obscure Spanish libraries and archives. Dr. Juan Gil and his charming wife, Consuelo Varela de Gil, directed me to a number of important manuscript sources that I would otherwise have missed.

A most important place for research in Central America is the Centro de Investigaciones Regionales de Meso-America, headed by Dr. Christopher Lutz. Dr. Lutz and his staff helped me a great deal during my research stays in Guatemala City and Antigua, as did Steven Webre, who is now on the staff of the Louisiana History Center. During my stay in Guatemala the director of the Archivo General de Centro America was Lic. Hernan del Valle Pérez. He and his associate Clodoveo Torres Moss, paleografo, were most cordial and helpful. Manuel Reyes Hernández, curator of the museo de Libros Antiguos in Antigua allowed me to use that collection of early Guatemalan imprints. Manuel Rubio Sánchez graciously furnished me with copies of materials from his own research files.

Members of the staff of the Newberry Library in Chicago, Illinois, were unfailingly helpful, particularly Dr. David Buisseret, director of the Hermon Dunlap Smith Center for the History of Cartography, Dr. Richard H. Brown, John Aubrey, Robert W. Karrow, Jr., and Paul Gehl.

Dr. Helen Wallis, head of the map department in the British Library and her assistant Sarah Tyacke introduced me to that great map collection and in addition made helpful suggestions about map holdings in other libraries. R. M. Haubourdin introduced me to the map collection of the Algemeen Rijksarchief in The Hague. Capitan de Corbeta Roberto Barreiro Meiro, director of the Museo Naval, Madrid, and Lola Higueras, chief of research, greatly assisted my work in one of the richest and most pleasant research libraries in Spain, perhaps the only such place that is always warm in winter and cool in summer.

Dr. Paul Smith of the National Marine Fisheries Service, Southwest Fisheries Center, arranged for me to accompany scientific parties around the Channel Islands and along the coast between San Diego and San Francisco. I am grateful to him for this help as well as for his advice regarding oceanography and fisheries. I also wish to thank Lloyd Farrar, port captain of the National Oceanic and Atmospheric Administration research vessel *David Starr Jordan*, Milton Roll, master of the ship, Manuel Ferreira, acting master, and the members of the crew who were unfailingly courteous and helpful to me.

Dr. Wayne V. Burt, emeritus professor, College of Oceanography, Oregon State University, arranged for me to travel on the O.S.U. research vessel, *Wecoma*, introducing me to coastal upwellings of the area north of San Francisco Bay. Dr. Burt also provided me with an introduction to Dr. Burney Le Boeuf of the Center for Marine Studies, University of California, Santa Cruz, who made room for me on an expedition aboard the research vessel *Ellen B. Scripps*, operated by the Scripps Institution of Oceanography. The expedition sailed along the coast and through the islands between San Diego and La Paz, Baja California, an area largely unspoiled since it was first seen by the sailors of the sixteenth century. During this expedition Dr. Le Boeuf, Captain Tom Beattie, and Dr. Claudio Campagna made many useful suggestions for interpreting the sixteenth century logs and reports.

The late Richard Pourade of San Diego allowed me to use the notes and photographs he gathered in his own research on the life of Juan Rodríguez Cabrillo. Dr. Mary Elizabeth Perry of the University of California at Los Angeles directed me to useful sources for information about sixteenth century Seville. Dr. Rubén Reina of the University of Pennsylvania allowed me free access to his collection of photocopies and transcripts from the A.G.C.A. and the A.G.I. Dr. Doyce B. Nunis, editor of the *Southern California Quarterly*, and Dr. Harwood P. Hinton, editor of *Arizona and the West*, have both given much valuable assistance with earlier pieces of this work. Mercedes Noviembre, librarian of the Biblioteca de Francisco Zabalburu in Madrid, Spain, allowed me free use of the rare books and manuscripts in that rich collection. Tanía Rizzo and Jean Beckner of the Honnold Library, Claremont Colleges, helped me find my way through the maps in the Henry Raup Wagner Collection. Sarah Hirsch, librarian of the Thomas Gilcrease Institute of American History and Art, gave much assistance in using the fine collection of Spanish manuscripts housed there. Sister Angela Woods helped me identify obscure religious allusions in the collections of the library at St. John's Seminary, Camarillo, California.

Finally, I wish to thank staff members of my own institution, not because their aid was any less valuable than that given by others, but because this is the customary order of things. Dr. Janet Fireman, David Debs, and William Mason helped me with many translation problems. Katharine Donahue, Kathryn Showers, and Lowell Herbrandson helped me with research questions and located obscure publications. Dr. Daniel Cohen identified for me the sea creatures mentioned in some of the accounts. Dr. Iris Engstrand, research associate at this institution and head of the history department at the University of San Diego, made many suggestions for improving the manuscript, as did Dr. Fireman and Donald Chaput. Leon Arnold, assistant director and on several occasions acting director, and Dr. Craig Black, director, arranged research time and encouraged me to continue the work.

Financial assistance for this project came from a number of sources. Mr. and Mrs. E. Hadley Stuart have been generous friends. The

Newberry Library, the Huntington Library, and the Los Angeles County Museum of Natural History Foundation all provided research funds. Several trips to libraries and archives in Guatemala, Mexico, Spain, England, Portugal, and the Netherlands were financed through grants from the Giles W. and Elise G. Mead Foundation; without that aid, none of this would have been possible.

However, the research is mine, the opinions expressed here are mine, and if there are any errors, they unfortunately are mine also. I hope there are none.

Juan Rodríguez Cabrillo

Chapter 1
From the Kingdoms
of Spain

SANTA ROSA ISLAND lies a few miles off the coast of Southern California. In the spring of 1901 a lone archaeologist wandered along a solitary stretch of the windswept dunes that mark the island's beaches. Kicking over a broken stone metate, he saw some curious scratches on the reverse side. He was unable to make sense of them, but he nevertheless cataloged the stone and photographed it. A description and photo later appeared in his report.[1] The stone itself was tucked away in the University of California museum collection at Berkeley, waiting for the day when another anthropologist would insist that the marks said "JRC" and that the stone had once graced the burial place of Juan Rodríguez Cabrillo, whose epic voyage marks the beginning of recorded history in California.[2]

Cabrillo is a name familiar in California, found on monuments and roads, schools and drugstores, maps and guidebooks. But few Californians understand this man's place in western history or know why his name adorns the landscape.

Juan Rodríguez Cabrillo led the first European expedition to the shores of Upper California in 1542, visiting Indian villages, noting the flora and fauna, and scouting for a place to settle. The 1543 account of this journey is the oldest written record of human activity on the West Coast of the United States. First published a hundred years ago, the manuscript has been translated and republished many times since then.[3]

The man himself is as mysterious as that piece of broken stone found on Santa Rosa Island. Few are aware of his role as soldier, sailor, shipbuilder, slaveowner, miner, and author, the first secular author published in the New World.

At the time of his death in 1543, the estate of Juan Rodríguez Cabrillo was one of the richest in Central America, destined to be fought over by his heirs and his enemies for another three-quarters of a century. The legal cases arising from these disputes have produced thousands of pages of documents[4] that now make it possible to know more about Juan Rodríguez Cabrillo than ever before, though not nearly enough to satisfy all our curiosity.

No one knows with certainty the place of his birth or the names of his parents, whether he came from a noble line or from poor but honest parents. He was probably not a hidalgo nor even descended from respectable lineage, or he would have said so. And if he had neglected to mention the fact, his heirs would not have been so shy.

Hidalguia was acquired by performing some great service for the crown. Hidalgos maintained horses and arms, supported a retinue of relatives and servants, and compiled a record of military service.[5] Almost any noble work was possible for a hidalgo, but such a man could not perform manual labor or engage in a trade. Instead, he had to be ready at a moment's notice to defend the realm or otherwise to enhance the royal estate.

Once acquired, *hidalguia* could be handed on from one generation to the next.[6] Juan Rodríguez Cabrillo achieved this status by his own merits, as his descendants successfully claimed. His unknown parents apparently had no such claim to honor or wealth.[7]

For centuries historians have maintained that Cabrillo was Portuguese. In fact, that is one reason he is known by the final surname, Cabrillo, as the Portuguese would call him, rather than Rodríguez, which modern Spanish usage demands. Today many

American historians who have studied the matter are convinced he was a Spaniard.

The present confusion grew out of a brief reference in Antonio de Herrera's multi-volume history of the Spanish conquests in the New World. Writing in the last part of the sixteenth century, with a mass of original reports and documents at his disposal, Herrera compiled a summary of Spanish achievement that is still considered authoritative after nearly four centuries. Usually meticulous in details, Herrera was nevertheless careless with some of his facts. His reference to the nationality of Juan Rodríguez Cabrillo is one of these errors.

In his brief account of the voyage to California, Herrera said that Viceroy Antonio de Mendoza[8]

> named as their captain Juan Rodríguez Cabrillo, Portuguese, a person very skilled in seamanship. One ship was named *San Salvador*, and it was the flagship. The other was the *Victoria*. Bartolomé Ferrer went as chief pilot, while Bartolome Fernández was also a pilot. The masters were Antonio Carrera and S. Remo.

Herrera called Juan Rodríguez Cabrillo a Portuguese, which no one had ever claimed before, but he missed the well-known Portuguese origins of the captain and pilot Antonio Correa (Carrera).[9]

Portuguese pilots were in great repute at the time. Such a man would be mentioned in dispatches. His name and nationality would be important information for any book on seafaring. It is not difficult to imagine Herrera as a weary author, revising his manuscript for the second or third time, deciding that it was important to say one of the men was a *portugués*, but carelessly placing that word next to the wrong name. Even easier to imagine is that a thoughtless printer allowed his attention to wander just long enough for the word *portugués* to fall into line behind the name Cabrillo instead of Correa.

American historians have been able to recognize such an error, but the historians of Portugal remain unconvinced. Chief among these writers was the Visconde de Lagoa, who consulted archival sources in Portugal and Spain without finding real evidence that Juan Rodríguez Cabrillo came from Portugal. Lagoa did find a number of Portuguese soldiers and seamen in New Spain named Juan Rodríguez, but that name was as common as is John Jones in the United States. Lagoa also found dozens of Spaniards named Juan Rodríguez in the same lists, but he decided not to mention this.[10]

Instead, he compiled a series of genuine and supposed references to Juan Rodríguez Cabrillo, then substituted the Portuguese spelling of the name for the Spanish in all his references to these old manuscripts. He made it appear that João Rodrígues Cabrilho was a name well documented in Spanish archives, though no one has ever yet found a sixteenth-century source with this spelling in it. If Juan Rodríguez Cabrillo was indeed Portuguese, neither the man himself nor his friends nor his relatives nor even his enemies seem to have mentioned the fact in the hundreds of pages of testimony that document the family's *calidad* (quality) and *limpieza de sangre* (purity of blood).

In recent years a number of scholars tried to locate Cabrillo descendants in Portugal, or a Cabrillo birthplace, or even a family named Cabrillo, but without notable results. A Portuguese historian, Celestino Soares, finally admitted that "the name Cabrillo is not known in Portugal." Nevertheless, Soares continued to insist this great explorer was Portuguese.[12]

In 1955 Maurice Holmes tried without success to locate "material relating to Cabrillo" in the Portuguese national archives. He found none and concluded that there was no proof for the assertion that Juan Rodríguez Cabrillo was Portuguese.[13]

Many surnames of the sixteenth century were derived from the name of a town, a province, or a region. The practice was particularly common among people of humble or rural origin, who often had no surname at all until they left their native villages and emigrated to America. Some historians, Portuguese and others, have guessed that Cabrillo was such a name.[14]

The problem for Portuguese historians is that there is no province or region in Portugal named Cabrillo. There are several Portuguese villages named Cabril and a few Spanish places with similar names. In both countries there are mountains and rivers named Cabril or something like it, as well as towns and other geographic locations named Cabrilla, Cabrillanes, and Cabrillas.[15] But not Cabrillo.

In an effort to solve the problem Joan M. Jensen traveled through Portugal in 1966 for the Cabrillo Historical Association of San Diego. She visited every village named Cabril, and she failed to discover any valid evidence about the origin of Juan Rodríguez Cabrillo. But so strong was the Portuguese tradition that she came home "much more convinced that Cabrillo was Portuguese and that he indeed came from one of these villages."[16]

More recently, in 1973, W. Michael Mathes checked pertinent historical and genealogical sources, reviewing arguments presented by writers who insist that Juan Rodríguez was Portuguese. Mathes found listings for 124 persons named Juan Rodríguez who immigrated to the New World before 1542, none of them named Cabrillo or Cabrilho.[17] Looking at the claims of Portuguese historians, Mathes found that they often misrepresented the facts in "a desperate attempt to prove a thesis rather than present objective evidence." After weighing all the evidence he could find, Mathes concluded that "there exists considerable doubt as to the nationality of Juan Rodríguez Cabrillo and, in fact, there is much to indicate he was not Portuguese but Castilian."[18]

Portuguese scholars for the most part have ignored Mathes' argument. When they discuss the very many skilled Portuguese navigators who served the Spanish crown, they still include Juan Rodríguez Cabrillo in that group.[19]

Government bodies have joined individual scholars in the dispute, but with even less success. Both the United States government and the state of California have asserted that Juan Rodríguez Cabrillo is Portuguese.[20] The government of Portugal, of course, agrees, but Portuguese agreement stops short of total harmony. Not one but two villages in Portugal named Cabril claim to be the birthplace of Juan Rodríguez Cabrillo.

The Camara Municipal de Montalegre insists that Juan Rodríguez Cabrillo was born in the nearby village of Cabril.[21] Further south, near the city of Castro Daire, citizens in another village named Cabril point to one of the oldest buildings in town as the very spot where Juan Rodríguez Cabrillo was born.[22] Obviously, at least one of these groups is wrong.

Convinced of the justice of their cause, the members of the Montalegre city council ceremoniously issued a proclamation in 1978, saying that "Joao Rodrigues Cabrillo" was born in Lapela, a barrio of their own village of Cabril. What is the evidence? Well, "in Lapela there exists a 'house of Galego' a name attributed to João Rodrigues Cabrillo."[23]

This is an obscure but not insignificant point. Juan Rodríguez Cabrillo discovered a port called Navidad on the Colima coast of Mexico. For years it was thought that Navidad was also called *"el puerto de Juan Gallego"*, presumably another name for the discoverer. As it turns out, the port of Juan Gallego is some distance up the coast from Navidad, and Juan Gallego is clearly not Juan Rodríguez Cabrillo.[24]

The word *Gallego* means a native of Galicia, the region of Spain just north of the Portuguese border. Supposing for the sake of argument that Juan Rodríguez Cabrillo was also called Juan Gallego, would a man who called himself Juan Gallego be Portuguese? In apparent response to this and other queries the Montalegre city councilmen declared that "João Rodrigues Cabrillo" must have "emigrated to Galicia where is married and became related to Spanish nobility, then departed to join the seafaring expeditions that explored the coast of America."[25] This is the wildest of all the stories. It has no basis in fact.

All that we know with certainty comes from a brief statement by the grandson of Juan Rodríguez Cabrillo. In sworn testimony given on December 4, 1617, Gerónimo Cabrillo de Aldana said:

"My paternal grandfather, Juan Rodríguez Cabrillo came [to the New World] from the Kingdoms of Spain in company with Pánfilo de Narváez."[26]

Narváez himself is something of a mystery man, even though he was a hidalgo—well known and well connected. Uncertainty cloaks his birthplace and early life. Is it not inconsistent to expect a man of humble origins to mention his place of birth, when men like Narváez, who had reason to be proud of their families failed to do so? In any case, poor men never did.[27]

Narváez was a good friend of Gonzalo Fernández de Oviedo y Valdez, official historian of the Indies. Oviedo called Narváez a "hidalgo who came to these parts with only a sword and a cape, searching for adventure." Oviedo thought it unnecessary to name the man's birthplace.[28]

Bartolomé de las Casas, who knew the explorer well, said Narváez came from Valladolid.[29] Herrera, the historian of the Conquest, writing decades afterwards, wrote snappishly that Narváez came from Tierra de Cuéllar and "not as some say from Valladolid." The argument seems unimportant now, but Herrera thought it offered an explanation for the eagerness of Narváez to serve in Cuba with Diego Velázquez, who came from Cuéllar.[30] That is a little ahead of the Cabrillo story, and anyway, as Las Casas said, Valladolid is very close to Cuéllar.[31]

Narváez first appears in the record in Jamaica in 1509 with Juan de Esquivel.[32] Testimony given by the wife of Juan Rodríguez Cabrillo in 1552 confirms the fact that her husband was in the Indies about the time Narváez was serving in Jamaica: "He came to these Indies more than forty years ago."[33]

During these early years Narváez and Velázquez became close friends. In 1511, when Velázquez was sent to pacify Cuba, he invited Narváez to organize a cuadrilla of thirty skilled crossbowmen to go along. Narváez obliged.[34]

Possibly both Juan Rodríguez Cabrillo and Diego Sánchez de Ortega, his close friend and future brother-in-law, were part of the

2. *Juan Rodríguez Cabrillo served as a crossbowman in the Spanish conquest of the Aztec empire. He later commanded his own company of crossbowmen in the conquest of Guatemala. (Historical Model Collection, Natural History Museum of Los Angeles County.)*

force, serving as pages, for Rodríguez was too young to be a fighting man. But whether in Cuba or elsewhere, they must have served aboard ship and in battle with Narváez before going to Mexico. In 1519, shortly after their arrival, both men commanded cuadrillas of crossbowmen. A young man with a quick mind, a strong arm, and a capacity for slaughter could earn such a command quickly, but not without battle experience.[35]

The royal historian Herrera argued later that Narváez preferred to lead men from the "tierra de Cuéllar." If so, then Juan Rodríguez and Diego Sánchez may have been natives of Cuéllar, moving later to Seville, where the family of Diego Sánchez made its home.[36]

Seville and the surrounding provinces of Andalusia furnished more than one-third of the emigrants to the New World during the first decades of the sixteenth century. A steady stream of immigrants from the Andalusian hinterlands and elsewhere flowed into Seville, the staging area for trade and communication with the Indies. These new *sevillanos* in turn often moved on to the Indies and claimed Seville as their place of origin. Juan Rodríguez doubtless came from Seville, but might not have been born there.[37]

Sixteenth-century Seville had the third largest cathedral in all Christendom. The major commercial street, Sierpes, twisted to an end near the plaza that fronted the episcopal palace and the adjacent cathedral. While merchants negotiated on the steps of the sacred edifice, urchins begged and stole and raced along the chained walkway. Some were children of prostitutes abandoned by penniless mothers. Not knowing their proper age, and lacking even a family name, these tough little outlaws had to fend for themselves. The luckiest found a merchant household to take them in and let them work for their keep.[38] Juan Rodríguez Cabrillo seems to have found such a place in the home of his friend, Diego Sánchez de Ortega.

Diego's father, Alonso Sánchez de Ortega, was an important merchant in Seville, who sent cargoes to the New World and contracted to assemble provisions for the fleets that sailed there.[39] Did he send his son Diego to the New World to act as his agent and send the young Juan Rodríguez as a helper? Perhaps. The record is incomplete, but the evidence fits. Juan Rodríguez was in the New World by 1510 or shortly thereafter. He did not know his exact age, and he had no family connections. He added Cabrillo to his name a quarter century later simply as a way to distinguish himself from the mass of men named Juan Rodríguez.

Of the masses of men named Juan Rodríguez several came with Narváez and signed the famous Cortés letter of 1520; two of them were Juan Rodríguez de Sevilla and Juan Rodríguez, *ballestero de Narvaez*. Two or three others were simply called Juan Rodríguez. One of these men was Juan Rodríguez Cabrillo. None of the men was listed as Portuguese. The same list of men who served with Narváez also contains the name of Diego Sánchez de Ortega, the close friend of Juan Rodrguez Cabrillo.[40]

Modern Spanish usage designates the first surname the patronymic and the second name the matronymic. Portuguese does just the reverse. Since the name Cabrillo is nonexistent in Portugal, Portuguese historian Celestino Soares decided that Juan Rodríguez Cabrillo had a Portuguese father and a Spanish mother.[41] There is a certain logic to the argument from the Portuguese viewpoint, but it has a fatal flaw. Soares assumed that sixteenth-century Spaniards followed modern usage, which they did not.[42] The records are filled with the names of soldiers and settlers who did not use the surname of either parent. In many families one child would take the surname of the father, while another used the mother's surname.

The sons of Juan Rodríguez, for example, were known as Juan Rodríguez Cabrillo, after the father, and Diego Sánchez de Ortega, after the maternal uncle.[43] The older son later began to call himself Juan Rodríguez Cabrillo de Medrano, apparently after a rich relative. His sons, the grandsons of Juan Rodríguez Cabrillo, were named Alonso de Medrano and Gerónimo Cabrillo de Aldana.[44]

This chaotic individualism reached an extreme in the family of Alonso de Luarca, a fellow conquistador of Juan Rodríguez Cabrillo.

Alonso and his wife, Ana de Elgueta, had seven sons. One of them took the matronymic, while the others chose names of various other relatives. None of them took the name of their father. The oldest son and heir was named Cristóbal de Santizo, while two others bore the names Alonso Alvarez de Santizo and Diego de Santizo. Two sons were named Juan del Fontín and Pedro del Fontín. One son was called Federico de Perena, after his maternal grandfather, and the youngest had the name Hernando de Elgueta, his mother's surname.[45] Surnames in the sixteenth century were as much a matter of choice as given names are now.

Some historians argue that Cabrillo is a nickname, and perhaps it is. Bernal Díaz del Castillo, who wrote the most detailed firsthand account of the Conquest, gave numerous examples of this practice.

Geronimo Mejía, he said, was called *Rapapelo* (the Scalper), because he was the grandson of a thief. Pedro de Solís, was called *Tras la Puerta* (Behind the Door) because he was a sneak. The wife of Juan Perez was called *La Vaquera* (the Cowgirl) for reasons Díaz preferred not to explain. Even the clergy was fair game. One priest was immortalized by Bernal Díaz as the Blowhard.[46]

All this makes it more than possible that Juan Rodríguez himself had a nickname. But the etymology is not very satisfactory. The closest Spanish derivatives seem to be *cabra* (goat) and *cabrón* (cuckold), neither of which is the sort of name a man with pretensions to hidalguía would claim for himself.[47]

The earliest record showing his use of the name Cabrillo is dated 1536. It is not in the handwriting of Juan Rodríguez.[48] In fact no documents have yet been found with the full signature, Juan Rodríguez Cabrillo, though he referred to himself by that name at least once.[49]

He could write and was good at it. This is clear from a report of the earthquake in Santiago, Guatemala, in 1541. The account was almost certainly written by Juan Rodríguez Cabrillo, who was out of the city at the time but arrived a few days later to pen the brief, terse, but moving story of the horror that had descended upon the capital city.[50]

An *interrogatorio* of August 1541 also was written by him in the same spare but forceful prose.[51]

These records offer strong evidence that he had a good, practical education, no knowledge of the classics, but the ability to put his ideas down on paper and have them understood. Several of his friends later testified that Juan Rodríguez was an experienced seaman before he went to Mexico with Narváez.[52] Others testified that by 1543 he was a pilot and navigator of considerable repute.[53] These jobs demanded a good basic education: reading logs and manifests, writing instructions and reports, preparing charts, making astronomical computations. All were daily tasks for ship's officers in the sixteenth century.[54] Many men of that century could count and could sign their own names. Some could read, though fewer were able to acquire the knack of writing.[55] Juan Rodríguez Cabrillo could do all these things and do them well.

In the records of the Archivo de Protocolos de Sevilla there are entries for many young men named Juan Rodríguez, at least one of whom was an agent and broker in the islands of the Indies. The earliest entry is dated 1509,[56] when Juan Rodríguez Cabrillo was scarcely ten or twelve years old. Similar records, dated 1515, show that Diego Sánchez, son of the same merchant, sailed to Española on business for his father.[57]

This Juan Rodríguez and this Diego Sánchez are not the men in whom we are interested, but they had much in common besides their common names. These two had connections with the armies and fleets of the Indies. They were merchants and investors. They had practical educations and the same experience in oceanborne commerce that Juan Rodríguez Cabrillo received in his early years. Personal letters from such merchants and brokers of this era give a good idea of daily life among New World entrepreneurs.[58]

These *factores* were typically young and industrious members of the powerful commercial families of Seville, sent to the Indies with a cargo of goods for sale or trade. Their letters contain no pretensions to scholarship, no allusions to classics or Scripture. The messages are brief and direct, all business, but clear and homey nonetheless. The writers were men of the Conquest, but businessmen as well. The Conquest was in part a business venture, one in which governors, merchants, and soldiers invested goods and money. Each expected to receive a share of the profits, though these were usually slow in coming.[59]

Consider the letter of a merchant who complained that he could not sell his goods because the soldiers had not yet received their shares of captured gold.[60]

> I wouldn't want to forget to write that at present you should not send me any merchandise whatever, even if they should give it to you gratis on the steps of the Exchange, because you cannot retrieve the money as quickly as you would think, no matter to what lengths you go. And so I beg you under no conditions send goods; indeed I will not receive them, to avoid giving a bad account of them.

There are many other examples of this close military business alliance, showing that soldiers and merchants were often the same people. In one case several businessmen gave Cortés four thousand *pesos de oro* plus the same value in supplies for his expedition to Mexico. Bernal Díaz del Castillo invested goods and money in the various trips he took to Tierra Firme and the islands, before he joined the great expedition of Cortés.[61]

There were risks in such an arrangement. Goods were lost or damaged, sometimes confiscated, and often sacrificed at bargain prices. Listen to a report from Santo Domingo:[62]

> Sir, I have come to terms . . . on 90 per cent for all undamaged goods, and for what is damaged irreparably, whatever it costs in Santo Domingo. I consider this a good arrangement, sir. . . . I have done this, so approve it; I swear to God that if I had not made this arrangement,

I would have had to sell for much less. Not a man in camp
would have dared buy any of it, if I hadn't given it to him.

This was the sort of business training Juan Rodríguez received in
the New World. His early military education took place in Cuba
with Narváez about 1510 or 1511. A brief look at this campaign
also reveals something about the opportunities he might have had
for experience in gold mining and shipbuilding, as well as military
affairs. In addition, the conquest of Cuba tells a good bit about the
character of the men who earned their fortunes in the Indies.

Christopher Columbus had reached the shores of Cuba on his
first voyage and touched there again when he returned in 1494.[63]
During the next few years the island was visited by other Spanish
vessels. By the turn of the century Spanish navigators reported having sailed completely around the island.[64] In the next decade both
Spanish government officials and New World adventurers became
interested in the possibility that Cuba might contain gold mines
and other resources worth exploiting.

This is the reason Diego Velázquez was sent from Española to
explore Cuba in late 1510 or early 1511. With a force of three hundred men he built a log fort at Baracoa, naming the settlement
Nuestra Señora de la Asunción. Within a few months he was reinforced from Jamaica by Pánfilo de Narváez and an assault force of
thirty crossbowmen, each one served by his own Jamaican slaves.[65]
One of the soldiers or one of the slaves carried smallpox with him,
and the disease became a secret ally in conquering the natives,
though Narváez hardly seemed to need such assistance.[66] This was
the expedition that was to survey and conquer Cuba.

Bartolomé de las Casas, at that time chaplain of the expedition,
witnessed one grisly incident that seems to have marked him for
life. Whether it was typical of the whole campaign is a matter for
speculation, but there seems to be no doubt that it happened pretty much as Las Casas described it.[67] Young Juan Rodríguez was
surely present and can scarcely have been untouched by the events.

One evening after a long and thirsty march in the interior, Narváez and his army arrived at the village of Caonao, where the Indians greeted them with food and calabashes of fresh water. Thus refreshed, the Spaniards were invited to enjoy a fish dinner prepared by the villagers. While the soldiers ate, the natives looked on, examining the horses—those peculiar animals the Indians had only heard about but not seen—and marveling at the dress and equipment of the Spaniards. As the curious villagers pressed closer, a soldier suddenly drew his sword and began hacking away at the bystanders. This was a signal for all to join in the slaughter, killing young and old, men and women, even domestic animals.[68]

No one knows how many Indians were killed. Las Casas said in one book that there were more than two thousand Indians in the town, plus a number of others carrying baggage for Narváez.[69] Later, he said that three thousand Indians were killed. No one has ever accused him of understatement. But the numbers, whether two thousand or three thousand, are less important than the atrocity itself. "I saw such terrible cruelties done there," Las Casas said later, "as I had never seen before nor thought to see."[70] It was a bloody massacre, and for reasons detailed by Las Casas, so obviously premeditated, that the priest abandoned the expedition then and there. He marched off in anger, cursing Narváez with a holy passion: "You and your men," he said, "can go to the devil."[71]

There are no surviving descriptions of any other battles, but there must have been others equally gruesome. Las Casas credited Narváez himself with killing two thousand Indians. The other three or four horsemen in his force slaughtered an additional eight thousand, and countless others were killed by the footsoldiers.[72] Even if the totals are exaggerated, as the enemies of Las Casas say, the Spanish campaign through Cuba was a bloody horror. Disease took an added toll, no one knows how much, though the worst was yet to come. The *encomienda* system, instituted after the Conquest, was the biggest killer of all.[73]

The *encomienda* was a form of personal service and tribute that originated in Spain but received some peculiar refinements in the

New World.[74] Through this system proprietors or *encomenderos* received certain villages as encomiendas, with the right to demand goods or services or both as annual fees (*tasaciones*). In exchange the encomenderos were supposed to provide the villagers with religious instruction and protection from their enemies. Innocuous sounding, perhaps, but in practice the system became a vicious substitute for slavery.

For example, any Indians who failed to acknowledge Spanish authority when formally required to do so, or who later rose in rebellion against the crown, could be branded as slaves and marched in cuadrillas to serve in the fields or the mines.[75]

Las Casas later wrote of seeing entire Cuban villages with no men left to work the fields. He saw women so undernourished they were unable to nurse their babies, so that within a period of three months seven thousand infants died.[76] During the same period, he said later, more than seventy thousand children, whose fathers and mothers had been sent to the mines, died of hunger."[77]

Those who were sent to the mines fared no better than those who stayed at home. The royal chronicler Oviedo saw them standing all day in muddy mountain streams, panning for gold. Given little food or rest, the Indians serving in these cuadrillas quickly sickened and died.[78] As Cuban slaves became scarce, Indians from other islands and blacks from Africa were brought in to replace them. Those who survived the ocean voyage seemed hardier than the Indians, but they also suffered from exhaustion, malnutrition, and disease. Much gold was gathered, as Oviedo later reported in his official history, but the human cost was immense.[79] In this atmosphere Juan Rodríguez trained for the Conquest.

Las Casas himself was an encomendero.[80] So was Diego Holguín, who served with Juan Rodríguez in Cuba and later went with him to Mexico and Guatemala.[81] So was Hernando Cortés. Bernal Díaz was promised an encomienda but was too restless to wait for one. "Diego Velázquez, the governor of the island of Cuba, who was my kinsman, promised to give me some Indians as soon as there were any available," he said, "but I did not care to be kept waiting until this should happen."[82]

Instead, Díaz and his friends, among them perhaps Juan Rodríguez, joined an expedition to the mainland, buying and equipping ships for this purpose in Cuba. Some sort of shipbuilding facilities had already been established at the present site of Havana, at that time called *Puerto de Carenas*,[83] where Juan Rodríguez may have had his first experience in building ships. No one knows how extensive these shipyards were, but the name itself gives us an idea. *Puerto de Carenas* means a place where ships are careened, or hauled ashore for repairs, and Las Casas reported seeing many ships rebuilt there. Díaz mentioned that ropes, cordage, cables, anchors, and water casks were available from local merchants.[84]

In 1516, after Narváez went to Spain and asked for permission, the crown authorized New World colonists to build their own ships and carry on trade among the islands.[85] By the time Hernán Cortés began recruiting men for his mainland expedition in 1518, trained shipwrights were easy to find.[86] This doubtless means that ships were being built in Cuba well before 1518. Materials and skilled workmen were readily available, and Díaz and his associates doubtless used them,[87] building a busy shipyard at Puerto de Carenas well supplied with materials needed to equip and repair ocean-going vessels.

Well before Cortés took an army to Mexico, Díaz and his friends had ample opportunity to gain experience in navigation, seamanship, and ground warfare. Armed with arquebuses and crossbows, they battled natives who wore thick cotton armor and carried lances, slings, bows, and arrows.[88] In 1518, when Governor Diego Velázquez decided to send a major expedition to the mainland, dozens of qualified soldiers and seamen were available. There was a rush to enlist, and Bernal Díaz himself went along with the rank of ensign.[89]

At the time of this appointment Bernal Díaz del Castillo was about twenty years old, with four or five years of military experience.[90]

Diego Holguín was twenty-six, had served in the conquest of Cuba, and had perhaps participated in other Caribbean expeditions.[91] Francisco López was about sixteen.[92] These men were the companions of Juan Rodríguez Cabrillo in the Conquest of Mexico—young men, experienced in seafaring and war, though not yet skilled enough to be numbered among the important leaders of the expedition.

In later years when recalling the exploits of Juan Rodríguez Cabrillo, Francisco López spoke of him in the way a younger and less experienced man would speak of someone older and more skillful.[93]

> This witness knew the late Juan Rodríguez Cabrillo during the conquest of Mexico, after the Indians expelled the Spanish from the city. During those days this witness saw him carry out his orders both as a soldier and as one charged with preparing material and fittings for the *bergantines* they were building in order to reconquer the city by way of the lake of Mexico. This Juan Rodríguez was a man of the sea, and he understood that sort of work.

Bernal Díaz considered himself an authority on land warfare and claimed some knowledge of seamanship, not an unusual combination in those days. Years later, when he was involved in writing his account of the Conquest, he recalled that Juan Rodríguez had come to Mexico as an experienced soldier—a crossbowman—and also as an experienced seaman,[94] implying that he gained his experience in those early forays in which Díaz was involved.

The birth records of Juan Rodríguez have not been found, but we do not have to guess his age. According to the *Historia Verdadera* of Bernal Díaz, he was old enough and experienced enough to serve as captain of the detachment sent to prepare and transport naval stores for the *bergantines*.[95] This means he was at least in his twenties when he went to Mexico, as were Díaz and Holguín.

By the time he sailed to California in 1542, Juan Rodríguez was old enough to command a fleet, run a shipyard, serve as *justicia mayor*, own rich mines and encomiendas, and have several marriageable daughters. On the other hand, he was still young enough to lead troops into battle.[96] This seems to describe a man in his forties, mature, no longer eager for adventure, but still able to command with vigor and enthusiasm. In 1537 he said he was "more than thirty-five years old."[97] We can suppose he was born around 1498 or 1500 and not be far wrong.

Summing up what we know about his early life, it appears that Juan Rodríguez Cabrillo was born in Spain, probably in Seville, but perhaps in Cuéllar. He came to the New World as a boy, a tough one who could make his own way. He served with Pánfilo de Narváez in the conquest of Cuba. As a merchant-adventurer he learned to read, write, keep accounts, and sell goods at a profit. He also learned something about military affairs and became a skilled crossbowman and a mariner. By the time Cortés went to Mexico, Juan Rodríguez was qualified to command a group of men in the achievement of a critically important military objective. Earning the confidence of his superiors and the loyalty of his subordinates, he played an important role in the greatest European military adventure in North America.

Chapter 2
Captain of Crossbowmen

FOLLOWING THE BLOODY march through Cuba, Governor Diego Velázquez and his field commander, Pánfilo de Narváez, sailed for Spain in July 1515 to report in person to the king. This was part of a developing ritual for successful commanders, who could expect a sympathetic hearing at the court when they requested political and economic favors for themselves and their friends.[1]

Velázquez in particular wanted royal approval for his scheme to fit out armadas and look for new islands to conquer or even a new region on the mainland. The mainland settlement at Castilla de Oro (Darien) was already providing considerable income to the crown. The royal treasury was also enriched by the Cuban tithes, fines, and custom duties, and especially the royal share of the newly mined Cuban gold.[2]

Velázquez and Narváez had proven themselves in Cuba, and they would doubtless do well elsewhere. Royal approval of the Velázquez plan was a certainty. So after spending a few months in Spain and without waiting for the official documents, Velázquez returned to Cuba and began sending out expeditions to look for other rich lands. By late fall 1518 two reconnaissance parties had returned with news of rich, hostile, and heavily populated regions in Yucatan.[3]

Even before the second expedition returned, Velázquez began the process of launching a third and much larger armada to exploit the new finds. Bernal Díaz had been in the second fleet, serving under Juan de Grijalva. Along with most of the other men he also enlisted in the new expedition, under the command of Hernando Cortés.[4]

The armada was small but impressive: a fleet of eleven ships, the largest only a hundred tons and the smallest a launch or *bergantín*; an army of 500 men and 50 sailors; a labor force of two hundred Indians, several black slaves, and a few native women; sixteen horses; and ships crammed full of supplies and trade goods, bought mostly on credit.[5]

Before the fleet left Cuba, Cortés and Velázquez were at odds. The governor wanted to remove his captain. Cortés seemed just as determined to cut his ties with Velázquez, and this he did when his army arrived on the Mexican mainland.[6]

After a preliminary search along the Yucatan coast, Cortés selected a site for a permanent base. With proper formality he founded a new town, La Villa Rica de Vera Cruz, to use as his headquarters. Appointing a *cabildo* or ruling council for his new town, Cortés had the council elect him *justicia mayor* and *capitán general*. He then dispatched a letter to the king, describing the country they were exploring, criticizing the supposed duplicity of Velázquez, and on behalf of all the men in his army asking the king to approve his independent command of the Mexican expedition.[7]

Through a combination of treachery and daring Cortés and his troops then swept through the Mexican provinces, defeating Indian armies and gathering a vast force of Indian allies for a final march on the capital. Reaching there on 8 November 1519, Cortés and his army scarcely paused to enjoy the food and women and rich apartments furnished by the Aztec emperor, Montezuma. There were other matters to think about.[8]

The Aztec capital, today's Mexico City, was perched on several islands in the middle of Lake Texcoco, a broad, shallow body of water. The islands of Tenochtitlán were connected with the mainland by narrow causeways and bridges. The city was a trap, one that Montezuma could spring simply by cutting the bridges, but one Cortés could avoid simply by building a few small ships. The vesssels would provide emergency transport for the army. More than this, Montezuma would see a Spanish fleet at first hand. His previous knowledge of Spanish seamanship had depended on the awestruck descriptions and vivid paintings brought back by his emissaries from Vera Cruz.[9]

As best they could, the messengers of Montezuma described the guns, the armor, and the horses, the thousands of Indian rebels who supported Cortés, and the ships that had brought the Spanish invaders from across the ocean. Before Montezuma could do much more than ponder these reports, Cortés had dismantled his armada at Vera Cruz, then ordered that the sails and rope and iron work be brought forward for use in building a small inland fleet. The ship carpenters who had stayed behind in Vera Cruz soon arrived with spars, rigging, and timber and set to work building four bergantines.[10]

These were small boats that could be propelled with oars or a sail. Cortés spoke of bergantines as *fustas*.[11] Either word means a small, open sailing vessel. Some insist the boats were of substantial size—perhaps forty feet in length—but the evidence is not convincing.[12]. Bernal Díaz described one ship in the original armada as being "very small, like a bergantine," as though that settled the matter.[13]

Petrus Martyris Angleria, a member of the Council of the Indies, writing from interviews and official reports, described the ships in somewhat more detail. The bergantines, he said, were little vessels, capable in a pinch of ferrying twenty men at a time to the mainland, along with their horses.[14] Thus, the total capacity of all four boats working together was somewhat more than a hundred men, including crew and rowers.

Some authors have misconstrued Cortés' own brief description to mean that the four boats would carry the whole army of three hundred men and a score or more horses at one time.[15] What he actually said was: "We could put three hundred men on the mainland and carry the horses any time we wished." Not the same thing at all.[16]

While Cortés was ensconced in Mexico in uneasy but sybaritic splendor, Velázquez stormed about the Cuban capital, seething with indignation at the man's insubordination. Stories and letters, official and unofficial, reported that in the few months since leaving Cuba Cortés had found immense wealth and was appealing to the king to recognize his independent rule.[17] Velázquez sent his own appeal to the king, then began to outfit another fleet to deal with Cortés.

This new fleet was even larger than the earlier ones: nineteen ships, fourteen hundred soldiers, ninety crossbowmen, eighty horsemen, and seventy arquebusiers. This body was led by Pánfilo de Narváez, who had just returned from Spain.[18] Among his men was the young crossbowman, Juan Rodríguez Cabrillo, who was then a captain or soon to be one.[19]

Narváez also brought twenty cannons and two master gunners, along with huge quantities of powder and shot.[20] Supplies doubtless consisted of the same sort of cassava bread and salt pork that Cortés had carried, along with such merchandise as swords, daggers, oil, vinegar, and cheese, trade items that had made Cortés sometimes seem like a merchant to his own men.[21]

By all accounts the expeditions of Cortés and Narváez left Cuba nearly barren of men and supplies. One Cuban merchant complained to his partner in Spain: "Because 1,200 men have left this island for Yucatan . . . there are few people to sell to."[22] Among the soldiers who sailed for Mexico with Narváez were several of the men who knew Juan Rodríguez Cabrillo and later went to Guatemala with him.

Among these soldiers was twenty-year-old Sancho de Barahona, who told everyone he would rather serve in the army of Cortés. Infuriated by the man's disloyalty, Narváez clapped him in irons and kept him on starvation rations for the remainder of the campaign. One or two other men were imprisoned with him, apparently for the same offense.[23] Was Juan Rodríguez one of these? There is reason to think so, as we shall see.

Another man who knew Juan Rodríguez in the army of Narváez was Diego Holguín. This thirty-year-old conquistador had been in the conquest of Santo Domingo in 1506, then had marched across Cuba with the crossbow army of Pánfilo de Narváez.[24] Others were Juan de Espinar, about eighteen years old, who said he met Juan Rodríguez when the Narváez armada formed in 1519;[25] and Pedro de Ovide, about nineteen years old.[26] Francisco López, a crossbowman about twenty years of age, arrived on the Mexican coast a few weeks after Cabrillo, sailing on a supply ship that the unsuspecting governor Velásquez sent with victuals for the army of Narváez.[27] A final companion, whose age we do not know, was Diego Sánchez de Ortega. Within a year or so Diego Sánchez commanded his own company of crossbowmen.[28]

The Narváez invading force landed near Vera Cruz in the last days of April 1520. After two weeks of fruitless negotiations with the emissaries of Narváez, Cortés marched out of Tenochtitlán to meet his new adversary. His trusted lieutenant, Pedro de Alvarado, remained behind with 140 less dependable men to guard their royal prisoner, Montezuma.[29]

Then followed more diplomatic maneuvering with Narváez, who was camped with his army at Cempoala. This was mostly bluff and bluster, for neither commander was seriously seeking a peaceful solution. Finally, in a brilliant and daring night attack, the outnumbered army of Cortés infiltrated the Narváez encampment.[30]

It was pitch dark and raining. Much of the opposing army was indoors trying to stay dry, convinced that the tiny army of Cortés could not do much against their vastly superior force. But luck was on the side of Cortés.[31]

When the attack came, Narváez found his artillery useless. His gunners had sealed the touch-holes of his cannons with wax to keep the powder dry, and the guns could not be fired. As his horsemen stumbled out into the driving rain, they found that Cortés had sent men to sneak into the corrals and cut the saddle girths. It was not just luck and cunning that made Cortés the victor. His army fought under a death sentence, proclaimed by Narváez, whose own force was overconfident, ill trained, and poorly motivated. The battle did not last long. Narváez was badly wounded, and his army was destroyed.[32]

Thus, with a quick stroke Cortés defeated his newest rival and added several hundred soldiers to his own invading army. Most of the men were glad to join Cortés, for many men in both armies had been friends in Cuba. Cortés treated them generously, ordering the return of their horses and weapons and promising them a share of the riches that would soon be captured. Those few who showed any serious reluctance to join Cortés were sent away for supplies or to explore distant coasts.[33]

Cortés ordered special treatment for Sancho de Barahona and his companions.[34] If Juan Rodríguez was one of these men, that fact could explain how Juan Rodríguez managed to command a cuadrilla of crossbowmen for Cortés when he had so recently served in a hostile army. This might also help to explain why Barahona and Rodríguez were later granted half shares in one of the richest encomiendas in Guatemala—but more about that later.

While Cortés and his men were winning an important victory on the coast. Alvarado and the remainder of the army were caught in a steadily worsening military situation in the capital. The Aztecs seemed to have found a new courage plus the determination to be rid of the Spanish invaders. These former friends turned sullen and hostile, and there were other clear signs of an impending attack.

When Cortés heard of this development, he hastened back to the capital with his heavily reinforced army. Ignoring advice from some of his lieutenants to camp on the shore of the lake, he marched across the causeways and on 24 June 1520 he entered the city, where a worried Pedro de Alvarado gave him a hearty welcome.[35]

Two weeks later the military situation had deteriorated so much that Cortés decided to abandon the city, only to find that he would have to fight his way out. With thirteen hundred soldiers, including horsemen and musketeers, and an additional two thousand Tlascalan troops, plus baggage, servants and their wives, and children, it was a risky undertaking. The Aztecs removed the bridges from the causeways and dug the channels wider and deeper.

To lead the retreat Cortés made Pedro de Alvarado commander of a special guard of a hundred and fifty Spanish soldiers and four hundred Tlascalans. This unit had charge of a portable timber bridge to stretch across the gaps in the causeways. After the rest of the army had fought its way across each section of causeway, Alvarado and his men were to bring the bridge forward to the next break and repeat the process. Another Indian guard was to bring up the artillery, which was of no real use on the retreat.[36]

Cortés had charge of the advance guard. Alvarado's men put the bridge into position about midnight of 10 July, and the army began to make its way out of the city toward the town of Tacuba on the western shore of the lake. Once the Aztecs saw what was happening, their squadrons attacked in such overwhelming numbers that the bridge had to be abandoned, choked as it was with baggage and boxes and bodies.[37]

Most of the crossbowmen and musketeers were in this beleaguered group. Bernal Díaz says they lost most of their weapons at the bridge.[38] Juan Rodríguez was one of the few who managed to fight his way out of the city, perhaps with Pedro de Alvarado, who abandoned his post at the bridge under circumstances that Díaz thought questionable. With four other soldiers Alvarado made his way forward and reported to Cortés that the rest of his command was dead or captured.[39]

The retreat lasted for five days. During that time, according to Bernal Díaz, more than nine hundred Spanish soldiers were either killed or captured and sacrificed. A thousand Tlascalan auxiliaries met a similar fate. All the artillery was gone, the bergantines destroyed, crossbows and muskets lost. Díaz said that most of the dead and missing were men from the poorly trained army of Nar-váez, who loaded themselves down with Aztec gold before the retreat, then found they could neither run nor swim.[40]

3. Indian carpenters helped build the bergantines used by Cortés during the Con-quest. (Diego Durán, Historia de las Indias de Nueva España, plate 30. Huntington Library.)

Cortés lost little time in regrouping his badly mauled army, gather-ing supplies and recruits where he could. When one ship was sent by the unsuspecting Governor of Cuba, Diego de Velázquez, the captain was tricked into surrender, and Cortés had more rein-forcements, including eight soldiers with "six crossbows, much twine for making bowstrings, and one mare."[41] Other ships arrived from Spain or the islands, laden with all sorts of trade goods—gunpowder and muskets, crossbows and crossbow cords, horses, arms—and more recruits for the army.[42]

Piles of unused ship fittings in storage at Vera Cruz were brought forward to Tepeaca, where Indian slaves were being branded and assigned to cuadrillas or labor battalions. Cortés had decided to build an entire fleet of bergantines for recapturing the Mexican capital. More than a thousand Indian bearers were required just to carry the shipbuilding materials inland.[43]

The supply train brought everything necessary for building a fleet: pieces of iron and long threaded bolts to fasten the timbers together; anchors, sails, and rigging; tow and cables; and the hammers, saws, augers, chisels, and other tools needed for building ships. Experienced blacksmiths and even one man who was "half a blacksmith" were assigned to work in the forge. From the ships themselves came huge cauldrons for melting pitch. Vast battalions of Indians were assigned to cut timber. While this work was yet under way, Cortés decided to move the army and the shipyard to Texcoco, where the lake was close and the town easily defended.[44]

Indians did not know how to harvest resin and prepare it for use in caulking the ships. Therefore, Cortés selected four seamen who knew the process, assigned them a cuadrilla of Indian slaves, and sent them to the pine forests near Huexotzingo. Juan Rodríguez was the man in charge of the operation.[45]

In a section of the *Historia Verdadera*, that was probably written

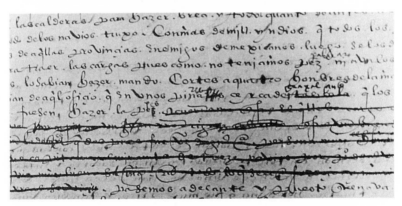

4. In the manuscript history of the Conquest of Mexico by Bernal Díaz del Castillo, the section describing the services of Juan Rodríguez Cabrillo has been crossed out with heavy ink lines. (Archivo General de Centro América.)

about 1564, Bernal Díaz said: "The man who had charge of the work and went as captain was Juan Rodríguez Cabrillo."[46] On a different occasion that same year Díaz said that Juan Rodríguez was "one of those whom Captain Hernando Cortés ordered to prepare pitch for building the *bergantines*."[47] His accounts seem to be the only ones that mention names.

Other chroniclers tell a similar story without giving the names of any of the men. According to Francisco López de Gómara, Cortés "sent to Vera Cruz for sails, rigging, nails, rope and other materials stored there from the ships he dismantled. And because they lacked pitch and it was neither known nor used in all the land, he ordered certain Spanish sailors to go and make it on a mountain near the city." Gómara's information came from Cortés, whose account is almost exactly the same.[48]

Seemingly, there were a number of ways to harvest pine resin, the most common involving a knife slash around the trunk. The

wound exuded a resinous substance which was collected in small earthern pots or, more crudely, in a hole cut into the trunk of the tree. The cuts in the wood healed very quickly, and the Spanish found the bleeding process could be prolonged by building a fire at the base of the tree to keep the resin warm and running.[49]

After the sap had stopped running, the trees were usually cut down and chopped into billets. These short pieces of wood were then placed in a crude furnace cut into the side of a hill, lined with tiles, and covered with more tiles or with sod. There was a shallow bowl at the bottom to collect the molten material and a gun barrel for use as a drain pipe. The wood was cooked for several days until the tar began to gather at the bottom of the furnace. This mass of hot pine tar was then drained off through the spout and collected into tubs or jars for final processing.

Bernal Díaz says the resin was cooked in great pots, probably the tar pots from the ships that brought the army from Cuba.[50] This was the final step in the process of making pitch. The boiling resin was mixed with animal fat—usually beef tallow—and then painted onto the hull of the freshly caulked ships.

The problem for Juan Rodríguez was this. There was no beef tallow in Mexico. The Aztecs had no herds of cattle, and the Spanish had brought none with them. Men accustomed to slaughter soon found a solution to the problem. The pitch makers butchered the bodies of dead Indians and rendered the human fat into tallow.[51]

Oviedo, the official chronicler of the Indies, gave the following account, quoting Licenciado Alonso Suaso:[52]

> This gentleman assured me that he had information which he knew to be true concerning the thirteen bergantines that were built in order to command the lake approaches and put the city under siege. They had no oil or tallow for tarring the boats. As a substitute they used human fat, from the hostile Indians they had killed, of whom there were a great

number besides those I have told you about. I have also heard other trustworthy gentlemen deny this and say it is false. But since it is common knowledge that the Indians would eat one another perhaps they also furnished such tallow for this most essential work, the construction of the bergantines. Not to make too much of the matter, I myself have known Christians to use such fat for medicinal purposes, and so I don't wonder that, lacking proper tar for their ships, they would use such an unguent and remedy in order to bring about a victory.

Gómara told a similar story. Though he was not an eyewitness, in later years he served as chaplain to Cortés and doubtless had much of his information from the commander of the expedition and other important officers. Here is Gómara's version:[53]

The bergantines were calked with tow and cotton, and from lack of tallow and oil . . . they were sealed, according to some, with human fat (not that men were killed for this purpose) taken from those who were killed in war. This was a cruel thing to do, repulsive to the Spaniards, but the Indians, who were inured to sacrifice, were cruel and cut open the bodies and extracted the fat.

Strangely enough, Bernal Díaz did not object to this story, as he did to so many of the other details of Gómara's history. If his uncharacteristic silence is something less than an absolute endorsement of the story, it seems nonetheless to be an indication that Díaz thought the incident to be completely unremarkable. It was so typical of what he saw and did in the conquest that he would not attempt to deny it.

Somewhat more than a century later the Dominican friar Thomas Gage lived in Guatemala, where Bernal Díaz had written his history. The descendants of Bernal Díaz, Juan Rodríguez, and many other conquistadors lived there, with stories of the conquest still current among them, still forming the basis for their many petitions for royal favor.[54]

Gage heard the human-tallow story and accepted it as true. This is considerably less than absolute proof that the story is true, for Gage seldom avoided an opportunity to slander the Spaniards or the Catholic church of which he was once a priest. In spite of all this, it appears that Gage's information was derived at least in part from family stories current in Guatemala in the 1620s, stories that were believed by the children and servants of the men who conquered Mexico.[55]

There is no way to be certain that Juan Rodríguez did or did not use human tallow to make pitch for the ships. But Oviedo thought he did, and Gómara thought so, too. Judging from their accounts, it seems likely that he used such tallow, but unlikely that the Spaniards collected it themselves. Instead, they probably relied on Indian workers, who did much of the lumbering and ship construction under Spanish supervision.

If true, the story tells a good deal about the character of Juan Rodríguez Cabrillo. He was, as we have seen, a young merchant and adventurer with a fair education. But he did not scruple to perform deeds that other men could scarcely bring themselves to discuss.

One man would say only that Juan Rodríguez had charge of work essential to the successful launching of the great inland fleet. Francisco López, who knew him in Cuba, said that Juan Rodríguez furnished "certain supplies and materials for the bergantines that they built." The reason Rodríguez was chosen for the work was that "he was a man of the sea and understood it all." The taciturn López also admitted that he was one of the conquistadors who worked with Rodríguez.[56]

Once the ships were built, they were immediately disassembled and brought to Texcoco for reassembly. Here they were caulked, and the seams were covered with that grisly brand of pitch.[57]

There may have been as many as 50,000 men—mostly Indian soldiers and laborers involved in transporting the ships from Tlaxcala, a trip that took the slow-moving column four days to make.

It was another four months before the ships were finished and in the water. Nonetheless, the work finally ended.[58]

On Sunday April 28, 1521, the thirteen bergantines floated slowly into Lake Texcoco, where a chaplain blessed the boats, while the ships' gunners fired a salute from the falconets mounted on the forecastles.[59]

The bergantines seem to have been about the same size as those four built and lost earlier in the conquest, perhaps thirty or more feet long and eight feet wide. There were twelve men to handle the oars plus another twelve with crossbows and muskets to do the fighting. Thus, most of the 194 musketeers and crossbowmen were assigned to the boats, where as Díaz said, they were safer and got more of the booty.[60]

Juan Rodríguez may have served in the boats, or he may have been one of the eighteen crossbowmen and musketeers assigned to Pedro de Alvarado's command. He may just as easily have been in the division commanded by Cristóbal de Olid or the one led by Gonzalo de Sandoval.[61] It is now impossible to know.

All that can be said with certainty is that Rodríguez fought well during the siege and that "he came out wounded," as his son testified later.[62] This may have happened when one of the bergantines was ambushed, and all the men either captured or wounded. It could have happened on another occasion when a ship was caught fast on stakes hidden under water and again all were wounded. It could have happened during the battle on the causeways or at some other time during the four month siege.[63] The details are unknown.

What is known is that the siege ended with a daring raid by the bergantines. In one quick stroke the Aztec leader Cuauhtemoc and all his entourage were captured, and the army surrendered unconditionally. The date was 13 August 1521.[64]

The flood tide of victory immersed the army in such a wave of riotous celebration that even the confirmed womanizer Bernal Díaz was scandalized. But this unbridled debauchery lasted only a brief time. When the men discovered how little treasure there was to divide and how small a portion Cortés alloted to them, jubilation turned to sullen discontent. Partly to end the grumbling and bickering among his troops, Cortés sent out a series of expeditions to conquer and occupy distant provinces. Juan Rodríguez played an important role in several of these new conquests.[65]

One of the areas under severe Indian pressure was the region south and east of Tepeaca, which the Spanish had renamed Segura de la Frontera, and placed under the command of Francisco de Orozco.[66] In October 1521, while other armies were being sent elsewhere, Orozco at Tepeaca was reinforced with a dozen horsemen, eighty other soldiers, and an army of Indian allies and ordered to subdue the rebellious Mixtecs in Oaxaca.[67]

Juan Rodríguez served in Orozco's campaign probably as one of Orozco's mounted officers. He appears to have grown more than moderately rich in the conquest of the Aztec capital, for an ordinary soldier could not afford a horse. However, the testimony on this point is unreliable.

Francisco Sánchez served with Rodríguez on the campaign and later testified briefly about it. The whereabouts of his original signed deposition is unknown, and the several known copies have some discrepancies.

In a copy of the original document which was sent to Spain in 1565 or thereabouts, Sánchez is quoted as saying that Juan Rodríguez served in the campaign "with his person, arms, and crossbow."[68] This wording is somewhat redundant and doubtless the result of a copyist's error.

The Sánchez testimony was copied again in 1617 from the original signed copy in Guatemala. Once more a copy was sent to Spain, while another was kept in the Guatemalan archives, where it is today. Both the Guatemalan copy and the Spanish copy of this later version say Juan Rodríguez served on the campaign "with his person, arms, and horse." This is the usual phrase for describing the military service of a hidalgo, which is the rank claimed by the heirs of Juan Rodríguez.[69]

According to Bernal Díaz, horses in the conquest "were worth their weight in gold."[70] What Díaz meant is that no ordinary *peón* in the ranks could afford the upkeep of a horse, much less the purchase price. Several other comrades testified that Juan Rodríguez served with Orozco in Oaxaca, but none mentioned his exact military status.[71] This means he was not one of the commanders, but he was certainly an officer of some rank.

Orozco's army surrounded the main body of Mixtec forces in the fortified city, Itzquintepec. Cut off from food and water and threatened by a well organized army of cocky veterans, the Mixtecs surrendered within a few days. Repeating the action taken in Mexico, Orozco founded a provincial capital at Ciudad Oaxaca and assigned men to garrison the place.[72]

Situated among fertile fields and laced with streams that were astonishingly rich in gold, Oaxaca was immensely attractive to the Spaniards. Several soldiers asked for encomiendas in the region and settled there. But Juan Rodríguez seems to have felt there were better things to come, richer provinces to conquer, more honors to be sought in battle.[73]

Cortés offered him an encomienda with a comfortable living, but Rodríguez refused it.[74] Instead, he enlisted in a new armed force that Pedro de Alvarado was leading into Tututepec, the coastal region just north of Tehuantepec.[75]

Having left Mexico early in 1522, Alvarado's army made a leisurely march through the countryside, stopping to collect reinforcements from among Orozco's idle troops in Oaxaca. With two hundred foot-soldiers, twenty horsemen, and a large contingent of Indian allies, Alvarado easily subdued the outlying towns. By the time his army reached Tututepec, the cacique and his people were ready to surrender without striking a blow.[76]

Then the plunder started, almost a rerun of the tragic scenes from the conquered city of Mexico. And Alvarado was hard to please. Even when the townspeople brought him rich presents of gold, and made a special set of solid gold stirrups for his horse, Alvarado was not sastisfied. Instead, he imprisoned the cacique on a pretext, extorted a great ransom and additional gifts worth more than thirty thousand pesos in gold, and then deliberately allowed the man to die in jail.[77]

Afterwards Alvarado gathered the settlers who had come with him from Oaxaca, founded a new town called Segura, and gave the surrounding villages to selected members of his army. Pausing to quell a minor rebellion among some of the soldiers who were left with nothing, he requisitioned a great quantity of gold for Cortés and the king and marched back to the capital.[78]

Dissatisfaction quickly spread among the settlers when Alvarado left. Many of them deserted Segura and returned to Oaxaca. As Spanish numbers dwindled, the native Mixes and Chontales staged a series of bloody raids on the remaining Spanish holdings. Alvarado and his army, including Rodríguez, returned to subdue the province once again. This time the Indian defeat was overwhelming. Settlers came back, and by mid-century Cuidad Oaxaca was said to be the second most important city in New Spain, though the population was largely Indian.[79]

During much of this time Cortés was in Pánuco on the east coast of Mexico with another army, attempting to hold the province against various Indian leaders and Spanish adventurers. Once the region seemed secure, he ordered Pedro de Alvarado and Cristóbal de Olid to organize expeditions for a march on Guatemala and Honduras. Both armies were ready by August 1523, Alvarado's being the larger with eighty horsemen, two hundred footsoldiers, and a considerable force of Indian allies.[80]

Juan Rodríguez, according to the testimony of his family and friends, served on this and later campaigns as an armed horseman and commander of a cuadrilla of crossbowmen. A fellow soldier, Juan de Valladolid, testified later that Juan Rodríguez was one of the principal officers or *capitanes* in Alvarado's army, and he probably was.[81]

Bernal Díaz said that he saw Juan Rodríguez serve as one of the captains of Pedro de Alvarado.[82] However, his reference is pretty clearly to the period around 1538 or 1539, when Díaz moved to Guatemala, and not to earlier service by Rodríguez as a captain.

The family of Juan Rodríguez later said various things about his rank, none of them very clear. In one place the son of Juan Rodríguez said, "He was held in great esteem by all the adelantados and the captains who were his associates on those campaigns" through Mexico and Guatemala.[83]

In another reference, the son of Juan Rodríguez made much of the fact that his father's close friend and associate in these same campaigns was Diego Sánchez de Ortega, the man whose sister Juan Rodríguez would marry.[84] Diego Sánchez in his own bid for royal patronage, claimed to have served somewhat earlier with Olid as "leader of a company of crossbowmen." Sánchez evidently did not lead his own company in Alvarado's army but instead seems to have served under Juan Rodríguez. Perhaps his future brother-in-law was one of those officers to whom Sánchez referred when he said, "I did everything the captains ordered."[85]

As in Mexico, the Spanish invasion forces were able to take advantage of ancient feuds between the Indian groups occupying Central America. While the Quichés and Tzutuhils put up a stubborn fight against the Spanish invader, the Cakchiquels sent troops and supplies to help Alvarado in the conquest of these historic enemies. Once this was accomplished Alvarado and the Cakchiquel lords found they had nothing in common. This time the Tzutuhils and Quichés joined Alvarado to crush Cakchiquel resistance.[86]

In addition an invisible ally was at work from within, sapping the resistance of the people who were about to come under Spanish attack. Scouts sent earlier by Alvarado to look at the country and perhaps even the ambassadors dispatched by Montezuma in his frantic quests for assistance had brought plague and smallpox to a population totally lacking immunity to these diseases.[87]

Perhaps a third of the Guatemalan highland population perished in fierce epidemics before Alvarado and his army set foot in the country. Many of the weakened survivors fell victim to minor ailments while Alvarado and his army were just beginning their occupation.[88]

The bulk of Alvarado's invasion army was made up of the same Tlaxcalan and Cholutecan auxiliaries who had made it possible for the Spanish to conquer Mexico. These Indian allies first fought alongside their Spanish overlords, then stayed to organize the cuadrillas, run the gold mines, and direct the encomiendas of the new Spanish ruling caste.[89]

Just as Alvarado completed preparations for the Guatemalan campaign, trouble broke out again in Pánuco, and it was not until December 1523 that the army finally began to march on Guatemala. His army consisted of twenty horsemen, three hundred footsoldiers, including a hundred and thirty crossbowmen and arquebusiers, and twenty thousand Tlaxcalan and Cholutecan allies.[90]

For at least a dozen years Juan Rodríguez followed Alvarado and his lieutenants through the Central American provinces. According to the later testimony of his son and his fellow soldiers, Juan Rodríguez helped "conquer every part of the provinces of Guatemala and Honduras." More than that, "Juan Rodríguez was one of those who conquered and settled the city of Guatemala and the province of Vera Paz, San Salvador, and Nicaragua."[91]

The fierce independence of the Indians, the mountainous terrain, the shifting alliances among Indians and Spaniards, and the insatiable Spanish thirst for wealth all help to explain why the conquest of the Central American provinces continued for such a long time. After a series of bloody battles Alvarado destroyed Utatlán, the Quiché capital, in April 1524. Accepting the surrender of the Quiché people, Alvarado had all the captives branded and sold into slavery.[92] The Quiché loss was doubly tragic because of the death of their leader Tecún Umán, who was probably the only man who might have saved what was left of Mayan civilization.[93]

Alvarado's army then marched on to the valley of Guatemala

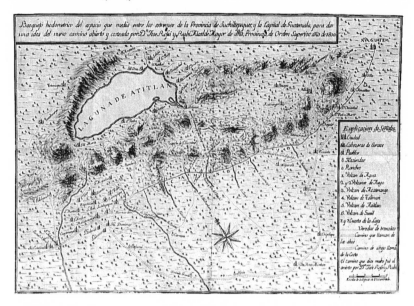

6. *This eighteenth century map shows the Laguna de Atitlán, where the Tzutuhil capital was located. (Museo de Libros Antiguos, Antigua, Guatemala.)*

where the Cakchiquels had their capital Iximché. Staying for a few days to rest his army in luxurious quarters at Iximché, he reorganized his forces and added new Cakchiquel recruits to the army. Financed by a levy on the Cakchiquel treasure houses, Alvarado next launched an assault on the Tzutuhil capital, Atitlán, which was situated on a nearly impregnable cliff above the lake of that name. His army defeated the Tzutuhiles in a pitched battle on the plain outside the city. The next morning Alvarado and his men marched on to occupy the hastily abandoned town. After a few more days of fighting the entire province was subdued.[94]

Returning to Iximché he received the surrender of the Tzutuhil leaders, demanding ransom in gold plus the usual levy of pretty girls for his troops. For himself Alvarado took the beautiful young wife of the Cakchiquel king, kept her husband in prison, and refused to release either of them until he was satisfied that no more gold could be extorted. By that time he was apparently tired of the lady anyway.[95]

Juan Rodríguez himself apparently took an Indian wife about this time, perhaps one of the extremely attractive Tzutuhil women who still beguile travelers with their delicate features and flashing smiles. Her name is unknown, but she lived with Juan Rodríguez for a number of years, bearing several children, among them at least three daughters. In 1548 these three daughters, nameless now, were listed as the wives of conquistadores. One was already a widow with several children of her own; another had three children; the third was childless, perhaps a newlywed.[96]

During the rest of the spring and summer Alvarado marched on through what was to become known as the province of San Salvador.[97] In one of their apparently endless bloody battles his army took the town of Acajutla, which had the only decent harbor in the province. But the whole campaign was indecisive, and in July 1524 the army came back to Iximché to regroup.[98]

On 25 July 1524, the feast of St. James, Alvarado made the conquest official. Iximché was declared to be the capital of Guatemala, with the name of Ciudad del Señor Santiago.[99] On 12 August a hundred men were registered as citizens. The name of Juan Rodríguez was twenty-ninth on the list.[100]

Chapter 3
Citizen of Santiago

SANTIAGO, THE NEW capital of Spanish Guatemala, was either a fine city or a spartan military encampment. There are two possible opinions on the matter. In his letter to Cortés, Pedro de Alvarado said the new capital looked like a typical Spanish town.[1] It may have done so, but the soldiers lived outside Iximché.

On the outskirts of the city, Alvarado gathered his army. The soldiers who had Indian mistresses, children, and servants built individual houses to accommodate them. Others bunked together in military fashion. Their dwellings were crude buildings, with forked poles at each corner to support the roof beams. Walls were made of cane plastered with mud, and there were grass roofs to keep out the rain. This was not so much a typical Spanish town as an army camp made up of temporary shelters, tents, and pavilions.[2]

Santiago remained a moving army camp for the next several years, while the army marched back and forth across Guatemala, San Salvador, Honduras, and Vera Paz, conquering and reconquering the country.

Within a few weeks of the founding of Santiago, Alvarado and his Cakchiquel friends were well on the way to becoming enemies. His constant attempts to extort more gold placed the Cakchiquel lords in such a quandary that they finally ordered a secret, nightime

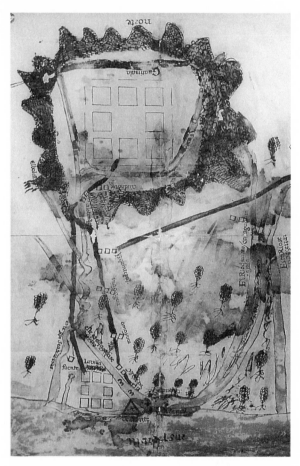

7. In this map of the late sixteenth century the scale is hopelessly distorted, and dimension indicates the importance of the town, rather than size or distance. The grid in the center shows the city established after the earthquake in 1541. The original site of the city is marked "ciudad vieja" at the foot of the Volcan de Agua. The port of Iztapa lies at the confluence of the rivers. The trees probably mark the locations of cacao groves. (Archivo General de Indias, Seville, Spain.)

evacuation of the capital. Once they had fled, Alvarado turned to the Tzutuhils and Quichés for help in catching and conquering his former allies.[3]

A large force under Pedro de Alvarado's brother went back to reoccupy San Salvador, and a provincial capital of that name was established in December 1524.[4] Meanwhile, Alvarado determined to abandon Iximché, and sometime during 1525 the capital was relocated at Olintepeque. After a few months the army moved again, and in March 1527, the capital was at Comalapa.[5]

During this time the army conquered vast stretches of country and seized huge quantities of goods and precious metals. Indians taken as prisoners were branded as slaves and sold, often to work in the placer mines, where many died from hunger and exposure.[6]

While all this was going on, Cortés with another army was trying to conquer Honduras. In 1525 Cortés ordered Pedro de Alvarado to come to his assistance. Arriving there early in 1526 with a small volunteer force, Alvarado found that his chief had returned to Mexico and expected him to follow.[7] We know Juan Rodríguez was with Alvarado on this campaign, as his friends and relatives later swore that he served in the conquest of Honduras.[8] Pedro de Alvarado went from Honduras to Mexico, and by September 1527 he was in Spain to answer charges of mismanagement and misappropriation, leaving his brother Jorge to direct affairs in Guatemala.[9]

The Spanish army in Guatemala was encamped at this time in the Chimaltenango Valley.[10] Some of the soldiers had been fighting more or less constantly for a decade. They were ready to build on the house lots, to till the fields, and to graze their animals on the pasture lands that settlers were supposed to have. In fact, they insisted on it.[11]

This semi-rebellion started with an attempt by the cabildo of Santiago to collect back taxes. The soldiers were indignant. They lacked all the benefits of city life but nonetheless were being asked to pay municipal taxes. It was too much. There seemed to be no end to the war. Three years after the formal founding of the city they were still wandering around the country, living in temporary shelters.

Many men simply said they would give it all up and return to Mexico City, where comrades were living in comfort. Moving swiftly to stem the tide of dissatisfaction, Jorge de Alvarado directed that a search be made for a permanent townsite.[12]

Until the sixteenth century the Spanish government had given little or no attention to urban planning. As a result many New World settlements were poorly located, and some had moved several times from their original sites. Finally, in 1523 a series of new ordinances emerged, outlining basic principles for town planning in the New World.[13]

Jorge de Alvarado at first appears not to have been overly concerned about these new royal decrees. Instead, he directed the new location for Santiago should have the same attributes as the townsites in the islands and in New Spain.[14] But during the next few weeks someone brought the new rules to his attention, and he appointed a committee of ten or so to inspect and report on the two most likely places for a permanent city. A dispute arose almost immediately.[15]

Hernando de Alvarado, brother of the captain general, urged that the city be located at Tianguecillo, an old Indian town that still contained many habitable buildings. He gave several reasons for his choice, the most prophetic being that the other site was "a land of volcanoes and sandstone, where the earth trembles greatly because of the fire belching from the volcanoes."[16]

This other place, Hernando de Alvarado's "land of volcanoes," was an ancient village site in the Valley of Almolonga. Firewood, timber, stone and fresh water were available in abundance at Almolonga. In contrast to the broad plains surrounding Tianguecillo, the Almolonga site was at the very base of an active volcano, with others in the immediate vicinity. But the surrounding fields were lush and green, and the original inhabitants had abandoned the place. Gonzalo Dovalle, *alcalde ordinario*, gave the view of most of the citizens when he said: "In the opinion of all the Spaniards and all the natives this is the best place in Guatemala."[17]

So the order was given, and the city was established in the Valley of Almolonga on 22 November 1527.[18] Four days later Juan Rodríguez and twenty other men were received for the second time as citizens of Santiago. However, one of the city officials, Sancho de Barahona, was not eligible to hold office, and questions arose about the legality of all the proceedings in which he had taken part.[19]

Consequently, on 18 March 1528, after new civic officials were duly elected and installed, Juan Rodríguez and a number of others were made citizens of Santiago for the third time. They were also officially given the *solares* or house lots that had been assigned to them when the city was laid out, as well as the agricultural and grazing lands each had taken in the valley.[20]

It is not possible to locate these lots and farm lands now with any precision. Early records have been lost, and the townsite itself was only recently rediscovered.[21] Nonetheless a good deal is known about this city which Juan Rodríguez helped to found.

Santiago in Almolonga was built around a central plaza, which had at one corner ruins of a stone-paved ball court from the Indian city that once occupied the site.[22] The governor's house was on the south side of the plaza, the uphill side. The church, soon to become the cathedral, was built around the corner, facing the plaza. Most of the important citizens also had their homes in the area south of the plaza. If we can believe the description left by Juan Rodríguez, this was a district of "fine homes." The cathedral and bishop's house, he said, were better than any in the New World, except those in Mexico City.[23]

In spite of this glowing tribute by one of its leading citizens, the city was somewhat less grand than might be imagined. While public buildings were usually of stone construction, most of the homes were built of adobe. Some walls were nothing more than a lattice work of reeds plastered with mud. Most roofs were thatched.[24]

As a horseman Juan Rodríguez received a larger allocation of land than footsoldiers received. The cavalryman's *solar*, called a *caballeria*, measured six hundred by three hundred feet. That of a footsoldier or peón was called a *peonia* and measured only three hundred by a hundred and fifty feet. Similarly, the farm and grazing land for a cavalryman was six hundred paces wide along the riverfront by fourteen hundred paces long, and this was the grant Rodríguez received.[25]

After a few months of settling in, many of the citizens began to demand clear title to their lands, claiming that their service as citizens during the previous five years satisfied the residence requirement of the law. Members of the *cabildo*, or city council, were not certain what to do. Ultimately they decided to give a conditional title to every citizen, with a clause stating that the five-year residency requirement must be satisfied if that had not yet been done. Juan Rodríguez received conditional title to his city property and rural land on 18 January 1529.[26]

Rodríguez also held several encomiendas that eventually produced income making him one of the richest men in Guatemala. The most valuable of these encomiendas was Cobán, which he and Diego Sánchez de Ortega shared jointly with Sancho de Barahona.

Cobán lies in a province which the Spaniards at that time called *Tezulutlán*, Land of War, because the inhabitants simply refused to surrender. When the province was later handed over to Bartolomé de Las Casas and his fellow Dominicans, the priests used peaceful means to convert the Indians and changed the name to *Vera Paz*, True Peace.[27]

In 1530 an army under Diego de Alvarado invaded the province and partially subdued it. Not much is known about this expedition, beyond the fact that Cobán was one of the prizes of war. The Dominicans always insisted that Cobán and Vera Paz were never really pacified. Nevertheless, there is ample evidence to show that Rodríguez, Sánchez, and Barahona lived there for several months of each year and enjoyed good incomes from their *encomiendas*.[28]

The earliest evidence comes from Diego Sánchez himself, who testified on 28 July 1531: "I hold and possess in the name of his majesty the pueblo of Xocotenango and Acatenango with half of the pueblo called Cobán."[29]

In April 1530 Pedro de Alvarado returned from his long journey to Mexico and Spain. He had in his possession a royal appointment as adelantado of Guatemala. With this in hand he was completely independent of his old commander Cortés. Among his entourage was a scholarly priest who would soon be made bishop of Santiago, Francisco de Marroquín.[30]

Some years later Marroquín gave a deposition in which he recalled that shortly after his arrival in Guatemala Diego de Alvarado conquered Vera Paz. According to Bishop Marroquín: "It is well known that the adelantado gave the town of Cobán as an encomienda to Juan Rodríguez and his [future] brother-in-law Diego Sánchez de Ortega."[31]

Surrounded as it was by hostile Indians, Cobán nonetheless had something the Spaniards wanted—rich gold placers.[32] In fact the gold is what led Alvarado to send an army there.

In July 1529 the cabildo of Santiago took official note of the fact that Diego Sánchez had made the first rich gold discovery in the region. A few months later the *cabildo* forbade any citizens to go out looking for gold, since their services were required for military campaigns. Diego Sánchez "and his companions" were exempted from this rule.[33]

It is not difficult to imagine Diego Sánchez and his companions, Juan Rodríguez and Sancho de Barahona, leading a cuadrilla of Indian slaves into Tezulutlán. With their *bateas*—large bowls with handles projecting from the sides—the Indians panned the streams for gold[34] and struck it rich. Very rich. Their triumphal return to Santiago nearly coincided with the return of the newly named adelantado. Pedro de Alvarado, who was always looking for more gold and more adventure, then sent Diego de Alvarado to conquer the area and subsequently granted Cobán to the three companions.

Much of this is speculation, since the *cabildo* records after 1530 are missing.[35] But the facts fit the story. Sánchez and Rodríguez

ꜰ Sacaſſe oʒo de otra manera En los ꜱꝛios ⱬ ⱥrroyos, o lagunas de

8. *The typical gold mine in sixteenth-century Guatemala was a placer, where Indians panned for gold, using bateas, or bowls with long handles. (Oviedo MS, HM 177, Huntington Library.)*

came to Mexico with Narváez, were imprisioned along with Barahona and later released by Cortés, who rewarded them for their loyalty.[36] That rich encomienda of Cobán was another reward from an equally grateful adelantado. The impressive gold discovery and the subsequent conquest, coming so soon after Marroquín's arrival, explain why the bishop could remember that grant so vividly thirty years later.

Juan Rodríguez lost little time in exploiting the encomienda. A Mexican Indian named Alonso Rodríguez was his overseer. This man later testified under oath about the early days, saying that he lived in Cobán for three years collecting tributes for Juan Rodríguez. He collected as tribute payments ornamental feathers, chickens, corn, and chiles. Alonso Rodríguez saw some of the Indians go to work in the mines Juan Rodríguez operated at Tecucistlán, a town whose environs were immediately adjacent to the region of Cobán.[37]

Whether these mines were the same as the ones owned by Juan

Rodríguez on the Rio de Uzpantlán is uncertain; nonetheless, the slaves in the Uzpantlán placers received their supplies from Cobán.

9. *The Indians lived in wooden huts, not greatly different from the dwellings of sixteenth century Spanish peasants. (Oviedo MS, HM 177, Huntington Library.)*

The Indians of Cobán also prepared food and cared for the living quarters of his cuadrillas in the gold placers. For every Indian who wielded a batea in the placers, three or four more were needed to dig gravel, to carry supplies, to prepare food and manage the living quarters. Since each cuadrilla numbered eighty or ninety people,[38] Rodríguez could very well have had several hundred Indian slaves and servants working in his gold diggings, an enormous burden for the people of Cobán.[39]

Another Mexican Indian, called both Juan Ximínez and Juan Xúarez in the records, later said through an interpreter: "He served in the cuadrilla of Juan Rodríguez in the mines, taking out gold.

He saw how the Indians of Cobán served Juan Rodríguez as his very own servants. They brought him beans, corn, chiles, and salt, as well as earthenware pots and griddles and bowls for the use of the Indians who worked in the mines."[40]

When Xúarez or Ximínez served in the mines near Cobán, much of the surrounding country was still unconquered. Through his interpreter he said: "He heard the Indians of Cobán say that the people of Tezulutlán kept pestering them to stop working for the Spaniards, threatening them, and calling them women, and saying they would have to kill them."[41]

Another Mexican Indian, called simply Juan had an even closer relationship with Juan Rodríguez than did Alonso Rodríguez, overseer of the cuadrilla. Juan said: "He was a *vecino* of Cobán in those days. He saw all of the *vecinos* paying tribute to Juan Rodríguez Cabrillo . . . in the form of corn, chickens, honey, chiles, and beans for the slaves that Juan Rodríguez Cabrillo had in the mines. The witness himself paid no tribute as a *vecino* of the town because he had charge of the town and lived there with Juan Rodríguez."[42]

It was common practice for encomenderos to live part of the year on their encomiendas and give them personal supervision. Often this meant moving a good part of the household to the encomienda. Bernal Díaz reported that he even took his own bed when he went to visit his distant properties.[43]

According to Bishop Marroquín there were a hundred Spaniards in Tezulutlán in the early years, enough men to conquer and occupy the country "almost up to the North Sea." Most of the Spaniards left when Alvarado began to prepare his armada for the trip to Peru, but according to Marroquín, the country was not totally abandoned.[44] Rodríguez, for one, still lived there part of the year, perhaps drawing gold from the mines, but certainly getting materials for the fleet he soon began to build on the Mar del Sur, the Pacific coast of Guatemala.[45]

In the summer of 1532, with news arriving daily about the fantastically wealthy conquests being made in Peru, Alvarado began to assemble a fleet on the Mar del Sur, intending to sail for Peru. On 1 September 1532 he wrote to the king describing the eight-ship armada he had just finished assembling.[46]

The flagship was a galleon of three hundred *toneles* called *San Cristóbal*. Another, called *Santa Clara* was a hundred and sixty *toneles*. Two others were slightly smaller. There were three caravels, sixty *toneles* and smaller, and a fifty-ton tender to serve the whole fleet.[47] Several years later in an unusually frank moment Alvarado confessed that these were poor ships—*flacos navíos* he called them.[48]

It is not certain who built the ships. Alvarado reported only that he had "a great number of carpenters, caulkers, and masters" to help with the work. Juan Rodríguez probably had little or nothing to do with the construction of this fleet. This is clear from his 1541 description of Alvarado's ships. While referring to these ships and describing his work with Alvarado's second armada, Rodríguez gave no indication that he might have had a role in building the earlier fleet.[50]

The probable reason for this is that Juan Rodríguez was on his way to Spain to find himself a wife. The gold discoveries at Cobán had made him rich, and his partner, Diego Sánchez de Ortega, had an unmarried sister back home in Spain. The girl was Beatríz Sánchez de Ortega. Her father was Alonso Sánchez de Ortega, citizen of Seville.[51] Nothing is known about her early life, except that her education did not include learning how to write.[52]

Details do not exist, but we can imagine that Juan Rodríguez stayed in Spain for as long as a year, courting Beatríz Sánchez, visiting the scenes of his youth, and purchasing supplies to take back to his estates in Guatemala. He probably also bought sails, rigging, iron work, instruments, tools, medicines, and other things for the ship he intended to build when he returned to Guatemala. He doubtless also purchased great quantities of material for trade with the army in Peru. He also certainly visited old friends and handled business and legal matters for himself and his comrades back in Guatemala.

Rich though he was at the time of his marriage, Juan Rodríguez was well past thirty, tough and rugged. And if he looked like the other scarred and wounded conquistadores, he was not very handsome either. In his own account of the city of Santiago, Rodríguez identified some of his friends and neighbors by their wounds and deformities. Blas Fernández was "the blind man," and Francisco Flores was "the cripple."[53] One young woman who came to Santiago from Spain to find a rich husband, was shocked when she saw what they looked like. According to her: "They look like they have escaped from hell, they are so badly maimed. Some have lost a foot, others a hand; others have no ears; others have one eye; others half a face. The handsomest has been scarred once or twice or three times."[54] Even Alvarado himself was crippled, with one leg several inches shorter than the other as a result of a battlefield injury.[55] Even so, Alvarado had no trouble finding a second young wife. Rodríguez seems to have fared just as well.

Although the marriage record has not yet come to light, there is abundant testimony that allows us to establish a date with near certainty. On 19 May 1552 Bishop Marroquín said that Juan Rodríguez and his wife Beatríz arrived in Santiago nineteen years earlier, having just come from Spain where they were married. To confirm the accuracy of his recollection, the bishop said he had known Juan Rodríguez for twenty-two years—ever since the bishop first arrived in Santiago in April 1530.[56]

In his depositions and correspondence Bishop Marroquín was always precise and accurate, particularly about dates. Moreover, there is a good deal of support for his recollection of the time Rodríguez and his bride arrived in Santiago. Gara López said in May 1552 that Juan and Beatríz had been married in Spain about twenty years earlier. Gonzalo Ortíz said at the same time that he had known both for about twenty years—since the time Juan Rodríguez had brought Beatríz back from Spain as his wife.[57]

Some of the most useful evidence comes from Alvaro de Paz, *mayordomo* for Alvarado. Paz said he first arrived in Santiago about

December 1533 or January 1534. Juan Rodríguez and his wife Beatríz were already living there. The testimony of these witnesses seems to establish the fact that Juan and Beatríz were married in Spain in late 1532 or early 1533. They arrived in Santiago by summer, 1533, and settled down in the house Juan Rodríguez owned there.[58]

Very likely the Rodríguez home was a large and complex establishment, a *familia* or *casa poblada* in the phrase of the day. Conquistadores who had the means were expected to provide food, clothing, and shelter for a vast assemblage of relatives, servants, distantly related family members, and friends less fortunate than themselves. This numerous household included natural children borne by Indian wives before the arrival of the wife from Spain, poor relatives, impoverished gentlemen, military aides, dependent maiden ladies (either orphans or children of other conquistadores), protégés, friends, Indian servants, and slaves. When the oldest son married, his wife and children were also expected to live at home.[59]

The *casa poblada* was not a casual arrangement to be adopted or abandoned at will, but one that could be enforced by law. In 1527 a few of the conquistadores planned to leave the army and the city in their disgust at the failure to find a permanent location for the Guatemalan capital. When the others learned about this, they immediately petitioned the cabildo to force the men to stay and support their *casas pobladas*.[60]

Under ordinary conditions support of a *casa poblada* or *mucha familia* was considered to be a great honor, and the larger the establishment, the greater the prestige of the man who owned it. The status of a hidalgo and a caballero was gained not only by acquiring riches but by acquiring a reputation for doing the things a hidalgo was expected to do.[61]

All these things are implied in the carefully worded statements of friends and relatives about the merits and services of Juan Rodríguez. In a lawsuit in 1542 Beatríz, his wife, said: "Juan Rodríguez is a married resident of this city. He has a wife and children there and his *casa poblada*." Many of his friends confirmed this. Cristóbal Rodríguez Picon said: "Juan Rodríguez is married in this city and this witness has seen that he maintains his *casa poblada* and wife and children there." Diego López de Villanueva said: "Juan Rodríguez has been married for a long time. He has his wife and children and his *casa poblada* in this city. Whenever the need arose he has gone on wars and campaigns with his own person, his arms, and his horse."[62]

Cristóbal Salvatierra said the family included both legitimate and natural children.[63] Nícolas López said: "He always kept his house in this city of Guatemala with a wife and children and a great family .... He was held in high esteem and treated as a person of honor."[64] Pedro de Ovide said: "Juan Rodríguez Cabrillo supported his house and family in this city as an honored man with a wife and children."[65] Alvaro de Paz, the *mayordomo* of Alvarado said: "Juan Rodríguez supported in this city a house, a wife and sons, and a family" in the manner of a *hidalgo*, as claimed by his son.[66] The son said: "Juan Rodríguez supported his house, wife, and family, and in the Conquest he served His Majesty with his person, his weapons, his horse, and his retainers, and this was the way he was esteemed in these parts."[67]

The house itself, though it does not exist today, was very likely a "courtyard house" with a central patio. In such a building the visitor entered from the street, walking through the house to the patio, which had colonnades on three or four sides. Building materials were wood, stone, adobe, and plaster. Roofs were sometimes made of tile, though shake or thatch roofs were more common in Santiago. Buildings like the Rodríguez house had many rooms, but the dwellings were still crowded because so many people lived there.[68]

The establishment was supported largely by Indians. Those in Cobán furnished Rodríguez with chickens, maize, chiles, honey, beans, salt, earthenware pots and griddles, and ornamental feathers and in addition sent servants to his house in Santiago.[69] His encomienda at Xicalapa also furnished food. In 1549, after tributes had been drastically reduced, two Indians from the village were obliged to fish in the sea three days each week and deliver their catch to his family.[70] Comitlán delivered two dozen chickens and four dozen clay pots and griddles each year, and furnished two Indian servants as well.[71] Xocotenango delivered sixty *mantas* every four months and kept the Rodríguez house constantly supplied with three Indian servants.[72]

The tributes before 1549 were probably at least double these amounts. In addition, most encomenderos went out on regular slave raids to the unconquered Indian villages and brought back captives to work on their *milpas* or in the mines. There were enormous numbers of slaves, both adults and children. In 1529, for example, four hundred men and four hundred women were sent by the Cakchiquels to do construction work in Santiago. A like number worked in Alvarado's gold placers. These figures do not include the "tribute of boys and girls," which did not end until 1536,[73] nor do they include the slaves who worked for individual encomenderos. Rodríguez could very well have had several hundred Indian slaves in his cuadrillas.

The real money crop of that time was cacao. Xicalapa furnished 250 *xiquipiles* per year in 1549, but that was after the *tasaciones* had been reduced. According to the returns filed by his wife, Juan Rodríguez received five hundred per year in 1542 from the same pueblo.[74] He may also have had other tributary pueblos, such as "San Pablo Costa de Capotitán where there is much cacao and cloth."[75]

The pueblos of Tacuba and Jumaitepeque, which Rodríguez received in December 1540 were also claimed by Francisco de la Cueva. Rodríguez did not receive income from these pueblos during his lifetime, but the wording of the cedula indicates the limitless demands an encomendero could make on his tributaries. This document declared that the pueblos were totally the property of Rodríguez: "All the people must serve you in your house and estates and farms"

just as they had served the previous encomendero.[76] The same provision is found in the *cedula de encomienda* for the pueblo of
Cobán,[77] whose Indians did in fact work in his mines and farms,
as appears from the testimony of people who saw them do so.

All this made Juan Rodríguez a rich man, but just how rich we
do not know. In 1542 one man testified that Juan Rodríguez had
an annual income of 500 pesos from the repartimiento that he con-
trolled in Santiago, "while other citizens of this city just as honorable
as he receive much less." Lieutenant Governor Francisco de la Cueva,
his opponent in a lawsuit, claimed that Juan Rodríguez received
"more than seven hundred *pesos de oro de minas* in rent every single
year."[78] While these may be exaggerations, the sums are huge. Difficult to relate to present day money values, they still indicate that
Rodríguez had an enormous income from his encomiendas.

As soon as he returned from Spain, Juan Rodríguez began investing
huge sums in a Peruvian trading venture. In the Guatemalan port
of Acajutla he built a ship named *Santiago*. By the time it was finished
the vessel alone cost him three thousand *castellanos de oro de
minas*.[79] Pedro de Alvarado was just then assembling his own fleet
to sail for Peru, and perhaps for a trial run Rodríguez sailed down
to the Gulf of Fonseca, taking important messages to the adelantado. But Rodríguez was becoming cautious about involvement with
Alvarado, and when Alvarado sailed for Peru, Rodríguez returned
to Guatemala.[80] The prudence of this move was obvious a few
months later, in August 1534, when Alvarado returned home
without a fleet, having sold six of his ships to Diego de Almagro.[81]

The astonishing riches of Peru attracted merchants and investors
from all parts of the Spanish empire. Doubtless working with his
father-in-law, Juan Rodríguez brought a shipload of goods from Spain
for the Peruvian market and sent it with his cuadrillas to Acajutla
where the *Santiago* was lying at the dock. Spaniards in Peru were
consuming supplies at an enormous rate, paying inflated prices with
Inca gold. Rodríguez expected a profit of no less than five thousand
castellanos de oro de minas. The ten horses and mares would bring

twelve or thirteen hundred pesos apiece from the Spanish soldiers fighting in Peru.[82]

When Alvarado's remaining vessels rode into the harbor at Acajutla, the adelantado saw the *Santiago* in the river, loaded to the gunwales and ready to sail. Here were the makings of a new fleet and supplies for a new army. He promptly sent a message to Domingo del Castillo, master of the ship, saying he had taken title to the vessel. Before Rodríguez knew what was happening, Castillo had the ship at sea under Alvarado's orders, exploring new regions of the Mar del Sur.[83]

It would be interesting to know what Rodríguez said to the adelantado when he learned the ship was gone. Surely he was angry, because he would have made a good deal of money selling his horses and goods in Peru. Rodríguez probably demanded reimbursement. Alvarado doubtless recounted his past generosity and promised Rodríguez an ample share of any new discoveries made by the fleet. Rodríguez seemingly accepted this offer, since he had little choice, but just to be on the safe side he decided to put it all in writing.

Rodríguez wrote to Castillo, saying that the ship had been taken without his permission and that the master should definitely not surrender ownership of the vessel. Two years passed before *Santiago* returned. By that time it was in such poor shape that Rodríguez sold it to Alvarado for a hundred and fifty *pesos de oro de minas*. His claim for damage to the ship and the loss of profits on his goods remained unsettled, but by this time Alvarado had great plans for new conquests in which Rodríguez was to receive a share.[85]

There was, for one thing, the promise of a new encomienda in Honduras, partly a payment for military service but also a partial payment for the lost ship and goods. The new grant came about in 1536, when Alvarado led an armed force into Honduras and Higueras to help reinforce the beleagured Spanish outposts there. Juan Rodríguez was one of the captains in this force, as is seen from a document signed by Alvarado at Puerto de Caballos on 20 July 1536, when it looked as though the campaign was almost over.[86]

In this document Juan Rodríguez was made a citizen of Gracias á Dios, though that new capital was not yet established. He was also named encomendero of "the pueblo of Teota and Cotela, with all its señores, Indians, barrios, and fields."[87] Within a few weeks Alvarado sailed again for Spain, while some of the army returned home and others marched on to complete the conquest. It is not clear whether Juan Rodríguez was one of those who went home or whether he stayed to finish the conquest and take possession of his new encomiendas.[88] Teota and Cotela are not listed in any of the later testimony about his extensive holdings. However, the document marks one important change. From this time on Juan Rodríguez added Cabrillo to his name. The repartimiento of 1536 seems to be the earliest document to use this form.

Before leaving for Spain, Alvarado made another series of arrangements with Rodríguez. One of the reasons for Alvarado's new trip to Spain was to secure royal approval for his most recent plan to build a fleet and sail for the Moluccas. Since Juan Rodríguez Cabrillo had so much experience in building ships, Alvarado appointed him *justicia mayor* of Acajutla and ordered him to build the new fleet in that port city just south of Santiago.[89] Here is the way Juan Rodríguez described the incident in August 1541: "It has been perhaps six years since the *Señor Adelantado* went to Spain, and at the time he left he ordered that I should build him an armada while he was in Spain, and so I built it."[90]

Wealth, honors, estates, a new wife—Juan Rodríguez Cabrillo seemed suddenly to have most of the things he had come to the Indies for. He needed only a son to inherit his name and estates and make the years of conquest worthwhile. Beatríz took care of that matter very nicely by bearing him two sons. The oldest was called Juan Rodríguez Cabrillo after his father. The other was named Diego Sánchez de Ortega after his maternal uncle.[91]

The children were baptized and confirmed in the cathedral church at Santiago, where the good prelate performed the rites himself.[92] The original records have long since disappeared, but there is evidence that helps to establish their approximate dates of birth.

In a statement probably prepared during the first days of January 1564 the younger Juan Rodríguez Cabrillo said he was then twenty-eight years old, and a number of people testified that they knew this to be the case.[93] On 12 February 1579 Juan Rodríguez Cabrillo the younger said he was forty-three years old and a native-born resident of Santiago.[94] These two statements seem to place the date of his birth between 1 January and 12 February 1536.

Concerning his brother Diego Sánchez de Ortega, we know next to nothing, except that Diego was born after his brother Juan and before 9 August 1543, when his name appeared in a legal document. As his mother stated then, there were no other legitimate children.[95] It is possible that the two boys were twins, though the evidence on this point is vague and inconclusive. In fact, it consists of nothing more than a statement by the notary in 1543 that Juan and Diego seemed to be about the same age.[96]

Charged with building a huge fleet for the adelantado, the new *justicia mayor* of Istapa, Juan Rodríguez Cabrillo, began to spend a good deal of time in that steamy port on the Mar del Sur. His wife, children, and other members of his family also lived there from time to time, watching Rodríguez govern the town and direct the shipyard where Alvarado's great new armada was under construction.

Chapter 4
Merchant and Shipbuilder

ABOUT FIFTEEN LEAGUES due south of Santiago, where the river Michatoya meanders into the Pacific Ocean, lay the sixteenth-century fishing village of Iztapa. Little more than an open roadstead and partially blocked by a huge sand bar, it was still the best seaport on the coast of the Mar del Sur.[1]

The shoreline was steep, the tides were fast and strong and the channel changed frequently during the flood season.[2] The anchorage was so hazardous that two ships from Alvarado's first fleet were lost there during the winter storms of 1533.[3] Nonetheless, the port had a number of redeeming qualities. The river was navigable for some distance inland. There was an abundance of good timber nearby, as well as pita fiber for making cables and rigging. Neighboring villages could provide food at low cost. While the port was hazardous during stormy weather, it was perfectly safe most of the time.[4] And it was the only seaport in Guatemala.[5]

All these factors combined to make it a natural site for Alvarado's shipyard. Alvaro de Paz is supposed to have described the riverbanks near the port of Iztapa as "a larger and better location for a shipyard than anywhere else in the Indies."[6]

Further down the coast in San Salvador was another port, equally open to the weather. This was Acajutla, seaport for the cities of

Trinidad and San Salvador. A considerably less than perfect harbor, Acajutla featured a dangerous reef across the entrance to the bay, and ships stopped there only with great risk. Yet, interior roads in San Salvador were so poor that Acajutla was the only port where Salvadoran cacao and other produce could be loaded for shipment to Peru and New Spain.[7] In fact, this was the port where Juan Rodríguez rigged and loaded his ship *Santiago* in 1534, just before Alvarado seized the vessel for his own use.[8]

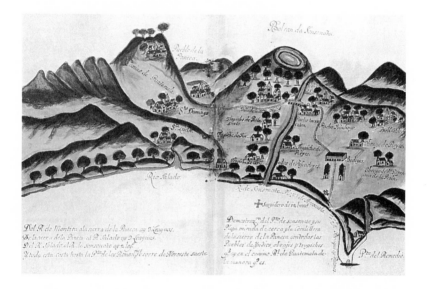

10. The beach at Acajutla, where the fleet of Alvarado was prepared for the great voyage of discovery. (Derrotero del Mar del Sur, HM 918, Huntington Library.)

The Guatemalan shipyard was located at Girabaltique, a short distance upriver from Iztapa. Here new ships were constructed and older vessels careened and refitted for Alvarado's great voyage of exploration.[9] A report sent to the king in 1589 said that in former times twenty ships were built in these yards, an apparent reference to Alvarado's first and second fleets, which numbered seven and thirteen vessels respectively.[10]

Alvarado's first efforts at shipbuilding were not very satisfactory. The labor force of Spanish and Indian workmen was not fully trained, and the materials were inferior to those available in Spain.[11] Consequently, when Alvarado sold his first ships to Pizarro and Almagro in 1534, he was unloading a fleet that was not really seaworthy. While he complained at the time that it was a forced sale at a low price,[12] he later confessed that the vessels were *flacos navíos*— poor ships.[13]

It was a common complaint. Shipbuilding in the sixteenth century was more an art than a science. The outcome of any construction project depended as much on the skill and experience of the shipwrights and the availability of materials as on the wishes of the owner or designer. One ship captain complained that "some ships start in the yards as small ones and end as large ones, while others start as large ships and end as small ones."[14] Ships were seldom built according to plan, and no two ships ever came out looking exactly alike. In Alvarado's first fleet one ship was a huge three hundred *toneles*, while the others were only half that size or less.[15]

The large vessel had much too deep a draft for the shallow anchorages in Guatemala.[16] When Alvarado planned his second fleet, he resolved to make the ships much smaller. In November 1535, he wrote to the Real Consejo de Indias that he was about to begin construction of three new galleons and one galley in his shipyard. Each vessel would be rated at a hundred tons and all would be equipped with oars "so they can sail in and out wherever they wish regardless of the currents and contrary winds." He had experienced sailors, skilled carpenters, and shipwrights ready to build the ships, and he expected to have the vessels ready for launching within a year.[17]

However, the plans could not be followed. Alvarado's expedition to Honduras and a disastrous fire in Santiago upset internal affairs in Guatemala and delayed ship construction for a year or so,[18] but the three galleons were eventually built and the galley as well.[19] Indian *cuadrillas* were again pressed into service, providing timber, iron, sails, cable, tar and pitch, and huge quantities of food for the shipwrights and black slaves working in the shipyard and for the Indian slaves engaged in producing raw materials.[20]

It was not easy to keep the work running smoothly. *Mayordomo* Alvaro de Paz found it was nearly a full time job locating and shipping the materials Juan Rodríguez ordered for the project.[21] Much of the timber was close at hand, but other supplies had to be brought from the interior provinces. The reliable Indian allies from Tlaxcala and Mexico were pressed into shameful servitude, "cutting and trimming timber and making pitch and rope and charcoal in order to build the ships and galleys and fustas." As they later complained to the king, this was a "greater burden than that endured by the children of Israel."[22]

Francisco de Torres, one of the first conquistadores and settlers in Guatemala, recalled seeing the Indians of Cobán bring pitch to Iztapa for the ship Juan Rodríguez was building for himself in the yards nearby.[23] But few liked to remember the shameful side of this story.

Istapa was a miserable town. The sailors and workmen eventually grew rebellious in their makeshift quarters, far removed from the comforts of the capital. Finally, Paz and Rodríguez sent out pressgangs and rounded up dozens of Indian women and girls to serve the men as bed companions, cooks, and laundresses.[24] Bishop Marroquín protested to no avail about "this most abominable affair," finally writing to ask the king to intervene. But by the time his letter arrived in Spain, the fleet was nearly ready to sail.[25]

Of the thirteen ships that eventually made up the armada, only a part actually belonged to Alvarado. Several of the vessels were owned by other conquistadores, who hoped to make money carrying supplies for the expedition and selling trade goods up and down the coast. Juan Rodríguez built and owned his own vessel.[26] Another was owned by Antonio Diosdado and a third by the partners Santos de Figueroa, Alvaro de Paz, and a third investor named

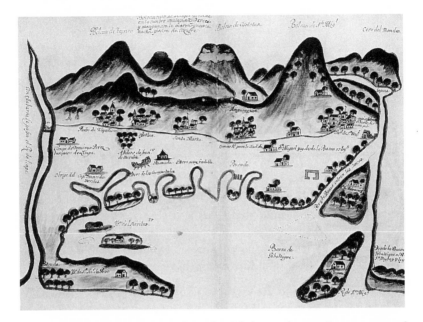

11. *Seventeenth-century view of the shipyard at Gibaltigue, where vessels were constructed for the Mar del Sur.*

Cisneros. Although they had religious names, these three vessels were usually known as *Juan Rodríguez, Diosdado,* and *Figueroa,* following the custom of the day in calling a vessel after its owner or master.[27] Other ships in the fleet were also called by secular names *Anton Hernández, Alvar Nuñez.*[28] Hernández was one of the pilots or masters, but Nuñez was part owner of his ship, along with Pedro de Alvarado.[29]

It is not clear whether the names of the vessels were actually painted on the hulls, as is now the case, but there is abundant evidence that sixteenth-century ships flew the banners and ensigns of their owners and their religious patrons.[30] Thus, each ship in the fleet Cortés built to besiege Mexico City carried one banner with the royal arms and another bearing the name of the vessel.[31] Similarly, *San Salvador*, the new ship owned by Juan Rodríguez "flew the banner of an *almirante* from the foretopmast as *almirantes* of the sea are accustomed to do."[32] The vessel also flew the arms of Alvarado and later those of Mendoza. The religious banner probably showed a crucifix and perhaps the words San Salvador.[33]

When Alvarado returned from Spain in 1539, he brought with him huge supplies of sails, rigging, ironwork, anchors, and other materials for the fleet. These were landed at Puerto de Caballos, and thousands of Indian conscripts were then forced to build a road and carry the supplies overland to the shipyard at Iztapa. It was a labor of many months, and whole regions were depopulated to organize cuadrillas, build the road, and transport the cargo from the Atlantic to the Pacific side of the country.[34]

Bartolomé de las Casas later wrote a brief but graphic description of the whole shipbuilding process:[35]

> He killed an infinite number of people in building the ships; from the north to the south sea a hundred and thirty leagues the Indians carried anchors of three and four *quintales*, which cut furrows into the shoulders and loins of some of them. And he carried in the same way much artillery on the shoulders of these sad, naked people; and I saw many loaded with artillery on those anguished roads. He broke up homes, taking the women and girls and giving them to the soldiers and sailors in order to keep them satisfied and bring them into his fleets.

In assembling his fleet Alvarado purchased several older vessels that were doubtless refitted with the supplies newly brought from Spain. He bought two of these in 1535, both galleons, plus a *bergantin*, that was either "large" or "small", depending on the person who described it.[36] Whatever its size the bergantín was nothing more than a service boat for the larger ships. Equipped with sails and oars, the bergantín was used to ferry men and materials to and from shore and to tow the larger ships in and out of port.[37]

One of the galleons was the *Santiago*, which Alvarado had con-fiscated from Juan Rodríguez in 1534. Originally built at a cost of three thousand *castellanos de oro de minas*, the ship was "decrepit, old, and broken," when Rodríguez got it back a couple of years later. "It was then worth no more than two hundred pesos de oro," Rodríguez complained. "I sold it later to the adelantado for a hun-dred and fifty."[38] These monetary terms are well known to scholars, but values have changed radically, and it is nearly impossi-ble to express them in modern terms. Still, it is clear that an expen-sive ship had deteriorated to such an extent that it was nearly wor-thless, with rigging rotten, sails torn and mended, and a hull rid-dled by shipworms.[39]

The other galleon was probably the one named *San Juan*. Along with a few other ships these two were hauled out of the water, replanked, and refitted with some of the shipchandlery newly brought from Spain.[40]

Descriptions of the old and new vessels in the fleet are meager. At one point a picture of the fleet was painted,[41] but it has disap-peared, and it is now impossible to know exactly what the vessels looked like. However, there is a good deal of circumstantial evidence that makes it possible to know more than ever before about the ships Juan Rodríguez Cabrillo ultimately took to California.

The entire fleet consisted of thirteen vessels,[42] of which seven or eight were built by Rodríguez between 1536 and 1540. This fact is clear from the testimony of several witnesses. In a letter to the king written in May 1535 Alvarado stated that he hoped to build "six or seven large ships."[43] Upon his return from Spain in 1539, Alvarado stopped in San Salvador and spoke to the historian Oviedo, telling him that he had built seven or eight ships on the Mar del Sur for a trip to the Spice Islands.[44] Diego Hernández, who served in the fleet, recalled in 1589 that "seven or eight ships" from this second fleet were built at the shipyard near Iztapa.[45]

On this fleet the quality of the work was high. Bishop Marro-quín told the king in 1537 that the ships in Alvarado's new fleet

were "built the best of any that sail the seas."[46] The historian
Remesal confirmed this opinion some decades later when he called
the fleet "the largest and best to sail the Mar del Sur up to that
time and for many years thereafter."[47] Not everyone agreed with
this estimate. Diego García de Palacio, writing in 1576, called the
vessels "very small ships."[48] But Diego Hernández, one of the men
who sailed in the fleet, said in 1589 that "three of them were very
large and had two decks."[49] Since they had two decks, these large
vessels were very likely galleons, as were the two other large ships
that Alvarado bought in 1535. Alvaro de Paz, whose memory may
have dimmed in thirty years, once said eleven of the ships were
galleons, the other two being galleys.[50] One of the new galleons
was the *San Salvador*, the ship belonging to Juan Rodríguez Cabrillo.

There is a good deal of circumstantial evidence concerning the
San Salvador. Even if Diego Hernández had not said that the ships
had two decks, that fact would have been obvious from information in other sources.

The manuscript account of the voyage to California, for example, has many references to the number of vessels in the fleet and
their size. This account is not a firsthand description of events that
occurred on the voyage, but rather a summary of several accounts
given by sailors after they returned from the trip. This is clear from
evidence given later by the notary, Juan León, and some of the men
he interviewed. León said he prepared a summary report by order
of the Royal Audiencia. Lázaro de Cárdenas and Francisco de Vargas
both said they made sworn reports for the viceroy, whose secretary
was Juan León. Rodríguez himself sent the viceroy a full report about
the newly-discovered land, and this account surely contained remarks
about the ships.[51]

Under Spanish law notaries interviewed witnesses, summarized
their statements, then read the information back to them for verifica-
tion. The resulting account was usually written in the third person, with occasional lapses to the first, preserving the sense and often
the words of the witness himself. This is exactly the style of the

manuscript account of the voyage to California, which summarizes statements by a number of men who made the voyage. One of these statements was the account written by or for the commander, Juan Rodríguez Cabrillo, before his tragic death.[52]

In this summary account the ship commanded by Juan Rodríguez Cabrillo was called the *capitana* to denote the flagship of the captain general, the commander of the fleet. Two statements in the account described the capitana as having a *puente* (a sterncastle), while the other ships had none.

The entry for Wednesday 15 November 1542 said: "*Los del otro navio pasaron mas trabajo y riesgo q̃ los de la capitana por ser el navio peqeño y no tener puente.*" The meaning here is that one of the ships was small and did not have a sterncastle (*puente*), unlike the flagship (*capitana*), which seemingly did have a sterncastle.[53]

For Wednesday, 28 February 1543, a similar entry read: "*Las mares . . . pasaban por encima de los nabíos que a no tener puentes.*" Here the meaning is that the seas washed over the ships that had no sterncastles. Thus it appears from this journal that the *capitana* had a sterncastle, while two or more others did not.[54]

A number of historians—Richard Stuart Evans, Alexander Smith Taylor, George Davidson, and Herbert E. Bolton—have translated the term to mean that a ship without a *puente* had no deck at all. It was simply an open boat. Henry Raup Wagner knew the meaning of the term but could not bring himself to use it properly.[55] The problem arises from the use of the words *puente* and *cubierta*, both of which mean "deck," but each in a somewhat different manner.

Antonio de Herrera, who wrote the first published account of the voyage, said in one place: "*El un navio alijó todo lo que llevaba, sobre cubierta,*"[56] The storm was so bad that one of the ships lost all the cargo that was being carried on deck. The ship in question was not the flagship, but a *navio pequeño*, or a small ship. "*Como no tenia puente, había alijado todo lo de cubierta, i hacía mucha agua.*"[57] Since it had no puente, the small vessel had lost everything carried on the *cubierta*.[57]

Obviously the meaning of the words *puente* and *cubierta* are important to an understanding of the construction data in the two detailed accounts. In the *Instruccion Nautica* of 1587, Diego García de Palacio gave a careful description of the construction methods and terminology used in ships of the time. The lowest level of a ship was called the *plan*. Each deck above that, including the main deck, was called a *cubierta*. The sterncastle or aftercabin was called a *puente*.[58]

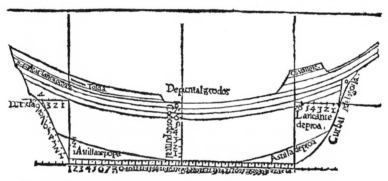

12. *This woodblock sketch shows the method used by Guatemalan shipwrights to compute the proportions of a ship's hull. The illustration is from the* Instrucción náutica *of Diego García de Palacio, who spent several years in Guatemala after the middle of the sixteenth century. (Huntington Library.)*

Other passages recorded in the summary journal describe the rigging of the ships in the fleet. On 27 February the ships ran all day to the west-northwest *"con los trinquetes baxos."* Some days later, with the storm still raging, the ships ran before the wind *"con los trinquetes baxitos."*[59] Both these phrases refer to the lower sails on the foremast. The following Sunday, still in the grip of the storm, they sailed before the wind *"con sendos papos de velas en los trinquetes."*[60] This means that each ship had a small stormsail on the foremast.

Herrera gave a similar description of the rigging used during the storm: *"En cinco dias corrieron docientas leguas, con los papahigos de los trinquetes.''* In five days they sailed two hundred leagues with only the lower sails on the foremasts.[61]

There is additional evidence about the rigging of the flagship *San Salvador.* Luis González, who was pilot on one of Alvarado's vessels, later testified as follows concerning this matter:[62]

> John R^s. Cabrillo went in his own ship which flew the banner of an *almirante* from its foretopmast . . . and this witness spoke with his pilot and knew it to be his ship.

All these references mean that each of the ships, large and small alike, was square rigged. The foremast was rigged with a topmast. The mainmast, therefore, had to have a similar rig, and there must also have been a mizzenmast, perhaps with a lateen rig.[63]

The only known report describing the entire fleet is that of Alvarado's messenger, Bernaldo de Molina, whom Alvarado sent to Spain with "a painting of the armada on canvas." On his way to Spain, Molina stopped in Santo Domingo and talked to Oviedo, the royal historian of the Indies. As always, Oviedo recorded the meeting: "He carried a painting, which he showed me, detailing the size and number of the ships in the adelantado's command; he talked about the fleet with me and with many others."[64] Both the written report and the picture would tell us a great deal about the *San Salvador* and the other ships in the fleet, but both documents have disappeared.

According to Oviedo, three of the ships were galleons of two hundred *toneladas* each. There were also "a very beautiful galley" and two little *fustas* or *bergantines.* "All the rest were [sailing] ships of a hundred *toneladas* or more."[65]

The *Santiago* was undoubtedly one of the two hundred-ton galleons, since it was chosen as the flagship of Alvarado's fleet and of the fleet that Ruy López de Villalobos later took to the Moluccas. This is the ship originally owned by Juan Rodríguez, perhaps built by him, and certainly rebuilt under his direction, using the materials Alvarado brought back from Spain in 1539.

The second two hundred-ton galleon was doubtless the *San*

Salvador. This vessel was the *almiranta*,[66] the ship of the vice commander of the fleet. Built and commanded by Juan Rodríguez Cabrillo, this vessel was later designated by the viceroy and probably by Alvarado as flagship of the armada that was to go up the coast of the Mar del Sur.[67] When the men returned, they agreed that all the ships on such voyages ought to be two hundred tonners, since the smaller vessels took too much of a beating in heavy seas.[68]

The third two hundred-ton galleon was apparently the *Diosdado*. Not much else is known about this ship, except that Bishop Marroquín later directed that the owners be paid its value out of the proceeds of Alvarado's estate.[69] *Diosdado* may have been one of the ships that sailed to the Moluccas with Villalobos, but this is not certain.

The galley was named *San Christóbal*. This vessel was later part of the Villalobos armada. The fusta or galeota was *San Martín*. The fragata or bergantine was *San Miguel*.[70]

All the other vessels were sailing ships. Alvarado called them *naos gruesas*, or big-bellied ships.[71] Their names were *San Jorge, San Antonio, San Francisco, San Juan de Letrán, Figueroa, Anton Hernández,* and *Alvar Núñez*,[72] called *Santa María de Buena Esperanza*.[73] The *Alvar Núñez* was very likely the one that was later called *Victoria*.

The galleons probably measured about a hundred feet in length, with sterncastles and forecastles. The hulls were relatively slim—about twenty-five feet of beam. Sterns were squared, and there was a good deal of taper or "tumble home" from the main decks to the tops of the sterncastles.[74]

The rest of the large ships were probably carracks, uncastled vessels. Like the galleons, they were squarerigged. These big-bellied ships would easily fit Alvarado's description, *naos gruesas*.[75] Their size probably varied somewhere between a hundred and a hundred and fifty *toneladas*.[76]

In November 1539 Alvarado wrote to the king saying: "I have prepared an armada to go on a voyage of discovery. It consists of twelve galleons and large ships, a galeota with twenty pairs of oars and a bergantine with thirteen." He expected final preparations to take some time and promised to send a full report once the ships were ready to sail.[77]

Before the new armada left to sail up the coast of New Spain, Juan Rodríguez Cabrillo took the *San Salvador* on a trading voyage to Peru.[78] If the ship carried the same cargo of horses and other supplies that the *Santiago* carried in 1534, the profits from that one voyage would have paid for the cost of the ship with a considerable profit left over. Horses in Peru at that time were worth more than a thousand *castellanos de oro de minas*, two or three times their value in Guatemala. The cost to Juan Rodríguez for building the *San Salvador* was four thousand *ducados*, somewhat more than the three thousand *castellanos de oro de minas* at which he had valued the *Santiago*.[79] In addition to repaying the cost of construction, the trip to Peru gave Juan Rodríguez a chance to train his crew and prepare himself for a long voyage of exploration.

Not that he actually intended to go on Alvarado's new expedition; his role in the voyage was really a last-minute sort of arrangement. Here is his own description of the matter.[80]

> The Adelantado kept after me, often begging me, that I should come with him in my ship as *almirante* of the armada. He said that he would reimburse me for my previous six years of service building the armada as well as for all the work I might later do in it. Because he kept begging and pestering me, I came with him in the armada as captain of my own ship and as *almirante* of the armada.

Once the armada was assembled, Alvarado took the fleet to Acajutla for final fitting and loading.[81] By midsummer 1540 everything was ready. The fleet sailed north late in August or early in September 1540. Alvarado had with him thirteen ships and more than a thousand men, many of whom had come with him from Spain in 1539.[82] Alvaro de Paz called it "the biggest gathering of men, arms, and horses ever seen in these parts." Some of the men talked later about places they had been, the people they had seen, and the things they had done on the expedition. Their accounts allow us to reconstruct events in some detail.

Juan de Alvarado, nephew of the adelantado, went along as *coronel* or miliary commander. Francisco Gíron, who came from Spain with Alvarado in 1539, said he was *alférez general* or second in command of the military forces. Both apparently sailed in the *Santiago* with Alvarado.[83]

Antonio de Figueroa said later that he went with Alvarado in the armada. Doubtless he sailed in the ship belonging to his father Santos de Figueroa.[84]

Bishop Francisco Marroquín also sailed with the fleet, as advisor to Alvarado and to his good friend Juan Rodríguez.[85] There were surely other priests in the armada as well, for the royal *cedula* of 1539 required Alvarado to send "clergymen and religious to teach and indoctrinate the natives."[86]

Martín Sánchez said he was master of the *Santiago*.[87] Lorenzo Hernández Barreda, and Gerónimo de San Remón were pilots on the ships that Rodríguez later took to California, while Antonio Correa and Bartolomé Ferrer were captains.[88]

Diego de Robledo, official notary of the armada recalled that in addition to men important enough to have their own horses and black slaves, there were a good many common soldiers.[89] Nicolas López de Yzárraga was *alguacil mayor*, or chief magistrate of the expedition.[90] Some men admitted that they served in much humbler capacities. Diego de Abuenza and Andrés Dubón said they were Alvarado's cabin boys or *pages*.[91] Antonio de Castellanos said he served in the armada,[92] as did Alonso de Torres,[93] Lázaro de Cárdenas,[94] Francisco de Vargas,[95] and Luis González.[96] Few of them them claimed to have held high rank. They were simply sailors or soldiers, as was Diego Hernández, who said he was supposed to go in the armada "with a gentleman," a relative of his named Hernán López Centeno, but "because of a certain problem, they did not go on that voyage."[97]

From Guatemala the fleet sailed first to Guatulco in New Spain to pick up additional supplies. No one has left a record of conditions on the ships, but there is an account written in 1544 by one of the Dominican friars who sailed from Spain to Chiapas with Fray Bartolomé de Las Casas. The author of this diary, Fray Tomás de la Torre, told a harrowing tale of seasickness, heat, thirst, vermin, and noxious odors from the bilge pumps, which ran almost continually when the ship was in heavy seas.[98] He gives a vivid picture of life on a sixteenth-century sailing ship.

"There are countless lice that eat men alive," wrote Fray Tomás, but that was not the worst of it. The sailors treated them shamefully. "They make us sleep below deck like Blacks. We sit or lie on the floor, and they step on us, not on our robes, but on our beards and mouths."[99]

The whole journey seemed to swing on a pedulum between grim comedy and stark tragedy. The sailors were either too ignorant or too lazy to do their work properly. The ship was poorly loaded, carrying too little in the hold and too much on deck. Consequently, the cargo shifted in a storm and the vessel nearly capsized. As the ship took on more water, barrels of cargo began to float in the hold. Soon, half the lower deck was under water, and the ship ran in such poor trim that passengers and crew crawled about, hanging onto ropes.[100]

There is no reason to think that Alvarado's fleet was so poorly manned, but conditions on board could scarcely have been comfortable. In addition to the sailors and soldiers and arms and equipment, each ship carried numerous Indian laborers and from six to a dozen horses.[101] Moreover, there were live sheep, pigs, and chickens to eat along the way.[102] Even without the animals, the stench was terrible. With perhaps a hundred people packed on board each vessel, plus horses and small animals, conditions in a stormy sea must have been intolerable. Fortunately for the men and women on the ships, the fleet took a coastal route, touching land frequently for fresh food and water. The first major port reached by the expedition was Guatulco, on the southern coast of New Spain.

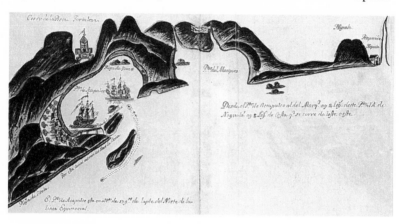

13. *The fragata* San Miguel *was beached for repairs at the port of Acapulco, shown here in an early seventeenth century view. (Derrotero del Mar del Sur, HM 918, Huntington Library.)*

Under the terms of his commission from the king, Alvarado was obliged to give Viceroy Mendoza a one-third interest in his expedition. Mendoza and Alvarado had agreed to these terms before Alvarado went to Spain. The two men must have had some additional communication about the matter in the two and a half years since the royal cedula was issued.[103] Nonetheless, when Alvarado tried to reprovision his ships at Guatulco, he was met by emissaries from Mendoza, who refused to allow him to take on supplies.[104] Just why is not clear. Perhaps it was an attempt to forestall Cortés, who had a side agreement with Alvarado and was prepared to provision the fleet with a huge load of biscuits, beans, and bacon, as well as cattle, sheep, pigs, and other supplies.[105]

This is not to say that the armada was poorly supplied when the fleet left Guatemala. There was evidently enough food for a leisurely journey up the coast of New Spain. After leaving Guatulco, the fleet stopped in Acapulco, largely, it seems, because one of the boats was leaking badly.[106]

This vessel was the fragata, *San Miguel*, which was beached for repairs in Acapulco. The problem was serious, and the vessel was still there at the end of November 1540. According to her pilot, Luis González, the *San Miguel* later sailed back to Guatulco and finally returned to Guatemala for a complete overhaul.[107]

Following the departure from Acapulco, Alvarado took the fleet north to the port of Santiago de Buena Esperanza in the province of Colima, arriving by the early part of November 1540. Again he tried to load supplies, and again Mendoza's agents prevented it. Finally, a conference was arranged at Tiripitío in Michoacán, about halfway between the coast and Mexico City. Viceroy Mendoza had his own advisers, while Alvarado was accompanied and advised by Bishop Marroquín.[108]

At Tiripitío it quickly became obvious why Alvarado had acquiesced so quietly to Mendoza's embargo on supplies. The Adelantado demanded and got a quarter interest in whatever discoveries might be made by the viceroy's own expeditions. These included the great land army the viceroy had recently sent to Quivira under the command of Francisco Vázquez de Coronado and the small armada he had sent to the mouth of the Colorado River under the command of Hernando de Alarcón.[109]

In return, Alvarado agreed to give the viceroy a half interest in his own expedition (instead of the third interest provided in the royal cedula) plus half interest in the fleet. The viceroy appears to have known that Alvarado did not own all the ships outright, even though Cortés and perhaps some others apparently thought he did.[110] In any case, the agreement clearly says that the viceroy would hold half interest in the vessels and supplies "in the same manner that the Señor Adelantado holds them."[111] Here it is possible to see the hand of Bishop Marroquín, reminding Alvarado that some of the vessels were not his to trade away.

In the final document, signed 29 November 1540, the partners agreed that supplies would be available at Acapulco in warehouses that the viceroy would build. The shipyard would be at Xirabaltique, where Alvarado agreed to have shops built and manned by skilled workmen.[112]

Alvarado and Mendoza also determined that a new harbor was needed to serve as home port for the fleet. Consequently, they sent Rodríguez Cabrillo to look for a new site, and within a week or two he discovered a fine port.[113] For a few days the place remained nameless, being called simply "the port of Colima."[114] Finally, Viceroy Mendoza landed there with his own vessels on 25 December 1540, so the port was called Navidad in honor of the Nativity of Our Lord.[115]

Despite Bishop Marroquín's apparent effort to protect the interests of the private shipowners, Juan Rodríguez objected vehemently when he learned the terms of the new agreement between Alvarado and Mendoza. Finally, with the help of the bishop, Rodríguez Cabrillo secured a new grant from Alvarado. On 20 December he was given the encomiendas of Tacuba and Jumaitepeque on the outskirts of Santiago, Guatemala.[116] These were rich pueblos, whose annual income of 600 pesos de oro[117] would surely have repaid Rodríguez for any expenses incurred in helping lead the expedition. Unfortunately, there was some difficulty about title to the encomienda, and legal action dragged on for more than a quarter of a century.[118]

None of this affected the expedition. The newly reconciled partners hastened to complete their preparations. The original plan was changed, and before spring, the partners decided to send two separate armadas. One, under the command of the Viceroy's relative Ruy López de Villalobos, was to take three ships and a galera and three hundred men and sail across the Pacific. The other, commanded by Alvarado's nephew Juan de Alvarado, was to sail with five ships and a fusta and another three hundred men, exploring the Pacific Coast to the north and west. Two additional vessels were to be kept in reserve for use as supply vessels in case some new and valuable lands were discovered.[119]

By this time Alvarado had decided not to go on any of the journeys himself, for he told the king that he intended to go back to

Guatemala as soon as the fleets were sent on their way.[120] Possibly he had never intended to sail any further. The seventeenth century historian Herrera said that Alvarado had gone with his fleet to Mexico only because Mendoza had asked him to come for a conference about the projected voyage of discovery. If this is so, then it is also possible that Juan Rodríguez originally intended to return to Guatemala at the same time as Alvarado.[121]

Other men may have had the same plans. Bishop Marroquín surely did not intend to be a permanent member of the expedition; he had come to Mexico only as an advisor to Alvarado. Yet even while the vessels and crews were being readied, the plans of the partners underwent substantial change. Both Alvarado and Mendoza were too restless to supervise preparation of the fleets. Instead, Juan Rodríguez Cabrillo took complete charge, while the partners themselves traveled around Mexico on various matters of business.[122]

In April a minor Indian revolt in Jalisco took a nasty turn for the worse. Suddenly Juan de Alvarado was needed elsewhere, and a new commander was named to head the coastal expedition. Orders signed on 29 April 1541 instructed Diego López de Zúñiga to sail up the coast in search of other well-developed countries where settlements could be established. The fleet chosen for this expedition seems to have included the three galleons and the fusta or bergantine. *San Salvador*—"everyone called the ship *Juan Rodríguez*"—was to be the flagship or *capitana*. As usual in these military-commercial ventures, the ships were to carry a big load of trade goods, perhaps one of the reasons the *Juan Rodríguez* was added to the fleet.[123]

Another armada was also ordered out, this one to be commanded by Hernando de Alarcón. With a small fleet of three ships Alarcón was to sail to the mouth of the Colorado River, which he had discovered a year or so earlier and named the *Buen Guia*. His primary orders were to establish contact with the land army of Francisco Vasquez de Coronado, but he seems also to have been ordered to establish a settlement on the Colorado.[124]

But before Alarcón or López de Zúñiga could set sail, a frantic message arrived, asking for help with the suddenly serious Indian crisis. Alvarado promptly stripped men, guns, and supplies from the fleet and headed for the interior. López de Zúñiga took a combined force of thirty calvalry and infantry to Izatlán. Alarcón with thirty additional infantryman went to Autlán. Rodríguez remained at Navidad where he hauled most of the vessels out of the water in order to keep them safe from shipworms.[125]

14. *An early view of the fighting in the Mixton War. Pedro de Alvarado is shown in the center of the illustration, about to be crushed by a horse at the Peñol de Nochistlán. (Shearman Collection, Natural History Museum of Los Angeles County.)*

The serious uprising quickly became a disaster. Regrouping his forces after a charge into the Indian lines at the Peñol de Nochistlán,

Alvarado was struck by a terrorized war horse. Rolling under the falling beast, Alvarado's body was badly crushed. He lingered for a few days in agony, then died.[126] The great plans of the partners fell into disarray.

Alvarado's men began to head back to their ships and set sail for Guatemala.[127] Perhaps in order to keep his own three vessels occupied and out of the clutches of Alvarado's men, Viceroy Mendoza sent Hernando de Alarcón to sail the ships up the Gulf of California in another fruitless attempt to contact the Coronado expedition. Francisco de Bolaños took a similar fleet some distance up the west coast of Lower California.

Earlier in the summer Alarcón was at Autlán with thirty soldiers but, like the other commanders, broke off the fight after Alvarado's disaster at the Peñol de Nochistlán and marched back to Navidad.[128] There has been some doubt that Alarcón made a second journey up the gulf, but the evidence seems to show that he did.[129] A sailor later testified that he saw both Alarcón and Bolaños sail out of the harbor at Navidad on the feast of the Virgin, September 8, 1541.[130] One fleet, he said, was heading *"para el ancón de la tierra,"* the same term Mendoza had used earlier in sending Alarcón to the mouth of the Colorado River.[131] Bolaños took the other fleet and explored "the land further up the coast," that is, the west coast of the California peninsula.[132] As though to settle any lingering doubts about these voyages, Mendoza later said that he had sent three expeditions up the coast in fulfillment of the agreement he and Alvarado had with the king. These expeditions seem pretty clearly to have been the two armadas of Alarcón and Bolaños that left in September 1541, and the later expedition of Juan Rodríguez Cabrillo.[133]

Having completed preparations for these voyages, Rodríguez himself sailed back to Guatemala. Before leaving he prepared a brief list of questions for the royal notary to propose to a selected list of witnesses, showing Alvarado's indebtness to him.

Alvarado had tried to pay the debt by granting Rodríguez the rich encomiendas of Tacuba and Xumaytepeque, but a problem arose which both men evidently hoped to solve upon their return to Guatemala. Francisco de la Cueva, Alvarado's brother-in-law whom he had appointed as lieutenant governor during his absence, refused to deliver legal title to Beatríz. Then, manipulating the record in a way that is still not entirely clear, Cueva managed to claim that he had taken the encomiendas for himself some weeks before Alvarado signed title over to Rodríguez.[134]

This move raised the kinds of questions that lawyers often refer to as interesting. Did Cueva have the right to grant an encomienda in Alvarado's absence? And if he did have this authority, could he grant one to himself? And if one or both of these things were possible, could Cueva, as lieutenant governor, lawfully defy the absent governor's order to deliver the titles to Rodríguez or his wife? These were questions raised by Rodríguez, but Cueva had his own. Did Rodríguez have the legal right to acquire additional encomiendas beyond those he already owned?[135]

Foreseeing a long battle in the courts, Rodríguez prepared his queries at Navidad in order to compile information for a permanent official record, *ad perpetua* [m] *rei memoria* [m], in the legal phrase of that day.[136] If Alvarado were alive this would not have been necessary, but he was dead and everything was in a state of confusion. The witnesses gathered in Navidad on 1 September 1541, but Rodríguez was in Guatemala by that time. As the royal official in Navidad explained,[137]

> Juan Rodríguez is busy preparing an armada for the viceroy and performing other appropriate services for His Majesty. For these reasons he cannot be present to examine and swear the witnesses. Therefore, Señor Don Luis [de Castilla, *justicia mayor* of New Spain] said that, since Juan Rodríguez empowered me to receive, swear, and question them, such action would be as valid as though he himself were present at the testimony, and so he gave me such complete authority as is required in these cases.

This statement is important because the rest of the record contains routine legal phraseology, seemingly showing that Rodríguez was in Navidad on 1 September 1541. In fact, he was in the port of Acajutla, Guatemala, where on 29 August he signed a power of attorney for his wife Beatríz, who had come to meet his ship.[138] Along with the passengers and cargo, Rodríguez seems to have carried in his ship an important letter from the viceroy to the *cabildo* of Santiago, as will become apparent in the story that follows.

After the disaster at Nochistlán Bishop Marroquín seems to have remained for a short time with Alvarado. But seeing that the campaign was over and the sailing of the fleet indefinitely delayed, he began his own overland trip back to Guatemala. Marroquín was in Chiapas conferring with the priests in that distant part of the province when a letter arrived from Viceroy Mendoza, telling him that Alvarado was dead.[139] In all probability Mendoza also enclosed Alvarado's brief will, naming Bishop Marroquín as one of the executors of the estate.[140]

The other executor was Juan de Alvarado, nephew of the adelantado, the governor's closest friend and advisor, and the general or *coronel* of the ill-fated expedition. On 10 August 1541 Marroquín wrote to the king, recommending that Juan de Alvarado be named governor of Guatemala and urging His Majesty to order Juan to marry Leonor, Pedro's daughter, and thus assure peace and harmony in the province.[141]

Somewhat earlier, 15 July 1541, Viceroy Mendoza had written to the members of the cabildo of Santiago, "ordering and directing" these gentlemen to accept Francisco de la Cueva as the new governor of the province.[142] Most of the influential citizens did not like Cueva, partly because of his unfair land dealings, but largely because he was fundamentally dishonest. As Bishop Marroquín later told the king, "He has no zeal for justice or interest in it and not much of a conscience.[143]"

Perhaps Viceroy Mendoza was not really serious in ordering the cabildo to accept Cueva as governor. If he were, he seems to have made the worst possible choice of messengers, Juan Rodríguez Cabrillo. The evidence for this is circumstantial but little short of convincing.

Mendoza's letter was dated 15 July 1541, but it did not reach the cabildo at Santiago until 29 August 1541, some forty-five days later. This was the day Juan Rodríguez signed the power of attorney for his wife Beatríz in the seaport of Iztapa, a short journey by post from the capital.[144]

Padre Remesal, who investigated the matter in 1615, was puzzled by the long delay in delivering the viceroy's letter. Remesal said that the letter could have been delivered by overland mail from Mexico in as little as twelve or fourteen days and certainly no longer than eighteen or twenty days. Why should it take two or three times that long? As Remesal said, there seems to have been "great negligence for such an important matter."[145]

Padre Remesal simply could not understand how anyone could be so careless. The answer, it seems, is that Rodríguez was the messenger. Although the news of Alvarado's death would precede him, Rodríguez did not want the official notice from the Viceroy to be delivered until he could discuss the matter with his friends in Santiago. Remesal and some later historians erroneously assumed that Mendoza's letter of 15 July was the cabildo's first news of the death of Alvarado. Even the viceroy knew this was not the case, as is clear from his own statement:[146]

> By the letters I wrote both to the bishop of this province and to Don Francisco de la Cueva, the lieutenant governor, you should already know that God Our Lord was disposed to raise the Lord Adelantado Alvarado to His Glory.

Remesal did not understand, as we now do, that Mendoza had written earlier to both Cueva and Marroquín and that Marroquín's copy of the letter arrived in Chiapas by 10 August. Cueva's copy of the letter should have arrived in Santiago within two or three days of that date.

But the viceroy's official communication to the cabildo of Santiago arrived much later, about the time it was read into the records, which was the same day that Juan Rodríguez and his wife were signing their own legal documents in Acajutla. It requires no great stretch of the imagination to picture Juan Rodríguez arriving in Acajutla a day or so earlier and sending the viceroy's letter to Santiago, along with his own messages to the bishop and the members of the cabildo who already knew and certainly shared his opinion of Cueva. If Cueva were to be appointed governor, the interests of Rodríguez and many other encomenderos would suffer.

It is not clear why Mendoza wrote the letter in Cueva's behalf. Perhaps he did it because the Cueva family was very influential at court.[147] Faced with a serious Indian war and threats of an official investigation of his own administration, Mendoza could use a few more friends at court. On the other hand Mendoza's letter was so half hearted that he scarcely seems to have thought he could force that unpopular governor on that notoriously unwilling and uncooperative group of old conquistadores. And his astonishing decision to send the letter with Rodríguez, as circumstances seem to indicate, meant that Rodríguez could deliver the letter at his convenience, thus giving his friends in Guatemala an opportunity to make their own plans for the appointment of a new governor.

Guatemalan officials met in Santiago at the end of August and for several days discussed all the ramifications of the problem. Marroquín and others still wanted to have a governor named Alvarado to keep the Indians in line. "His name alone," said Marroquín, "was enough to maintain peace in the land." Finally on 9 September 1541, they hit upon a happy compromise: Beatríz de la Cueva, widow of Alvarado, would be named governor *pro tem* by the cabildo. She would immediately reappoint Francisco de la Cueva as lieutenant governor, but this time she would reserve for herself the right to grant encomiendas.[148]

The members of the cabildo, accompanied by Bishop Marroquín

and Lieutenant Governor Francisco de la Cueva, then hurried to the adelantado's palace to ask his widow whether she would agree. She did so and immediately took her oath of office as governor, swearing on the cross that adorns the rod which is the symbol of the governor's authority. Immediately upon signing her oath of office, Doña Beatríz signed a second document, naming Cueva as lieutenant governor and giving him the *vara de justicia* as his emblem of office. In this document she specifically "reserved for herself henceforth the right to grant Indians, . . . and not [so empowering] the lieutenant governor nor any other person." The unhappy young widow then signed herself *"la sin ventura,"* the Unfortunate One.[149]

Cueva presented his documents at the cabildo meeting the following morning, 10 September 1541, and the *vara de justicia* was returned to him. A day later Beatríz de la Cueva, governor of Guatemala, widow of the adelantado, *La sin ventura*, was dead. Half the people in Santiago died with her.[150]

On 11 September 1541, at about two or three in the morning, the city of Santiago was devastated by a flood of water, mud, and rock and a terrifying earthquake. Alvarado's wife and most of the other people in his palace were killed. In fact most of the houses in the city were badly damaged or destroyed and hundreds of people died, including six hundred Indians.[151] The best account of this terrible calamity was written by a man known only as Juan Rodríguez, *escribano*. His story appeared in a little pamphlet printed in Mexico before the end of 1541. It was called *Relacíon del espantable terremoto que agora nuevamente acontecido en las yndias en una ciudad llamada Guatimala.*[152] It is the earliest secular publication known to have been printed in the New World, the first in a series of *relaciones* that marked the beginning of journalism in Spanish America.[153] Several authorities have identified the author as Juan Rodríguez Cabrillo.[154] It was an easy identification to make, as there was no one else in the city by that name.

The *Relación* was written by someone who knew the people in

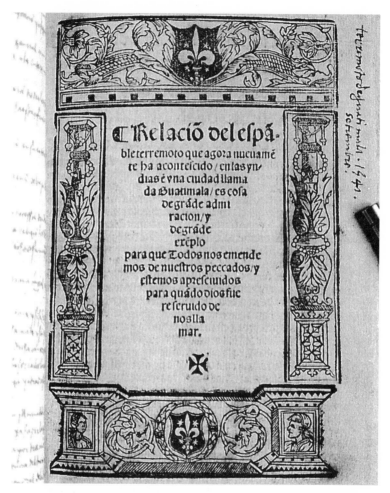

15. The report of the earthquake in Guatemala by Juan Rodríguez was the first secular publication in the New World. (Real Biblioteca de San Lorenzo de El Escorial, Spain.)

Santiago intimately but who was not himself an eyewitness. Instead, he arrived there shortly after the earthquake and flood, saw all the damage, interviewed witnesses, and therefore was able to tell much of the story in the first person plural. The writer did not lose his home or family in the torrent or have any other personal involvement in it.[155] All this fits Juan Rodríguez Cabrillo.

Bishop Marroquín, in his own report, went to some length to explain exactly why he was not able to save Doña Beatríz, whose house was just across the plaza from his own.[156] Rodríguez, on the other hand, made no attempt to give a similar explanation, doubtless because he expected his reader to know that he was in Acajutla with the few remaining ships of his armada.

The author of the *Relación* was a man accustomed to the use of military terms. Thus, he described distances as "four crossbow shots" or "three crossbow shots" or "half a crossbow shot outside the city."[157] These are terms that Juan Rodríguez Cabrillo, conquistador and crossbowman, would have used.

Moreover, the grammar and the vocabulary are typical of a man who was literate but not a polished writer. It may have been this lack of literary skill that led the printer to add *escribano* to the signature on the *Relación*.[158] Bishop Marroquín wrote a similar account to the king in October 1541 describing the same incident but with much greater clarity and in a finer literary style.[159]

There is an unsigned manuscript in the Archivo General de Indias in Seville which seems to be a clean copy of the Rodríguez *Relación*, but with some words, phrases, and sentences changed. Some of the changes may be liberties taken by a copyist, but at least one sentence in the Seville manuscript seems to preserve original wording that was changed for the printed version. The manuscript sentence reads *"Murio Robles el sastre con una amiga suya."*[160] The printed version translates as follows: "Robles the tailor died along with his *wife*," rather than with a "lady friend" as the manuscript version has it.[161]

It is possible to make a guess as to how the manuscript *Relación* came to be printed. Juan Rodríguez, commander of Alvarado's fleet, wrote the letter as a report to Juan de Alvarado, commander of the military force, who then sent a copy to the printer Juan Pablos.

Bishop Marroquín reported in November 1541 that Juan de Alvarado was on his way to Spain and that several reports about the devastation of the city had been sent to Spain also.[162]

From the account given by Bernal Díaz it is clear that Juan de Alvarado traveled via Mexico City where he was joined by young Pedro de Alvarado, a cousin or nephew and son of the Juan de Alvarado who was encomendero of Tiripitío in Michoacán.[163]

On their way to Spain, the two men stopped in Havana about the end of December 1541 and gave one or more copies of the *Relación* to Juan de Lobera, who sent one to the historian Oviedo in a letter dated 4 January 1542. After making a few editorial changes, Oviedo put the *Relación* in his *Historia general*,[164] where it has become known as a second printed version of the original Rodríguez story[165]. Juan and young Pedro de Alvarado then disappeared. Bernal Díaz wrote their epitaph: "There was never any more news of them. Some thought they were lost at sea or that the Moors captured them."[166]

Juan Rodríguez Cabrillo remained in Santiago long enough to move his household to the new site in the valley where the city stands today under the name Antigua.[167] Then, summoned by the viceroy, he returned to Navidad with his ship and began preparations for the voyage to California.[168]

Chapter 5
A New Expedition to California

WHILE THE SHAKEN survivors of the Santiago quake struggled to salvage what they could from the shattered city, Viceroy Antonio de Mendoza took to the field with a new army marching against the rebellious natives of Nueva Galicia. Within a few months the last rebels surrendered.

Scarcely stopping for breath, Mendoza then scurried about, collecting ships and men for the great expeditions he and Alvarado had wanted to dispatch a year earlier. Mendoza planned to send out two fleets. One was to sail up the northern coast. A second was to go directly west. They would meet in the islands of the western Pacific.[1]

With several boats from his own fleet, plus a dozen from the fleet assembled by Alvarado, Mendoza had more than enough vessels to send on these expeditions. In case these were not enough, the viceroy could count a good three dozen other vessels in service between various ports on the Pacific coast, any or all of which he could press into service to complete his contract with the crown.[2] This should have been sufficient to relieve him of worry, were he not confronted with the problem of title to Alvarado's fleet, plus an additional problem about the use of privately owned vessels like the *San Salvador*.

According to the will that Bishop Marroquín prepared for Alvarado the heirs were all to continue the enterprise, carrying out the agreements Alvarado had made with the viceroy and the crown to explore the coast and to sail to the Moluccas and the islands of *el Poniente*.[3]

The original heir of the Adelantado was Beatríz, *la sin ventura*, and she was dead. There were other possible heirs, including natural daughters and nephews, but they were reluctant to step forward and claim the estate.

The reason lay in a curious provision of Spanish law which stipulated that an heir acquired the debts as well as the assets of an estate. The prospective heir was allowed a brief time to study the matter, and he could refuse the inheritance, if he judged it would be a burden.[4] Mendoza later explained it this way to a friend:[5]

> There was no one who would assume title to the assets for fear of the debts, so no one was named heir of the *adelantado*. As a result, his ships remained in my possession, along with those I owned, plus the share of the contract very graciously granted me by His Majesty.

The investors who owned the ships named for themselves—the *Juan Rodríguez*, the *Diosdado*, and the *Figueroa*—may have been pleased with the news that Mendoza intended to send a fleet to sea after all. These men had invested heavily in Alvarado's original expedition, building and equipping the vessels and paying the crews who sailed their ships up the coast of New Spain. If the expedition were cancelled all this investment was lost. No one realized this better than Juan Rodríguez.

While in Navidad, just after the death of Alvarado and shortly before making his way back to Guatemala, he wrote about [6]

> the things the Lord Adelantado owes me. This is an obligation that he neglected to declare in his will because of his grave injuries . . . . I hope to be able to collect from his estate and his heirs.

Once back in Guatemala, Juan Rodríguez registered his claim with Bishop Marroquín, the executor.[7] It soon became clear to him that the estate was heavily in debt, and as a result Rodríguez and the bishop apparently came to terms. Juan Rodríguez would cooperate with Viceroy Mendoza, attempting to collect his own money and helping to pay some of Alvarado's other debts out of the expected profits from the exploring venture.

Consequently, when Mendoza summoned him to Navidad in the spring of 1542, Juan Rodríguez hurriedly gathered his ships, supplies, and men and sailed north once again. This was no easy task.

The annual succesion of wars and expeditions over the past decade and a half had decimated the Spanish and Indian populations in Guatemala. The recent earthquake had brought the economy of the country to the brink of collapse. There is not much mystery in the way Rodríguez managed to regroup his band of soldiers of fortune. His methods were established in two decades of conquest.

With a nudge from Las Casas, we can guess at the columns of Indian slaves carrying food and munitions; the herders bringing animals and caged fowl; the grinning soldiers herding Indian women and girls on board the vessels.[8] But this we know by inference and not from official records.

The younger Juan Rodríguez was a child five or six years of age when his father sailed away for the last time. When the young man described the armada in 1560, nearly twenty years of family reminiscence had erased all the lurid details from his mind. Here is what he said:[9]

> Juan Rodríguez took his own ship on that expedition, supplying at his own cost provisions, servants, arms, and horses.

A brief summary, this, but other details are available in scraps from here and there.

For example, the armada that Rodríguez took to California was seemingly larger than most writers have thought. The young

Rodríguez said his father "took his own ship" and "other ships" as well on that voyage to California.[10] Francisco de Vargas and Lázaro de Cárdenas, two sailors who were on the voyage, said Rodríguez had three ships in his armada; one of them recalled that there was also a *bergantín*.[11]

In detailed testimony given in 1560, Cárdenas said that he saw Rodríguez being given command of "his own ship and an armada of two other ships." It is very clear that Cárdenas intended to say the armada consisted of three ships, for he continued to refer to "the two other ships" and "the same two ships."[12]

The detailed account by Cárdenas helps to clarify the testimony of several other men, who incidentally were not on the journey. One of these, Nicolás López de Yzárraga, said in 1561 that Rodríguez had been sent "with two ships to discover the coast of Poniente."[13] On the same occasion another witness, Juan de Valladolid, said that Rodríguez went on the journey "with some ships."[14] Somewhat clearer is the statement by Juan de Aragón in September 1542 that Juan Rodríguez sailed "with other ships" to discover the coast of the South Sea.[15] No doubt we are supposed to understand all these men as saying that Juan Rodríguez Cabrillo had more than two vessels in his fleet.

In any case, the testimony of Lázaro de Cárdenas is confirmed by that of Francisco de Vargas, who also went on the journey, and who recalled in 1561 that the fleet had consisted of three ships, one being a *bergantín*.[16] As was seen earlier, the *bergantín* was a launch or service boat, probably the *bergantín pequeño* that was part of Alvarado's fleet in 1538.[17]

The Vargas and Cárdenas statements were made in 1560 in response to questions proposed by Cabrillo's son, who, of course, was not on the voyage. Their testimony was given before Juan León, the same notary who interviewed crewmen in 1543, after the armada returned to Navidad. León's job was to ferret out the truth. He obviously considered these statements to be consistent with those he had heard in 1543. Another early witness, Pedro de Velbas, testified under oath in Mexico in 1546 that he had talked to the mariners from Cabrillo's expedition and had seen their charts. The armada, he said, consisted of three ships:[18]

> The viceroy sent an armada of three ships to explore [the coast of] the Mar del Sur. They sailed along that [coast], as some of the mariners who went there marked on a chart, six hundred leagues higher than the point reached by Ulloa.

Several other sources confirm the size of the fleet—three ships. In 1547 the viceroy himself said that when the fleet returned from California, he sent the crews with three ships on a voyage to Peru.[19] One witness spoke of this armada as "another three ships,"[20] though a second seemed to say that the same crews went out again in the same three ships.[21] The main point is clear. There were three ships in Cabrillo's fleet. The royal chronicler, Herrera, was wrong when he said a half century later that Cabrillo had only two ships in his fleet.[22]

Just when Rodríguez received the viceroy's commission is not clear. It may have happened before his return to Guatemala. On 2 September 1541 the notary, Juan de la Torre, said Rodríguez was "busy supervising preparations for the armada of the Lord Viceroy and with other important business."[23] However, the notary did not call him captain general, but *mayordomo*. Therefore, it is more likely that Rodríguez received the commission in the first months of 1542 when he returned to Mexico.

Soon after his arrival, perhaps in early April 1542, Ruy López de Villalobos, a relative of the viceroy, arrived at Navidad bringing dispatches from the viceroy. Lázaro de Cárdenas, who accompanied Villalobos on the trip from Mexico City, described the event this way:[24]

> He brought here orders from the viceroy and the royal audiencia. They made Juan Rodríguez Cabrillo captain general for the exploration of the coast.

16. In this map of the Mixton War zone the port of Navidad is at the bottom, just
to the right of center. North is to the left. (Archivo General de Indias, Seville,
Spain.)

When Viceroy Mendoza summoned him back to Navidad in the
spring of 1542, the world of Juan Rodríguez was a shambles.
Alvarado's grand fleet was scattered, men and equipment gone. With
his own personal fortune seriously depleted by the disaster in Santiago, Juan Rodríguez must have toyed with the idea of not going
at all, but the riches to be discovered in a voyage up the coast reinforced his lagging determination to explore the northern reaches
of the Mar del Sur.

Mendoza seems never to have doubted that Rodríguez would
return. On 10 March 1542 he remarked in a letter to Spain that
the Bolaños expedition had met with disaster, and the dismasted
vessels were laid up *"en la ysla del Marques"* on the coast of Baja
California. Nonetheless, he wrote, "I have ordered two more ships

to be prepared so that the same voyage up the coast can be made this summer." These were the two ships that were to accompany the flagship *San Salvador.*[25]

Rodríguez also supervised the preparation of another fleet so that Villalobos himself could sail on his famous voyage to the islands of the western Pacific. The family and friends of Rodríguez later claimed that he "dispatched the armadas of Captains Villalobos and Bolaños," before leaving on his own journey.[26]

Henry R. Wagner called this "the one transparent error" in the document, since the facts seems to show that Villalobos left for the Moluccas after Cabrillo sailed to California.[27] Nevertheless, there is good evidence that the family's version of events is more or less correct.

Francisco de Vargas, one of the seamen who sailed with Cabrillo, told a story that seems to support the family version. Vargas said that after Bolaños and Alarcón left on their voyages in the fall of 1541, Rodríguez "took charge of the other armada, preparing it so that Villalobos might go, as he did, to discover the islands."[28]

Since Bolaños was marooned with his damaged ships on the coast of California and Villalobos was to take these vessels with him to the Moluccas, it was logical that Villalobos should lead the rescue party. He was undoubtedly the commander that Mendoza sent out in the spring of 1542 to bring back Bolaños. Francisco de Vargas is probably correct in saying that Bolaños returned before Cabrillo left for California but that Villalobos was still away.[29] During his trip to California Villalobos saw for himself the rich fishing grounds along that coast. He hoped to catch and salt a huge supply of these fish to use on his trip to the Spice Islands.[30] His report helped confirm Juan Rodríguez in his determination to feed his own crews from the local fishery.

The original journals of the expedition say that Villalobos left from the Puerto de Juan Gallego, and all modern writers have assumed this to be another name for the port of Navidad.[31] But Juan Gallego and Navidad are separate ports and none of the accounts confuses the names. The Cavendish map and other sailing charts show Juan Gallego as a port on the Colima coast some distance to the north of Navidad.[32]

17. *In this late sixteenth century map the port of Juan Gallego is shown on the coast of New Spain to the right of the tip of the California peninsula. (Cavendish Map, Algemeen Rijksarchief, The Hague.)*

The royal cosmographer Alonso de Santa Cruz, writing a few years after the voyage, gives additional information that helps to claify the point. Santa Cruz said that Villalobos did not depart from Navidad, at least not directly. According to his account, Villalobos[33]

> left the port of Navidad, which is on the coast of New Spain on the Mar del Sur. He went to Puerto Santo from which he left on his voyage the day of All Saints of 1542.

"Santo" is doubtless another name for Juan Gallego, as it appears in the same location as that port on some charts, although neither appears with great frequency on charts of the period.

In any case, the matter is conclusively settled in an anonymous account of the expedition by one of the men who went with Villalobos, perhaps the chaplain, Gerónimo de Santisteban. This account says that after leaving Navidad, Villalobos found his ships to be improperly ballasted. Rather than return to Navidad, he pulled his fleet onto the port of Juan Gallego to unload and rearrange the cargo, and it was some time before the ships could put to sea again.[34] The fact that he chose to refit at Juan Gallego rather than Navidad undoubtedly reflects a growing disillusionment with the port of Navidad, which Andrés de Urdaneta a few years later described as poorly situated, in an unhealthy region, with inadequate ship-building facilities.[35]

Alvarado and Mendoza planned that the two fleets would approach the Spice Islands and China in a sort of pincers movement. Villalobos was to sail directly across the Pacific, while Cabrillo would seek the same goal on a northwesterly route along the coast. If this seems to show a monumental disdain for geography, it did not seem so implausible at the time. No one then had any clear concept of the shape of the Pacific basin or of the great distances involved. It was generally assumed that North America was either an extension of the Asian mainland or very close to it and that the Especieria and the Moluccas were islands near this shared coastline. Thus when Cabrillo's men returned, they reported that the fleet had come very close to the coast of China, an opinion backed by prominent navigators who had themselves been to the Moluccas.[36]

Maps by Battista Agnese, generally thought to date from around 1550, show the coast of Central America and Lower California meanderning lazily westward and a little north toward Asia. California is not much further from Asia than it is from Central America.[37] Giacomo Gastaldi, apparently working with information from the Cabrillo expedition, drew a map of the Pacific in 1562 that shows Japan as almost an offshore island near the coast of

California, closer to North America than it is to Asia.[38] As late as 1600 a cosmographer confidently drew the California coastline stretching nearly due west to Asia, adding, almost as an afterthought, that the land was "yet to be discovered."[39]

More important for the Cabrillo expedition is a 1541 map by Domingo del Castillo, which confirmed this general impression of the coastline of western North America.[40] In his marvelously detailed representation of the California peninsula, Castillo drew upon the results of the Ulloa, Bolaños, and Alarcón expeditions, giving what was for the time a generally accurate picture of the coastlines of lower California.

With Castillo as piloto mayor Alarcón set sail from Navidad on 8 September 1541. Just as he was sailing away, Luis de Castilla arrived with orders cancelling the expedition. Castilla managed to stop only two of the ships, but the flagship was under sail and never turned back. Here is a 1547 account of Castilla's testimony on the subject:[41]

> One of the ships was outside the harbor and sailing away, and the others were about to sail. He took the men from the latter two ships, but the other was already at sea, and he could not bring it back. A small boat that he sent to call it back sailed all the way to the Puerto de Culiacán but could not catch up with it.

Domingo del Castillo was under orders to prepare a map of the coast. A note on the file copy of Alarcón's instructions says: "He will plot the entire coast on a sheet of paper, with each degree noted in its proper position."[42] Castillo's map, made on Mendoza's orders, is probably the first map to show the name California on the peninsula.

The Castillo map is now known only through the copy engraved for Lorenzana's *Historia de Nueva España*, published in Mexico in 1770. Henry R. Wagner has criticized the accuracy of Lorenzana's copy, especially the word California on the lower part of the peninsula.[43] Although Lorenzana modernized the coastline, Humboldt, who saw both the published copy and the original, seemed to think the copy was a faithful one, and he used both the copy and the original interchangeably.[44]

The Castillo map, made with data gathered on this expedition, plus the journeys of Ulloa and Bolaños, was surely included with the instructions that Villalobos brought from Mendoza to Juan Rodríguez in the spring of 1542. No copy of these instructions is known to exist, but they were very likely the same as those given to leaders of earlier expeditions to the north. All the early explorers carried very much the same orders. For example, the instructions sent by Cortés to Diego Hurtado de Mendoza in 1532 were repeated nearly verbatim to Diego López de Zúñiga in 1541.[45] There are similar parallels between Zúñiga's instructions and those given to Alarcón two days later.[46] If Juan Rodríguez was to have been the *almirante* on Zúñiga's voyage, as seems likely, then the orders to Zúñiga were his orders also.

There was no reason for Mendoza to change the orders when he decided to make Juan Rodríguez Cabrillo himself *captain general* of the fleet. Probably the only significant difference was that Zúñiga carried a special royal appointment as *contador* or the yet-to-be-discovered coastline and Spice Islands.[47] Juan Rodríguez Cabrillo had no such royal appointment, but was simply commander of the expedition.

Article one in the orders to Juan Rodríguez doubtless named the ships that he was to take with him. Two of the names we know, the galleon *San Salvador* and another ship named *La Victoria*. *San Salvador*, also called *Juan Rodríguez*, was a galleon of two hundred tons, the flagship of the expedition, and the personal property of Juan Rodríguez. The *San Salvador* was about a hundred feet long, with a high sterncastle and a lower forecastle. She had a slim hull—about twenty-five feet of beam—a square stern, and a good deal of taper or "tumble home" from the mail deck to the top of the sterncastle.[48]

18. *One of the few surviving pictures of ocean-going vessels built at the time of Alvarado's armada, this view shows six ships in a Portugese fleet of 1541. ("Roteiro de Dom. Joham de Castro," Cottonian MS, Tib. D. IX, British Library, London.)*

The ship *Victoria* was a smaller, round-bellied, square-rigged vessel of a hundred tons or so. Some writers, missing the meaning of *cubierta*, call the *Victoria* an open boat, which it was not. The ship had decks, but it was uncastled and miserable to man in stormy weather. By a process of elimination, we can say the *Victoria* was either the *Figueroa*, the *Alvar Núñez*, or the *Anton Hernández*, the carracks or naos gruesas that Alvarado called by the names of their owners.[49]

The *Victoria* was named after Santa María de la Victoria, the seamen's shrine in Triana, just across the river from Seville. The ship itself may very well have been the *Santa María de Buena Esperanza*, renamed to honor the patroness of Spanish sailors.[50] In the summer of 1542 Alvar Núñez reported that his ship, the *Buena Esperanza*, was with the rest of the fleet in the port of Navidad, where, presumably,

Juan Rodríguez had taken her.[51]

In addition to these vessels there were several bateles and the bergantín reported by Francisco de Vargas. Carrying a single mast and a lateen sail, these launches were in constant uses by fleets as they sailed along the coast. Close to shore, they served largely to ferry the parties sent to fetch wood and water. They also scouted out safe passageways for the larger ships into unfamiliar harbors, and carried men and messages between the vessels. On long runs out to sea they were either towed or hoisted aboard one of the larger vessels.[52]

The launch in Juan Rodríguez Cabrillo's armada was probably called *San Miguel*, the fragata or bergantín in Alvarado's fleet, with a lateen sail and auxiliary power from thirteen pairs of oars. *San Miguel* was not a particularly dependable boat, it seems Alvarado had to put her ashore in Acapulco to recaulk the seams then had to send her back to Guatemala for a complete refit. Two years later Juan Rodríguez Cabrillo had to put her ashore on the California coast after her seams pulled apart in heavy seas.[53]

The second and third articles in Mendoza's instructions required the leader of the expedition to make a detailed list of the men and weapons carried in the vessels. The list included at least two hundred names: four officers, twenty-five or thirty crewmen, and two or three cabin boys for the *San Salvador*, plus a couple of dozen Blacks and Indian slaves, twenty-five soldiers, at least one priest and perhaps a lay brother to assist him, and probably a few merchants and their clerks, about a hundred souls in all.[54]

The carrack carried fewer passengers and crew, perhaps a little more than half as many as the *San Salvador*, say fifty or sixty men. There may have been a second carrack, but probably the bergantíin was the third ship.

The bergantín or fragata was served by six or eight men, plus slaves or sailors under punishment to man the oars. In all there were about two hundred, and if there were two carracks in the fleet, perhaps 250 people on the Cabrillo expedition, a figure that seems modest in light of the earlier decisions to send three hundred men with the coastal expedition and another three hundred across the Pacific. In fact, the estimate may be on the low side.[55] About four years after the expedition returned, the royal treasuerer Francisco de Godoy said there were three hundred Spaniards in the armada.[56] A shipmaster named Jácome Ginovés said there were three hundred in the ships sent to Peru,[57] which, as we have seen, were likely the same ones sent to California.

Until the actual manifest is discovered in some unopened bundle of documents it will be impossible to be more precise. Of the people who talked about the expedition shortly after its return, none saw fit to give precise information on its size. Pedro de Velbas, for example, said in 1547 that Juan Rodríguez had a large armada "and many men in it."[58]

A vessel the size of San Salvador would have been equipped with two or three small pieces of artillery, in addition to the arquebuses and crossbows used by the soldiers for close combat at sea and ashore. The small weapons were probably issued to soldiers who had none of their own. These were charged against their individual accounts, the amounts to be deducted later from their shares in the proceeds of the expedition.[59]

Expeditions of this sort were quasi commercial ventures. The fourth article required all goods carried by merchants and other members of the expedition to be delivered to the master of the ship, both for safekeeping and to give the commander better control of relations with native tribes. Trade could take place only with his permission and only in the presence of the captain general.[60]

There were also articles requiring the captain general to keep a strict watch on the morals of the people in his care, and to see that the men showed proper respect for the priest assigned to care for their souls.[61] How closely these rules were observed is anyone's guess. The rules issued to Villalobos for his trans-Pacific voyage specified six months on a rowing bench in the galera for habitual blasphemy,[62] but Villalobos had been given much more detailed disciplinary rules than those that were issued in 1541 to the coastal expeditions. If the testimony of Friar Tomás de la Torre can be trusted, sailors were habitually rude and insulting to priests, and written rules probably did not change their attitudes very much.[63]

One thing is certain. The sexual mores of men in the armada were grossly deficient, even by the standards of the Conquest. Alvarado himself herded Indian women onto his boats and gave them to the sailors.[64] Surely, then, his men did not expect Mendoza's rule about public morality to be enforced with any great enthusiasm. On the other hand, licentious conduct was always illegal, and laws on this matter were enforced with vigor at certain times and places. The famous pilot Juan Fernández de Ladrillero, for example, was brought before the Mexican Inquisition in 1556 and publicly punished for blasphemy.[65]

Fernández was chief pilot of the Bolaños expedition, where he commanded the ship *San Gabriel*. He later told a story about reaching port after a heavy storm that helps us understand how the men conducted themselves:[66]

> We anchored in eight fathoms on a clean bottom, well protected from the northeast. Whereupon we all folded our hands and gave many thanks to God. So great was our devotion and our faces so troubled that we seemed more like friars in Holy Week than sailors in port.

Very probably the rules of conduct in Cabrillo's armada were enforced as rules so often are today, at the whim of the commander and in response to his perception of the need to tighten or loosen the reins of discipline.

More than twenty additional rules outlined the course the expedition was to take and the treatment of natives in any newly discovered lands. These are interesting largely because they very clearly fit the behavior of the Cabrillo expedition during the months spent in California.

Generally, the expedition was to adopt a guarded but friendly attitude toward the natives. If other vessels were sighted, the expedition was to avoid them and also to avoid doing anything else that might endanger the safety of the ships or the men. For example, if the commander had checked carefully and found the natives friendly, then the men might go ashore and make a full reconnaissance, taking careful notes about the people, their language and religion, the quality of the soil, the houses they built, and whether "the country is an island or mainland."[67]

This was a money-oriented venture, and special note was to be taken about trade goods, the things that sold well and items that sold poorly. Both Zúñiga and Alarcón had instructions to establish permanent settlements, if conditions seemed right. In this matter, as will be seen, the instructions given to Zuñiga were the same as those given to Juan Rodríguez Cabrillo. "If you find a good country where you can make a settlement as ordered, you should remain settled there," sending a part of the fleet to scout further along the coast, just in case an even better country might lie beyond.[68]

The instructions had a good deal to say about this settlement. Permanent camp should be far removed from large native towns, in order to avoid problems between the men and the townspeople. At the same time the commander was supposed to keep the men armed and to maintain a constant watch for surprise attacks. Drawing upon unhappy experience in Mexico and Central America, Mendoza ordered that the natives should be treated kindly and should not be divided into encomiendas "until the land is pacified."[69]

Finally, the commander was admonished to keep watch for any sign of the Coronado expedition and to leave messages from time to time for Villalobos and the "ships we are sending to the islands."[70] Not only did the planners underestimate the distance across the Pacific Ocean, they all clearly had little concept of the size of the North American continent, and they seemingly thought Coronado was heading northwest, rather than northeast.

The expedition to California was to be a major undertaking, not just a reconnaissance of the coast. Supplies enough to last two years were taken on board the vessels.[71] This does not mean there were two years of daily rations for every man on the ships, but there was a two year supply of such basic staples as wine, olive oil, hard bread, beans, salt meat and salt fish, all to be supplemented by fresh fish and food gathered ashore or traded with the natives along the way.[72] Those who could afford to do so carried their own food, especially officers and wealthy passengers.[73]

Diego García de Palacio, who lived for years in Guatemala and knew Pacific sailing intimately, wrote in some detail about this matter. The *despensero* or steward had charge of food supplies and the *fogón*, or fireplace. Cabin boys did most of the cooking and serving under his supervision. For the midday meal of the seamen, the boys set a large table on deck under an awning and served the men in groups of four: first a little stack of biscuits with a few garlic cloves to give it flavor, then sardines or cheese, with oil and vinegar to season the sardines. Each man received three mugs of wine. On Sunday and Thursday there was salt meat. Otherwise, meals were rounded out with cod or some other fish, plus beans, peas, or cabbage, and soup. In port the food was fresh and hot. Under sail it was likely to be salted, dried, hard, and often cold. While there was fire in the fogón, a boy stood by with a pail of water, because the whole ship was flammable, especially the sails and the rigging. Once the cooking was finished, the fire in the stove was quenched with a bucket or two of water, until the coals were reduced to a mess of soggy ashes.[74]

Seamen ate relatively well, for the time, but officers fared better. The four major officers of the ship—the captain, pilot, master, and the surgeon—ate together in their private quarters under the cubierta or half-deck. Their food was prepared by their own servants from private stocks, and included whatever fish, fowl, meat, vegetables, wine, and dried fruit they were foresighted enough to bring along.[75] Slaves probably ate whatever scraps they could find, supplemented by a daily ration of soup and bread. Not enough to live in comfort, surely, but sufficent to sustain life and strength.

From all the evidence given on the matter, it seems that the ships going to California were elaborately armed and equipped, with more men and supplies than anyone now supposes. The son of Juan Rodríguez said in 1560 that his father carried "servants, arms, and horses" on the voyage.[76] The *San Salvador* could have carried ten horses easily, the other ships fewer. Juan de Salazar said in 1547 that he saw the ships being loaded at Navidad with "oakum, iron work, hempen ropes and many other things, and cattle."[77]

He is also the man who said he saw skilled Blacks helping refit the vessels in the docks at Navidad. "It is well known, and moreover he himself saw *negros* bought and sent to the ships to help the craftsmen do their work." No doubt some of the same *officiales* who refitted the vessels also went on the ships as carpenters, caulkers, and sailmakers, accompanied by the same Black slaves who helped prepare the vessels for sea.[78]

Only a few of the men on the expedition are known to us today. These include Juan Rodríguez Cabrillo, commander of the expedition and pilot of his own ship, *San Salvador*; Gerónimo de San Remón, master of one of the ships, perhaps the *San Salvador*;[79] Bartolomé Ferrer, chief pilot of the armada and pilot of one of the other ships, doubtless the *Victoria*;[80] Lorenzo Hernández Barreda, also a pilot;[81] and Antonio Correa, master.[82]

Correa was a Portuguese mariner and probably commanded the bergantin, whose crew was headed by a master, rather than a pilot. He had experience in command of his own ship and was in fact named by Viceroy Mendoza to command a similar vessel when he returned from the Cabrillo voyage.[83] Ferrer was from the Levantine coast of Spain,[84] and Hernández was a Corsican. Lázaro de Cárdenas and Francisco de Vargas were both on the voyage, probably as merchants or as soldiers, as there is no evidence that they were experienced seamen.

Though royal orders required that two priests be taken on the expedition, we only know of one. This was Fray Julian de Lescano, an Augustinian monk, who testified in 1547 that he went to California with the armada.[85]

Details of the voyage are slim, coming to us from a summary report prepared in 1543, of which the extant version is nothing more than an abbreviated copy, plus a brief account published in 1601 by the historian Herrera. Both of these accounts are worth critical examination. First the summary report of 1543.

It is a disappointingly brief document, about eight folio pages in length, that summarizes the great bulk of what we know about the expedition. The original author was probably Juan León, notary of the royal audiencia of Mexico, who was ordered in 1543 to take down testimony from survivors of the expedition in Navidad and to put together an account of the journey. Years later he swore under oath that he made the investigation and composed a report as he was ordered to do.[86]

> This witness knew Juan Rodríguez Cabrillo in New Spain in the armada that he assembled there by order of the viceroy, Don Antonio de Mendoza, and of the adelantado, Don Pedro de Alvarado. First [Juan Rodríguez] went as *almirante* of this armada and then as captain, [sailing] along the South Sea coast of New Spain on a discovery of the lands that they sent him to discover, where he died. And this witness knows in addition what he learned in New Spain from a probanza that was made before this witness as notary, by order of the Royal Audiencia.

No one knows what happened to León's original report, which is not now available.

The origin of the report is naturally of great interest to historians, some of whom have attributed authorship either to Bartolomé Ferrer, who took command of the expedition after Cabrillo's death, or to Juan Páez, whose name appears in several places on the cover and the first page of the text.[87]

The argument in favor of Ferrer is disposed of most easily. The document does not bear his name, except in two places in the text. Neither he nor any of his contemporaries ever claimed that he wrote an account of the journey. Instead, this idea seems to have originated with H. W. Henshaw, who published the first English translation in 1879.[88] Henshaw doubtless took his cue from California's first history buff, Alexander S. Taylor, who seemed to think Ferrer might have been the author.[89]

There is a bit more evidence that Juan Páez was the author, though none of this evidence will stand close scrutiny. There was a man named Juan Páez living in Santiago, a notary, and a friend of Juan Rodríguez.[90] The document itself has the name Juan Páez on the cover and the first page. These few facts have been enough to convince some writers that Juan Páez of Santiago was a member of the expedition and the author of the account. As it happens, the Juan Páez in question died before the expedition got under way. We know this from a report of the destruction of Santiago in 1541, where he is called "Juan Páez, already dead."[91]

A stronger piece of evidence claims authorship for Juan Páez de Castro. This is much nearer to the truth of the matter, though still not the final answer. Juan Páez de Castro was royal chronicler of Charles V, and he gathered notes and manuscripts for a projected history of that monarch's reign. Many such documents were copied in his hand and bear his name at the top of the page or on a cover sheet. Some of these can be found in legajo 20 of the *Real Patronato* section at the Archivo General de Indias in Seville. Others exist in the royal library established by Philip II at El Escorial and are there clearly and prominently identified as the papers of Juan Páez de Castro. However, few of these are thought to be original compositions by Páez. Rather, they are original documents or copies gathered by Páez from various sources.[92]

Páez did not become royal chronicler until 1555. He had the report in his possession at one time, as the numbered notes on the document indicate, but he did not write it. It is not in his hand. The man who wrote the copy we now have is Andrés de Urdaneta. The report is in his handwriting.[93]

One of the leading navigators and cosmographers of his day, Urdaneta reached Guatemala in 1539 with Pedro de Alvarado to lead his expedition to the Spice Islands. Once he arrived in Mexico, however, Urdaneta decided that he would not go to the Spice Islands. After Alvarado's death, Mendoza again offered him command of the fleet, and Urdaneta refused a second time. No one knows why, though some think he was even then toying with plans to enter a monastery.[94]

Later in 1543, after the fleet had sailed, Urdaneta went as *visitador* to Navidad, where Juan León was interrogating the survivors of the expedition of Juan Rodríguez Cabrillo. Armed with the *vara de justicia*, Urdaneta could gather any information he wanted, use any official records, question any witnesses.[95] He very likely made his copy of the León report on this visit, also taking copies of the logs and charts. He still had these in 1559, when he began to plan his own trip to the Moluccas.

Collateral evidence shows that no copies of the expedition's logs and maps reached Spain before 1559. Before that date the royal cosmographers in Seville were unaware of the discoveries made on this journey. None of the place names were entered on the *padrón general*, the official maps kept at the Casa de Contratación. We know this by inference, since the original copies of these maps have not survived. Their general contents must be deduced from copies made by the cosmographers for wealthy patrons or friends of the king.

One of the most interesting maps in this group is the 1551 planisphere by the royal cosmographer Sancho Gutiérrez. Although Gutiérrez had access to all the maps and charts in the padron, his planisphere contains no firsthand information about the places visited by the expedition.[96] In fact, the earliest map to draw directly upon information brought back by the expedition of Juan Rodríguez Cabrillo is that of Andrés Homem dated 1559.[97] The Homem map and one published by Giacomo Gastaldi in 1561 or 1562 may be based on logs or charts sent to Spain by Urdaneta in 1559 or earlier to support his argument for a new attempt to find the return route across the Pacific.[98]

The atlases of Baptista Agnese made in the 1550s show some of the discoveries made by Juan Rodríguez Cabrillo, but they are pretty definitely based on those listed by Francisco López de Gómara in his 1552 *Historia de Indias*.[99] Gómara named only a few of the locations visited by Juan Rodríguez Cabrillo. He apparently thought so little of this explorer's accomplishments, that he failed even to mention his name or to locate the places on his own map of the Pacific.[100]

Even the cosmografo mayor of the Casa de Contratacion, Alonso de Santa Cruz, did not have access to the original expedition report until the late 1550s or the 1560s. His *Cronica del Emperador Carlos V* contains a rather lengthy reference to the Villalobos expedition plus some extended extracts from the Juan Rodríguez story of the destruction of Santiago, but no reference to the expedition.[101] As chief geographer he certainly would have included some mention of the expedition if dependable information had been available.

Instead, he seems to have had no more information than could have been contained in one of the regular letters from his friend Viceroy Mendoza. Something like this was probably Gómara's source also, very likely a letter borrowed from Santa Cruz.[102]

The man who had detailed information about the voyage, Andrés de Urdaneta, did not return to Spain until 1566, after completing his round trip across the Pacific. In the fall of that year he joined with other important cosmosgraphers in Madrid to render an official opinion about the exact location of the East Indies. Philip II had asked these experts to decide whether or not the Moluccas, the Philippines, and Cebu were included in the territory pawned to the king of Portugal by Charles V. This was a question of growing importance because of the obvious wealth of the western Pacific islands. This group appointed to study the problem included Chief Cosmographer Alonso de Santa Cruz and his cosmographer Sancho Gutiérrez, as well as Urdaneta and several others. After studying a number of documents, the group presented individual and joint opinions, none of which need concern us here. What does interest us is a series of notes made on the documents, particularly the notes on the account of Juan Rodríguez Cabrillo's expedition.[103]

The expedition report has a cover sheet with notations that look like this:[104]

De Ju° Páez

Relacion del descubrimi° q̃ hizo
Juan rrodriguez navegando por
la contra costa del mar del
sur al norte llebo dos navios*

myo

no ymporta   N°. 145

The words "myo" and "no importa" are in the handwriting of Sancho Gutiérrez. Notes by Gutiérrez on two reports about the Villalobos expedition seem to clarify his cryptic notes. On one of the Villalobos documents he wrote, "Visto por my Sancho Gu[tié]rez." On another that had no title page he wrote, *relacion del vidge que hizo desde la nueva españa alas yslas del poniente Ruy lopez de villalobos Año de 42 pororden del virrey Don antonio de mendoça.*[105] Apparently Gutiérrez studied these documents for his report on the location of the Moluccas. He judged the report on the journey made by Juan Rodríguez Cabrillo "not important," because it did not contain information about the location of the western Pacific islands.

On the reverse of the cover sheet, in a section of the page that may originally have been folded outward, is this note: "Ju° paez 46." Another series of notes appears at the top of the first page of text, looking somewhat as follows:

---

*Account of the discovery that Juan Rodríguez made, sailing along the outer coast of the South Sea to the north. He took two ships.

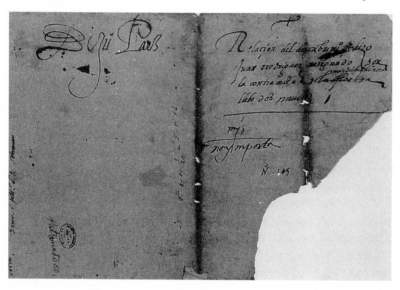

1542

de Ju° Páez

Navegacion del
mar del sur al norte

para el año de
1543

cespedes

19. *When the survivors of Cabrillo's expedition to California returned to Navidad,
they were met by Juan León, who compiled a report from the several accounts
given by members of the expedition. The copy shown here is a summary apparently made by Andrés de Urdaneta for his own use in charting a route
across the Pacific. (Archivo General de Indias, Seville, Spain.)*

The phrase in the left section above, "1542/para el año de/1543,"
is in a format and handwriting that appears in other documents
in the same legajo. These other documents usually have an additional notation, *"de los papeles que Trajeron de Sevilla de Santa Cruz"*
and *"de los papeles de la arca de Santa Cruz,"* showing that they were
part of the library of Alonso de Santa Cruz found packed in an
old leather trunk (*arca encorada vieja*) and sequestered by the crown

after his death.[106] These documents were later delivered to Juan López de Velasco in 1572 upon his appointment as royal historian and cosmographer.[107] However, the report prepared in 1543 by Juan León may not have been among these papers.

Some time before the end of the fifteen sixties the report came into the possession of Juan Páez de Castro, as is apparent from the name of Juan Páez written in several places on the manuscript. Páez was made *cronista oficial* or official historian of Charles V in 1555 and was considered "the best of the emperor's chroniclers."[108] Páez was in the habit of copying whole documents, making copious notes, and numbering these notes and documents. Some of his index sheets still exist in the library of El Escorial. When he died in 1570, his papers were sequestered by the crown, and later they were also delivered to the new royal historian and cosmographer, Juan López de Velasco. By 1574 Velasco had completed his *Geografía y Descripción Universal de las Indias*. His account includes a brief reference to the discoveries made by Juan Rodríguez Cabrillo, the first official account to do so. In his text Velasco repeated the erroneous statement that Cabrillo had only two ships.[109] This is a clear indication that the León manuscript, was in his hands, either from the estate of Santa Cruz or from that of Páez de Castro.

In the upper right-hand corner of the first page of text in this manuscript is the notation: *"Navegacion del mar del sur al norte cespedes."* This is a note by Andrés García de Céspedes, *cosmografo mayor* from 1596 to 1611. On the same day Céspedes was appointed to his post Antonio de Herrera y Tordesillas became *coronista mayor*. All official geographical records were delivered to Céspedes, as the document shows. Historical materials were given to Herrera.[110] Among the papers received by Herrera was a second report of the expedition led by Juan Rodríguez Cabrillo. This report apparently differed in some respects from the one that was delivered to Céspedes. Perhaps Herrera had a more complete version of Urdaneta's copy, while Céspedes received a summary.

Herrera's account of the trip appeared in two brief chapters of his *Historia general*, published early in the seventeenth century.[111] Herrera's account was the first to be published, and for centuries it was the basic printed source of information about the expedition. Herrera's errors about the nationality of Juan Rodríguez and the number of ships on his expedition have stimulated the writing of a lot of bad history, all based ultimately on Herrera's book and León's manuscript, and few agreeing with each other in detail.

So this sole surviving account of the Cabrillo expedition is based on a report compiled by Juan León in 1543 at the order of the Real Audiencia. Once León's report was finished, as we have seen, and largely to keep the sailors busy until needed for reinforcing Villalobos, Mendoza put the crewmen back on board their three ships and sent them off to Peru with a load of horses for sale in that newly-conquered kingdom. Many of them did not return, which helps further to explain our lack of information about the Cabrillo voyage.

The León report was itself based on at least three and perhaps as many as five original accounts. There appear to be about ten transitions in the present text, making it appear that the compiler skipped back and forth a bit from one source to another, as most compilers did then and still do today.

The document is incomplete, lacking the list of crewmen that was doubtless appended to the original. So it is not a verbatim transcript of León's summary, but a further condensation by Urdaneta, written in his hand. Despite these drawbacks the document contains much direct and indirect information about the expedition, the ships, the men, the places visited, and the methods of navigation.

Navigation in those days was not an exact science but an art. Pilots furnished their own instruments and maps and made their computations in individual ways. Thus, when we see abrupt changes in the accumulated latitude error in the document, we can assume that the latitude readings were drawn from accounts made by different navigators.

The first part of the account, covering nearly four months of the voyage and containing many first person references and descriptions of the country and its inhabitants is pretty clearly the work of the commander of the expedition, Juan Rodríguez Cabrillo, sometimes called in this part simply Juan Rodríguez, perhaps because in his report he signed himself that way. This section contains most of the material describing the countryside, the inhabitants, the houses, plants and animals, names of towns, and even a few native names for flora and fauna. Distances on land are often measured in arquebus shots, as a military commander might do, and little note is taken of winds and currents and sailing methods.

Several later sections are most concerned with navigational details. Style, content, and navigational data clearly identify them as the work of two different pilots. One section near the end of the document contains a number of references to prayer and other religious matters. This inevitably suggests that the source may have been the priest who accompanied the expedition, although the section could also have been written by a sailor frightened into an uncommonly religious mood by the severe winter storms that struck the coast of upper California.

The document is put together in the style and language typical of a sixteenth-century notary. There is no hint of emotion, no lingering over a polished phrase. This is simply a brief, terse summary of the main events of the voyage, by a man trained to ferret out the plain, unadorned facts from the accounts of witnesses whose recollections and points of view might differ substantially. This is not to say that the writer was always successful. His descriptions of the geography of Upper California are sometimes confusing, often contradictory.

Some parts were condensed by Juan León, but much of the summation was done by Andrés de Urdaneta, who left out those parts that seemed to him either uninteresting or unimportant. There is so much detail in the early portion of the narrative, and the final sections are so abbreviated, that it is clear the writer lost interest in the project as he went through the manuscript. The list of names originally appended to the manuscript by León was omitted when

Urdaneta made his own copy. The friar was more interested in the discoveries than in the crewman who went on the trip. And by the end of the manuscipt, he was very tired of the work. His fatigue shows in his handwriting, which got a bit larger, while the lines of text got a bit shorter toward the end of the manuscript.

Acknowledging all of these difficulties in advance, there is still enough dependable information to give us a remarkably clear picture of Juan Rodríguez Cabrillo's voyage to California.

Chapter 6
Discoveries in Lower California

WITH A TREACHEROUS southerly wind blowing across the bows, Juan Rodríguez Cabrillo led his fleet out of the harbor at Navidad at noon on Tuesday 27 June 1542,[1] nearly two years after first setting sail from Guatemala with Alvarado's great armada. The main objective of the voyage remained the same as ever; "to discover the coast of New Spain."[2] The pilots had studied and copied all the available charts and maps from the expeditions of Cortes, Bolaños, Alarcón, and Ulloa; problems had been discussed over and over. Discovery to them meant not something totally unexpected, for they thought they knew what to expect: a coast line that ran to the northwest all the way to China.[3] They expected to fill in the blank spaces on the maps and bring back reports of new trading opportunities and new places to settle.

Once out of the harbor, with a fair southeast wind, they made good time, sailing up the coast forty leagues or so to Cabo Corrientes, where they anchored late the next day. This first full day of sailing pretty well confirms the use by Juan Rodríguez of a league equivalent to 2.5 miles, more or less.[4] Contrary winds kept them from crossing the gulf for three or four days, but on 2 July they came within "sight of California," as the summary account puts it. On Monday the third of July they anchored off the "Point of

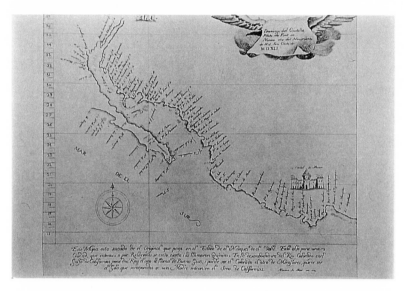

20. In 1541 Domingo del Castillo prepared a map of the coast of New Spain and
the peninsula of California as far west as the Cabo del Engaño, the limit of
geographical discoveries prior to the expedition of Juan Rodríguez Cabrillo. The
original of the map has disappeared. This copy was published in 1770 by Francisco Antonio de Lorenzana in his Historia de Nueva España. (Huntington
Library.)

California."[5] This is one of the earliest uses of the word California to designate a geographical location on the Pacific coast.

Fray Antonio de Meno had used the word a year earlier in describing the discoveries of the Ulloa expedition,[6] and Domingo del
Castillo very probably put the name on his map of the California
peninsula and the Pacific Coast of New Spain later that same
year.[7] The sense in the report of the expedition of Juan Rodríguez
Cabrillo seems to be that the word applies only to the tip of the
peninsula, which he calls the "Punta de la California."[8] In Herrera's
version of the voyage the armada arrived at the "Port of the Marqués del Valle [Cortés], which they called La Cruz, which is the
Coast of California."[9]

The name was also applied to a place on the coast in a description of the voyage given in the Mendoza visita of 1547. In this document Sebastián de Vora swore that he had "talked with many mariners who went on the voyage of discovery with Juan Rodríguez Cabrillo along the coast to the Bay of California."[10]

There is some evidence that Ulloa's men invoked the name California in a joking reference to the bay where Ulloa landed or to an island in that bay. The joke, if it was one, was on the conquistadors, for this barren coast bore no resemblance to that "earthly paradise" described by Ordoñez de Montalvo. In his novel about the adventures of a certain knight named Esplandián, Montalvo told about the inhabitants of an island named California, a place inhabited solely by women and ruled by a gorgeous queen, who allowed men on the island once each year or so for a ceremony of singular character. The island was "at the right hand of the Indies," and the ceremony was one aimed at continuing the race, not to put too fine a point on it all.[12] Womanizers of great initiative and enthusiasm, the conquistadors no doubt appreciated the story and perhaps repeated it frequently so that the story lost nothing in the telling.

Having all this in mind, it is easy to see how the conquistadors might remember very clearly Montalvo's name for the island California but be a little vague about its exact description. It is no surprise to see some of them calling California an island,[13] some a bay, some a point of land, and all doing so at more or less the same time and place. One map of the 1580s even placed California on the coast of Sinaloa,[14] but the men with Juan Rodríguez were not responsible for this. The expedition report used by Herrera placed the California landfall at "veinte i quatro grados largos," or "a generous twenty four degrees" of latitude.[15] George Davidson, who spent years surveying the Pacific Coast, has identified this place as Cape Pulmo, the easternmost point of land in the Baja California peninsula, latitude 23 degrees and 23 minutes.[16]

Just south of this bay is a small cove called Santa Cruz, with a good sandy beach, a stream of fresh water, and anchorage in ten fathoms close to shore.[17] This is the place Herrera called El Puerto del Marques del Valle, the same place that Sebastián de Vora called El Puerto de California. The armada rested here for two days and replenished supplies of wood and water. If they saw Calafia and her buxom maidens, they failed to make a note of it.

In this first landfall on the California coast, a well-known location visited several times by earlier expeditions, the latitude reading was in error by more than half a degree, and there was apparently no attempt to make a longitude determination. In fact, there are no longitude estimates for the whole expedition. The explanation for all this lies in the way navigation was practiced in the early sixteenth century.

Distances were measured with wooden floats or logs, traverse boards, and often by dead reckoning. Time was kept with an hourglass. The simple mariner's astrolabe could be used for a good approximation of latitude, and all these instruments were in use on the west coast of New Spain before 1540.[18] But the navigational instruments approved for use in Spanish ships were scandalously inaccurate, as many pilots were beginning to discover. Even the compass was undependable.[19]

Chief Cosmographer Alonso de Santa Cruz carried on a lengthy correspondence with Viceroy Antonio de Mendoza in an attempt to establish longitudes and compass declinations for New Spain. During the eclipse of the moon in 1539 Mendoza made observations in Guadalajara, while Santa Cruz observed the phenomenon in Toledo. From these data Santa Cruz concluded that Guadalajara was "6 hours and about four fifths of an hour" west of Toledo. He then concluded that this placed Guadalajara "a scant 105 degrees" west of Toledo. He estimated that Navidad lay two and a half degrees west of Guadalajara or 107 and a half degrees from Toledo.[20] In all these computations he erred on the side of generosity. Toledo is about four degrees east of Greenwich. Guadalajara lies in 103 degrees and 20 minutes west longitude, and Navidad is only a degree and a half farther west. Santa Cruz erred by placing Navidad about two and a half degrees farther west than it actually is, but this is not a bad calculation for a geographer whose smallest unit of measurement was a fifth of an hour.

Similarly, Santa Cruz and the other pilots in Seville generally agreed that the compass variation in the islands of the West Indies was about three points west of north. But Viceroy Mendoza assured him that he had observed the compass variation many times in Mexico and found it to be a little less than two points to the east of north.[21] Both men were wildly wrong,[22] a fact Santa Cruz may have suspected, when he confessed, "This confused me greatly."[23] Doubtless it confused the pilots on the Mar del Sur just as much.

The conclusion to be drawn from all this is that pilots in the early sixteenth century were not able to determine latitude, longitude, or direction with great exactness. Considering the crude and inaccurate instruments at their disposal, these early navigators were fortunate to be able to come within a degree or so of correct latitude. Most of them could only make a guess at longitude. They nearly always assumed their compasses to be several points in error. In fact, at just about the same time the expedition of Juan Rodríguez Cabrillo was leaving Navidad, a great argument was beginning at the Casa de Contratación, because the officially approved charts and instruments were made with so little attention to accuracy.[24] Even if the instruments had been more precise, the mathematical tables were not.[25] Moreover, many of the pilots did not know how to handle their instruments or keep them in good repair. Ulloa made this complaint about one of his own pilots, Juan Castellón, saying he did not keep his instruments carefully corrected and in good order.[26] As it turned out, neither of Ulloa's pilots made very accurate observations, and as they sailed farther north, their errors increased. The same thing happened on the voyage led by Juan Rodríguez, though his observations were somewhat more accurate than those of Ulloa at the higher latitudes.

After their first California landfall, the ships of the fleet rounded the tip of the peninsula, then sailed north and west along the coast for more than a month, following the route pioneered by Ulloa and Bolaños. For various reasons progress was slow. The northwesterly winds and a moderate northwesterly current often kept them from making much headway when sailing close to shore. The constant need for replenishing food and water supplies also retarded the ships. But the country was dry and unforested, the Indians lived in misery and want, and there was little temptation to tarry long in the bays and ports the Spaniards visited. Because the coastline was fairly well known from the previous visits of Ulloa (1539) and Bolaños (1541), the expedition discovered very little that was new or noteworthy on this part of the journey.

From the point called California the expedition sailed south and west to Cabo San Lucas, where the shore parties managed to find water. They saw no Indians, doubtless because the inhabitants went into hiding when they saw ships arriving along the coast.[27] Visits by two prior expeditions had been enough to convince the natives that the strangers were not bringing gifts.

Leaving the night of the seventh on the tide, the fleet sailed all day on the eighth and finally anchored the morning of July ninth about fifty leagues from Cabo San Lucas at the place Ulloa had named Punta de la Trinidad on Santa Margarita Island.[28] The passage was safe enough, but the country was forbidding. The whole coastline was mountainous, rugged, and barren. Even today nothing grows there but desert brush and cactus.[29] From the summary report it is apparent the commander was looking for that "good country where you can make a settlement." Clearly, this was not such a place.

Nonetheless, the commander anchored here for two days, waiting for a change in the wind, which blows all year from the northwest.[30] No doubt the fleet anchored inside the southern extension of Magdalena Bay, which is well protected, unlike the bay itself, where the wind blows across the sandspit at its northern end. These contrary winds were a continuing problem for the commander since his route was to the northwest, and his vessels could not sail close to the wind. The summary report calls these "west northwest winds,"[31] an indication that his pilots were using compasses that had been corrected for the use of ships sailing between Spain and the Indies, where compass variation was west rather than east.

In this passage and elsewhere the evidence is strong that his compasses registered too far to the west, by perhaps as much as a full point (11 1/4 degrees).[32] Few of the compass readings refer to quarter points, such as those that would be expressed in English as "West by North." This does not mean he used a sixteen-point compass. Rather, the summary report contains a simplification of sailing directions made by the notary who prepared the summary record of the journey. The standard Spanish compass had thirty-two points.[33]

On Thursday, 13 July, the armada sailed past the entrance to Magdalena Bay, a place Bolaños had christened Puerto de San Pedro. Bolaños had explored the area thoroughly and reported that no wood or water was to be found ashore, so the ships did not bother to anchor again, though the mouth of the bay is a beautifully sheltered spot. Continuing north, the armada rounded the rocky volcanic outcropping at Cape San Lázaro, then sailed with a favorable wind along that seventy-five mile sandy crescent of coastline to Point San Juánico, where they arrived on Wednesday the ninth.[34]

Here they went ashore and followed an Indian trail inland a distance of "about an arquebus shot" to a spring. The surrounding tableland was dry and barren, the place now called Punta Pequeña. Juan Rodríguez Cabrillo called it Puerto de la Madalena in honor of St. Mary Magdalen, whose feast is celebrated on 22 July. This was the first place named by the expedition, doubtless due to a suggestion from the priest who accompanied the armada.[35]

They left this spot on 20 July, heading now to the northwest, along another great crescent curve of coastline. Sailing very nearly against the wind, they made poor time, anchoring for the night behind the point Bolaños had named for Santa Catalina, now called Santo Domingo Point.[36]

For five more days they battled the winds, finally anchoring on July 25 in a large bay that they named Puerto de Santiago after St. James the Apostle, whose feastday it was. Wagner is of the opinion that the bay was very possibly discovered and given the same name by Bolaños, who arrived along this part of the coast in late November 1541, about the time of the feast of St. James Intercisus.[37] Undoubtedly, he is wrong. Juan Fernández de Ladrillero said the bay was called San Mateo by the Bolaños party.[38]

Inside the bay is a fine sheltered lagoon, where a few months earlier Bolaños and his crews found vast schools of fishes like those common along the Spanish coasts. These included flatfish (*lenguadas*), horse mackerel, (*caballas*), and sharks (*cazones*), or *follos* as they called them in Andalusia, plus "a great quantity of sardines just like those of Spain."[39] But even the Spanish love for seafood was not enough to keep the restless men of the armada in port. The wind had changed, and they were able to sail quickly around Abreojos Point.

The commander's note here says these are "very dangerous and treacherous shoals. They cannot be seen except when the sea breaks upon then." This is an interesting comment, as it is one of the few useful bits of navigational information in the first section of the manuscript. His calculations placed the rocks "a league from shore and in a full 27 and a half degrees," which is three quarters of a degree north of their actual location.[40]

By all appearances, this first section of the account was taken from the report prepared by Juan Rodríguez Cabrillo himself. Navigational details are largely lacking; the attention of the writer is directed ashore. He notes whether the land is dry or fertile. His use of "an arquebus shot" to measure distance is strongly reminiscent of the same sort of military terminology used in the *Relación del Espantable Terremoto*, where distances are given in crossbow shots. On a few rare occasions, the narrative retains the first person style of the original report, as though the copyist wanted to record the commander's exact words.[41]

On 26 July, after sailing nearly sixty miles, the ships anchored on the lee side of Asunción Point, a place marked by the first trees seen since leaving the Punta de California. "We named it Santa Ana," the narrative says, after the saint whose feastday it was. The surrounding hillsides were covered with trees when Cabrillo saw them, though this is not now the case. Vizcaíno reported seeing a "vast number" of sea lions (*zalophus californianus*) on a nearby islet. The men of the expedition doubtless saw them too, though this information is not included in the log. The animals still come there by the thousands (8,500 in 1979 and 2,400 in 1984).[42]

A day later the fleet anchored in a place the commander called Puerto Fondo because of its great depth, some thirty fathoms. This place is now called San Pablo Bay, and the anchorage is no longer as deep.[43] The log for this date contains the first mention of the great kelp (*macrocystus*) beds along the coast. Especially interesting was the "grass" that was clearly visible on the bottom (*phyllosphadix*).

Just beyond this bay San Pablo Point and surrounding headlands form a rock barrier, an arm of the Sierra Pintada that rises within a few miles to elevations of two and three thousand feet. Though these steep slopes provide shelter from the wind, sailing around the point can be a difficult maneuver, as the explorers discovered. Three times on 28 July the pilot tried to round the point, and each time the ships had to return to Puerto Fondo.[44]

Finally, on the last day of the month, the armada sailed around the point and anchored a day later within sight of Cedros Island.[45] "From California to here," said Juan Rodríguez Cabrillo, "we have not seen an Indian." The landscape was stark and uninviting. "This is high country, rough and brushy." They called the place San Pedro Víncula, again because it was the feast of that saint.[46]

Contrary winds kept them from approaching Cedros for several days, so they spent their time fishing and hunting for birds. "Because of contrary winds, we were on this island until the following Saturday. There are many fish that can be caught with a hook and many birds."[47] Finally, after beating first on one tack and then another, they managed to reach the Isla de Cedros on 5 August. They remained at this grand island until 10 August, taking on wood and water, looking for Indians, seeing signs of habitation, but failing to meet any of the people who lived there.

The vegetation in the sixteenth century was apparently much as it is today. Tall cedars and pines, some as high as sixty or seventy feet, covered the crests and western slopes of the mountains. The rest of the island was covered with grass, shrubs, and dwarf oak.[48]

Cabrillo said that the south shore of the island ran almost east-west. In reality it runs west northwest to east southeast. On the next day he sailed across Sebastián Vizcaíno Bay, which he called simply the ensenada, to Playa María Bay. Arriving on 12 August, he named it Puerto de Santa Clara in honor of the day's patron. His course, he said, ran northeast-southwest, while the coastline ran north northwest and south southeast.[49] In each of these determinations, his compass readings erred by about fifteen or twenty degrees too far to the west, partly because of magnetic declination, but also because he used the corrected compasses made in Seville, as noted earlier.

In this little bay the Spaniards found four Indians, who ran off when they approached. Again, because of contrary winds they remained here until the thirteenth, studying the land, which they found to be bare of trees, but unbroken and having both plains and valleys.[50]

When the journey resumed, the winds were light and they made slow progress for a couple of days. To avoid missing anything ashore, they anchored close in each night. Later in the week the northwest wind returned, and by Thursday the seventeenth they were buffeted by sudden rainstorms and shifting winds. Saturday they reached a small, rocky island, where they spent the night and then named it San Bernardo in honor of that Sunday's patron saint. The mainland had a very fine appearance, as Juan Rodríguez Cabrillo reported, with plains and nice valleys, a few groves of trees in some places, open country elsewhere.[51]

Sailing north from that barren little island, they passed Rosario Bay and Baja Point, which Ulloa had called Cabo del Engaño because he had not been able to sail past it in spite of repeated attempts. With fair winds, *San Salvador* and the other ships had no trouble rounding this sandy point, which they called Punta del Engaño, as though denying Ulloa's evidence that it was a great and dangerous cape where the direction of the coastline changed dramatically.[52] From this point onward Cabrillo and his men were entering uncharted waters, where no Spanish ships had been before.[53]

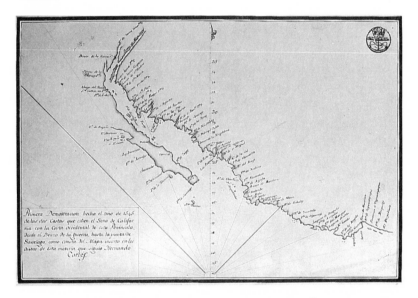

21. In this map of the California peninsula the Cabo del Engaño is at the far left. From this point the expedition sailed into unknown waters. (Museo Naval, Madrid, Spain.)

Sailing directly north, they landed at Cape San Quentin.[54] Here they remained overnight, then went ashore to take formal possession of the country, naming the place Puerto de la Posesión. The legal formality was conducted by "Captain Juan Rodríguez Cabrillo in the name of His Majesty and of the Most Illustrious Señor Don Antonio de Mendoza."[55] The formulary for such ceremonies is interesting, as can be seen from that used by Ulloa in 1539:[56]

> I Pedro de Palenca, public notary of this armada bear witness and true testimony to all the gentlemen who might see these presents (whom God Our Lord honor and preserve from evil) that on the eighteenth day of the month of September of the year thirty-nine the Very Magnificent Señor Francisco de Ulloa, lieutenant governor and captain of this armada, for the Most Illustrious Señor Marques del Valle de Guaxaca, took possession in El Puerto de Los Puertos en La Baya de Posesyon for the said Señor Marques and in the name of the Emperor our Lord, King of Castille, this place being in latitude twenty-nine and two-thirds degrees. Placing his hand upon his sword, he said that if there were any person who might contradict him, he was ready to defend what he had done. He cut trees with the [sword], moved stones from one place to another, and took water from the sea, pouring it upon the land; all of this being done as a sign of possession.

Juan Rodríguez Cabrillo, of course, would have substituted his own name for that of Ulloa, Mendoza's for Cortés, and he would have given the latitude as thirty-one and a half degrees. He was a bit more than a degree too high here in estimating latitude, and his compass reading for the previous day's sailing was also in error (north northwest, rather than true north). However, his measurement of distance for that leg of the journey was very nearly perfect, as it so often was. He said he had gone ten leagues, and the actual distance is a bit more than twenty-six miles.[57]

This Puerto de la Posesion was backed by "high and rolling mountains, and it has fine valleys. It appears to be a good place, though barren." This is a small and perfectly sheltered port, though extensive shoals make the approach treacherous. The wooden ships of those days could be drawn ashore on the sand and mud flats, so the armada spent five days repairing sails, filling water casks, and probably drawing the leaky fragata, *San Miguel* ashore, to recaulk the seams.[58]

In this port he found three large villages and some Indian fishermen.[59] Though most of them ran away, some of the men captured one, gave him some trinkets, and let him go, following the viceroy's instructions to be friendly. Their generosity paid off two days later, when they saw smoke at one of the villages and took a boat to shore. About thirty Indians came out to meet them. Two women and a boy were brave enough to go back to the ship with the Spaniards. For their trouble they were given some clothing and small gifts. Try as they might, neither the Spaniards nor their Mexican Indian interpreters were able to communicate with the Indians, even in sign language. The following day, Friday the twenty-fifth, the shore party met another groups of Indians at the watering place. Doubtless expecting gifts similar to those distributed the day before, these Indians led the sailors to a pool of fresh water and one nearby of salt. Using signs, the Indians of this group said they lived far inland and came from a large tribe.[60]

Five other Indians appeared on the beach that same afternoon and asked to be taken out to the ships. Their bodies were painted in black and white to resemble the jackets and slashed doublets of the Spaniards, decorations almost exactly like those seen by von Langsdorff at San José two centuries later. They said they had met bearded men who brought dogs and carried crossbows and swords and who looked just like the Spaniards. These men were some five days journey toward the interior. Certainly they had seen Ulloa and his men three years earlier, but on the off chance that they were talking of Coronado, Cabrillo wrote a letter and asked the Indians to deliver it to him.[61] A half century later the Indians told Vizcaíno a similar story about bearded men with firearms some distance away.[62]

The narrative gives a great deal of detail about these Indians, perhaps because Juan Rodriguez Cabrillo spent a good deal of ink on his own description. They were tall and well built. Some wore deerskins and possibly deerskin sandals similar to those worn in Mexico. They carried bows and flint-tipped arrows.[63]

After spending five days in port, repairing the ships, taking on wood and water, and making notes about the people and countryside, the fleet left on Sunday the twenty-seventh of August. They sailed slowly along the coast until the thirteenth, when a violent storm struck and they were driven almost all the way back to Puerto de la Posesíon. They hid under the lee of San Martin Island, a volcanic cone they had noted earlier and named in honor of Saint Augustine, whose feast is celebrated on 28 August.[64]

The island was and still is quite barren. The men of the armada met no Indians here but noted that the island was probably occupied, at least occasionally. They also found huge piles of driftwood, cypresses and cedar, as they then thought. The two "cow horns" they found here were probably horns of wild sheep that roamed over the rocks and craters.[65]

A few days later, Sunday, 3 September, they once again began sailing up the coast, this time with more success. By the following Thursday they were anchored in San Ramón Bay, and on Friday the eighth they were at Colnett Bay, which they named Puerto de Santa María in honor of the Virgin Mary, whose birthday is celebrated on 8 September.[66]

Some inconsistencies in the narrative at this point make it appear that the compiler switched sources, probably in order to shorten what he thought was a dull and repetitious story. One striking quality in the narrative is that the compass directions are suddenly quite correct. From San Martín Island the ships followed a course directly north along a coast that runs true north for a distance of seven leagues (nineteen miles) to San Ramón Bay and its large beds of kelp. There the coast turned to the northwest, and the ships followed it to Colnett Bay, just east of Cape Colnett.[67]

Most of the earlier translations have identified the expedition's name for this bay as San Martín, and with some reason. The manuscript calls it "san m" and "san min," the second abbreviation certainly being a Spanish abbreviation for Martín. However, the day of arrival there was one of the most important feasts of the Blessed Virgin. Moreover, at least one important sixteenth-century source (the 1592 Molyneux globe) locates a Santa Maria at this place. The word "min" could very easily be a mistaken reading of "m^{ia}." This is the standard abbreviation of Maria, and in any case, it is often impossible to distinguish between the letters "a" and "n" in sixteenth- century manuscripts and charts. For these reasons it seems likely that the manuscript is in error about the name.[68]

There is also an error in the departure date. The manuscript has the fleet leaving port on "Monday the eighth," an obvious error for the eleventh,[69] doubtless a result of switching manuscript sources. Peculiarities in vocabulary and style also argue for a change in manuscript sources. For instance, the mountains at Cape Colnett are said to "come from behind," a phrase that appears again on 16 November in a section that seems to be based on the report of Bartolomé Ferrer or one of the other pilots.[70]

In the spare and skeletal style of this part of the narrative, we see that the ships took on water here and perhaps recaulked seams opened during the stormy days at the end of August. The Spaniards stayed here for three days, again taking formal possession of the country, doubtless on the feast of the Virgin.

The Indians they met were robust people who wore no clothes, much like the people pictured in reports two centuries later, but carried bows and flint-tipped arrows.[71] There were forty of them in all. The Indians were not afraid of the Spaniards, and though natives and visitors could not understand each other, they entertained the explorers with a feast of roasted agave and fish. It requires little imagination to see why the Spaniards stayed so long. This was not only the largest group of Indians the expedition had met along the California coast, it was also their first encounter with genuinely friendly and generous people.

An Indian of ẙ Southermost parts of California
as Returning from Fishing & another on his Barklog

Two Californian Women, the one in a Birds Skin the other in that of a Deer

22 and 23. *Among the earliest pictures of California Indians are these women and the fisherman depicted in George Shelvocke's* Voyage Around the World, *published in 1726. (Huntington Library.)*

Leaving this place on the eleventh, the fleet sailed to Santo Tomás Point, fighting the wind all the way. They arrived on September 14, the feast of the Exaltation of the Holy Cross, and the explorers named the placed Cabo de Cruz. They found no wood or water at Cabo de Cruz, nor did they see any sign of Indians. None of this is surprising. The Santo Tomás River, prominently featured on maps of this coast, disappears into the sands just before it reaches the ocean, except during the very wettest months of winter, when it flows all the way to the sea.[72]

Two more days of hard sailing against stiff northwest winds took them only a few miles farther up the coast, but they began to note a dramatic change in the landscape. "Another sort of country begins here. It is red earth and better looking."[73]

Back with narrative of the expedition, we find the fleet on 17 September sailing into "a fine, sheltered port," where the approach lay between a small island and the mainland. The bay is now called Bahía de Todos Santos, and the island is Todos Santos Island. Cabrillo called the port San Mateo in honor of the apostle whose feast came on 21 September, when he must have performed the formal ceremony that declared the place to belong to the king of Spain and the viceroy of New Spain. There were no springs at the landing place, now the city of Ensenada, so the ships refilled their water casks in a small pool of rain water, while other shore parties went out for a look at the countryside.[74]

They found "a good country from the looks of things. There are broad savannahs, and the vegetation is like that of Spain." Some of the trees reminded them of ceibas or floss-silk trees, "except the wood is hard."[75] These may have been ash or sycamores, for ceibas are not part of the natural flora here.

Strangest of all, from our viewpoint, were the "flocks of animals, like cattle, that roam by the hundreds and more." From their appearance and gait they looked like the Peruvian "sheep" that Cabrillo had seen on his trip to the Inca country two years earlier. The problem with this description is that there are no animals native to California that have "long wool and small horns" and "broad, round tails." Very likely these were herds of pronghorn antelopes. Either the men did not see them up close, or the man who compiled the narrative made an error or an interpolation here. Cabrillo may have said that the beasts reminded him of the llamas in Peru; and Juan León, who knew what llamas were, may have added the phrase about the "long wool."[76]

The armada sailed again on 23 September and continued its journey up the coast, where the narrator saw "very beautiful valleys, groves of trees, and low, rolling countryside." On the twenty-sixth and twenty-seventh they passed the Coronado Islands, which they called Islas Desiertas. They estimated the latitude at thirty-four degrees, a bit more than a degree and a half too high. The mainland was "a good land, by its appearance, with broad valleys and with mountains farther inland." As more trees appeared, the landscape in places was covered with dense smoke, a result of deliberate burning by the Indians.[77] This aboriginal burning technique increased the harvest of acorns and grass seeds and improved the browse for deer, rabbits, and other animals. Planned burns were usually made in the fall, after the seed harvest.[78]

Thus, in three months of fairly pleasant travel the expedition had gone well beyond the places reached by Bolaños and Ulloa, checking every large inlet and bay, but nonetheless confirming the earlier conclusions that the country was too dry and barren for settlement. Cabo del Engaño, which seems to have stopped Ulloa in his tracks, had been an easy sail for the ships of Juan Rodríguez Cabrillo, and the men pushed their ships further north and west with renewed enthusiasm and vigor.

Chapter 7
The Discovery of Upper California

THE EXPEDITION CONTINUED TO sail north and west, and on 28 September the explorers discovered "a sheltered port and a very good one, to which they gave the name San Miguel," as the next day would be the feast of Saint Michael. This was the first landfall in the area that was to become known as Upper California. The name given to the new port seems to have caused some grumbling among the crew members, for San Miguel was the name of the small *fragata*. The crews of the other ships evidently demanded similar honor, so the next important discoveries were named after the other two ships, *San Salvador* and *La Victoria*.

The port named for the smallest ship in the fleet was San Diego Bay. Cabrillo estimated the latitude at thirty-four and a third degrees. After anchoring at the entrance to the bay, a party went ashore and found a few Indians, most of whom fled. For three of the natives avarice outweighed fear, and they stayed to receive some gifts. The presents must have been a disappointment, for that night, when the men went ashore to fish with a net, some of the Indians returned, armed with bows and arrows and shot three of the Spaniards,[2] but the wounds must have been minor, and relations with the Indians here soon began to improve.

The next morning another shore party rowed up the bay in a

boat, perhaps the *San Miguel*, sounding the depth of the water and looking for other natives. Spying two children on the beach, they landed, captured them, and brought them back to the fleet. They were talkative children, but try as they might, no one could understand the language, and signs were useless. Consequently, the commander gave the children some shirts, a very generous gift, and sent them back ashore.[3]

The good treatment accorded the Indian children seems to have strengthened the resolve of the adults. Three of them came out to the ships on the following morning and managed a lengthy conversation in sign language. They reported that further inland there were bearded men dressed just like those on the ships, armed with crossbows and swords. "They made gestures with the right arm as though they were using lances, and they ran about as though they were riding horses." According to the Indians, the bearded men had killed many natives. This, they said, was the reason they had fled in fear when Juan Rodríguez Cabrillo and his men approached them two days earlier. The Indians had a curious name for the Spaniards, who thought it sounded something like "Guacamal."[4]

This port, now called San Diego, was the finest on the West Coast and the first landfall made by Cabrillo in Upper California. During their five day sojourn here there was a great storm, but the fleet had sailed farther up the harbor and felt scarcely a tremor of movement.[5]

Leaving port on Tuesday, 3 October, the armada sailed slowly up the coast, noting many interesting valleys, broad savannahs, high mountains a few miles inland, and a great pall of smoke that told them the area was heavily inhabited. After two days of this, they sailed out toward some islands that lay about seven leagues, or twenty miles offshore.[6]

Reaching the nearest island on Saturday the seventh, they named it San Salvador, after the expedition's flagship. This is the island now called Santa Catalina. The second island (now named San Clemente) they called Victoria, after the third ship in the armada.[7]

They went ashore on the nearer one, San Salvador, and as the boat approached, a great crowd of armed Indians appeared. Shouting and gesticulating, the Indians made it clear that they wanted the strangers to come ashore. But the women suddenly fled, and for a time it seemed as though this might be a trap. Finally, the Indians put down their weapons, and eight or ten of them piled into a canoe and paddled boldy out to the ships.[8]

As usual, the commander gave the visitors beads and other gifts that pleased them. A little later all went ashore, the best of friends. As the narrative has it, "They felt very secure, the Spaniards, the Indian women, and everyone." During this brief visit an old man came up to the visitors and said that he had heard reports of bearded men dressed like the Spaniards somewhere on the mainland.[9]

Anxious to continue exploring the vastly improved coastline, Juan Rodríguez Cabrillo and his men made a hasty departure from the islands, and the next morning they were in San Pedro Bay. The burning chapparal raised such thick clouds of smoke that they named the place Baya de los Fumos (the Bay of Smoke). Cabrillo called this place "a good port and a good land with many valleys and plains and wooded areas." A few Indians came out to visit them in a canoe and repeated the now familiar story that bearded men just like the Spaniards lived somewhere to the north. Since this was Sunday, they decided to remain for the day in port.[10]

On Monday, the ninth of October, they left the Baya de los Fuegos (the Bay of Fire), as they also called it, and sailed a few miles up the coast. Seeing another large cove, they anchored overnight in what is now called Santa Monica Bay.[11]

On Tuesday the tenth they sailed up the coast another twenty miles. In one of the few direct quotations from Juan Rodríguez Cabrillo, the narrative gives a little glimpse of the countryside. "We saw an Indian town on the land next to the sea, with large houses built much like those of New Spain." On the beach were many fine canoes, each capable of carrying twelve or thirteen Indians. There were so many of these impressive vessels that the men christened the place Pueblo de las Canoas. This was very probably the large village at Mugu Lagoon, the same place visited half a century later by Vizcaíno.[12] Canoeloads of Indians came out to visit the ships and talk to the men. By this time the explorers were almost bored by the repeated story of bearded Christians marching through the interior. The local name for the Christians sounded to Spanish ears like "Taquimine."[13]

24. For various reasons a full report of the results of the Cabrillo expedition did not reach Europe until the late 1550s, when the viceroy of Mexico, Luis de Velasco, began to ask for permission to send a new fleet to the Islands of the West. In 1559 Andrés Homem seemingly drew upon this information to produce the first reasonably accurate depiction of the region explored by Juan Rodríguez Cabrillo. (Bibliothéque Nationale, Paris.)

The manuscript sources used by Herrera at the end of the sixteenth century led him to believe that these Indians were "gentle" people.[14] This did not necessarily mean they were pacifists, as we shall see, but they made Juan Rodríguez and his men feel so welcome that they distributed gifts here for the first time since leaving the island of San Salvador. This pleased the Indians so much that they repeated their stories about Spaniards who traveled in the interior, adding that they were near a great river and that they were only seven days' travel away.[15]

Realizing that these Spaniards could be from Alarcón's second voyage, Juan Rodríguez very nearly decided to send two men to find out whether these persistent reports were true. Finally, he decided not to do so, and instead dispatched another letter in care of some Indians who were going in that direction.[16]

For the next few days the expedition sailed along the channel that runs between the nearby islands and the mainland, an area known now as the Santa Barbara Channel, with a southern extension called the San Pedro Channel. The islands themselves are now named the Channel Islands. Juan Rodríguez later called them the Islas de San Lucas, after the Apostle Luke, because he took formal possession of the islands on the feast of St. Luke. He seems to have recognized that these islands can be subdivided into two groups, those near Santa Barbara being in one group of San Lucas Islands (now called San Miguel, Santa Rosa, Santa Cruz, and Anacapa), and those near San Pedro (now called Santa Barbara, Santa Catalina, San Clemente, and San Nicolas) constituting the "other islands of San Lucas."[17]

The main narrative of the expedition is almost hopelessly confusing and repetitious at this point, having been derived from several sources, each account somewhat different from the other. The seeming contradictions are probably due to the fact that the various islands and the towns on the mainland were visited on different days by various vessels in the expedition. As a result, what purports to be a list of village names in the narrative for 15 October is really a composite of several lists, with a good deal of repetition. The same holds true for a second list of that date, as well as the list dated 1 November, one following comments made for 3 January 1543, and one dated 12 January. For more than a century historians have disputed the exact locations of these places. But now with more information available than was previously the case, it is possible to clear up some of the confusion and to be reasonably certain about the whereabouts of the expedition.

On Friday the thirteenth the ships sailed further up the channel. Passing Quelqueme (Hueneme), Misinagua (Ventura), and Xuco (Rincón), they noticed the Anacapa Islands on the port side.[18] From Indians who came out from the mainland they learned that these were uninhabited. The mainland was a country of broad savannahs, dotted with groves of trees. Passing the Rincón, where the lowlands of Carpinteria begin, they anchored on Saturday the fourteenth at Carpinteria Valley, a place that was both "very beautiful and filled with people, a level country with many trees."[19] This proved to be one of the most pleasant spots on the voyage. Indians in canoes swarmed out to the ships with newly-caught fish to trade with the men of the armada. There were so many canoes at Xuco that it was like another Pueblo de las Canoas. As a result they called this one Pueblo de las Canoas also, and then gave the same name to all the villages in the area, from Mugu to Xuco and beyond, a province that the Indians called Xucu. Xuco was the "*primer pueblo de las canoas*," or the chief town in that group. The Indians of the Pueblos de las Canoas became "great friends" of the Spaniards, at least for the time.[20]

Sunday, 15 October, the armada continued its slow voyage up the heavily populated coast, passing Coloc (or Alloc, as it was also called in the text), in the Carpinteria estuary, Xabagua (or Xagua) near present Montecito and, Cicacut (also called Ciucut, Xocotoc, and Yutum) near present Santa Barbara. They anchored for the night four of five miles west of Goleta Point. Since the Indians in this place brought them so many fresh sardines, they called the villages in the area Los Pueblos de Sardinas. This was a different province with the additionally confusing name of Xexu, and Cicacut was the chief village.[21]

On 16 October the fleet sailed further westward, passing Potoltuc (also called Partocac, Paltatre, and Paltocac), Anacbuc (also called Nacbuc), and Gwa, the latter two of which were located on small islets adjoining the mainland. They stopped for the night at two villages, now called Dos Pueblos, but then named Quanmu or Quiman.[22]

The next day, Tuesday the seventeenth, they continued sailing west, still encountering canoeloads of Indians with fresh sardines to trade for the beads and other gifts the ships carried for that purpose.[23] Anchoring for the night off Gaviota Pass, they noted the Indians still clothed themselves in skins, still tied their hair in cords, with little daggers of flint, bone, and wood stuck into the braids. As with the Indians in Xucu, these people knew about maize or *oep*, but did not raise it themselves. Some alleged that there was corn in the interior and "cattle," or elk, which they called *cae*. Juan Rodríguez Cabrillo said the country was "more than excellent." It was obviously that "good country where you can make a settlement" that Mendoza had ordered him to find.[24]

The wind blew stronger on the morning of 18 October, as the ships of the armada neared Point Conception. Sailing west, as they were, the coastline appeared so long and low that it reminded the sailors of a galley, so they named it Cabo de Galera. As the northwest wind freshened, the ships found it impossible to sail around the cape . Coming about, they headed south toward the Channel Islands, landing and taking possession on San Miguel. In a singular failure of imagination they named this island La Posesión, still calling the whole group Las Islas de San Lucas, as we have seen. The sudden foul weather forced the ships to remain for a week in the islands, anchored most of that time in the harbor at La Posesión, the place now called Cuyler Harbor on San Miguel Island.[25]

While anchored here the captain made some effort to sort out the geography of the islands, most of which had been visited by one or another of his vessels while the rest of the armada made its way along the coast. At every island, cape, and point visited by the flagship, the captain general took possession in the name of the king, "naming them and placing markers there." We have this from the testimony of Lázaro de Cárdenas. Cárdenas also confirmed a fact that was common knowledge among the men but somewhat muddled in the summary report we now have: that the principal island in the San Lucas group was called Capitana.[26] This was the familiar name of the expedition's flagship, which was more formally called *San Salvador* and less formally called *Juan Rodríguez*.

As though to add to our confusion, the Spaniards also called this island La Posesión, just as they did the one we now call San Miguel and probably others as well. No wonder the compiler of the expedition's narrative got so many place names confused! Historians formerly thought San Miguel was the only one with the name, but a careful reading of the sources makes it clear that the island called San Salvador also was "one of those called La Posesión."[27] It was also called Juan Rodríguez and Capitana.

The island variously called San Salvador, Capitana, Juan Rodríguez, and La Posesión was so clearly marked on Cabrillo's maps and so clearly identified by the official marker Cabrillo and his men placed there in 1542 that it was still easily identified twenty-three years later, when Andrés de Urdaneta and Rodrígo de Espinosa made their pioneering voyage back across the Pacific from the Philippines. Friar Andrés, as we have seen, knew about the island in about 1559 when he wrote that San Salvador was in latitude "thirty-four degrees or more," the location Juan Rodríguez Cabrillo had given it[28] and the latitude it bears on the Homem map.[29] When Urdaneta and Rodrígo de Espinosa arrived there in 1565, they calculated a more nearly correct latitude of thirty-three degrees and twenty-six minutes but still recognized the island as San Salvador.[30] This near pinpoint accuracy is typical of the superior navigating accomplished by Urdaneta and Rodríguez. It is also a testimony to the quality of the records and charts brought back by the expedition of Juan Rodríguez Cabrillo.

By Wednesday, 25 October, when the storm abated, they were in the harbor at San Miguel, one of the islands named Posesión. From this point it was possible to see the Cabo de Galera, but there was insufficient wind to take them around the point. Instead, they drifted in the entrance to the channel, so that when a heavy storm struck again at midnight the onshore wind very nearly blew them aground. On the evening of the twenty-sixth, with a fresh breeze from the south, the fleet was able to round the cape and explore the coast for a few leagues north of Point Arguello. But the treacherous winds and the strong west-flowing currents kept driving them toward the rocky coastline, and they were unable to land at the village they called Nocos (near present Jalama).[31]

The Indians told them stories of a great river to the north, and one of the accounts has given a name to the river, el Rio de Nuestra Señora.[32] The river in question was probably the Rio de Buena Guia, named by Alarcón in honor of Nuestra Señora de Buena Guia whose motto was on Mendoza's coat of arms. Some of Ulloa's men thought the river flowed into the Pacific as well as the gulf, and Alarcón had said it reached the sea and "those islands," presumably the Spice Islands.[33] Of course, it did neither, but the expedition was doubtless instructed to look for evidence and settle the matter once for all.

After several days of fighting the elements, the ships turned back toward the channel villages, finally coming to rest just about midnight of 1 November at a village below Cabo de Galera. Because it was the Feast of All Saints, they called the village Todos Santos, but the natives called it Xexo. The next day they sailed on to the Pueblos de Sardinas, anchoring at Cicacut, where they stayed for a few days taking on wood and water.[34]

The Indians at Cicacut were delighted to have the Spaniards back. The canoe masters came on board, dressed in their official capes and followed by Indian oarsmen. Indian musicians brought out their pipes and rattling reeds, and the sailors played Spanish bagpipes and tambourines. Dancing and feasting began. The elderly woman who was chief of this province stayed on board the flagship for the next two nights, along with a good many of her loyal subjects.[35] These Indians were party-goers of great dedication, it would seem. Father Juan Crespí reported a similar celebration at the same place two centuries later. With a few details changed, it could very easily describe the party of November 1542.[36]

> In the afternoon the chief men came from each town, one after the other, adorned according to their usage, painted and loaded with plumage and some hollow reeds in their hands, to the movement and noise of which they kept time with their songs and the cadence of the dance, in such good time and in such unison that it produced real harmony. These dances lasted all afternoon, and it cost us much trouble to rid ourselves of the people. They were sent away, charged with emphatic signs not to come in the night and disturb us; but it was in vain, for as soon as night fell they returned, playing on some pipes whose noise grated on our ears.

Finally, a squad of soldiers was sent out with some small gifts, telling the Indians that they were no longer welcome, and that if they came again the reception would not be so pleasant. Juan Rodríguez and his men also loved a party, it seems, for they remained at the Pueblos de Sardinas until Monday, November 6.

The Indians here lived in round dwellings, made of reeds tied to a wooden framework over a dirt floor.[37] Herrera printed a report of the expedition that describes these dwellings as having "dos aguas," a gabled roof from which water drains in two directions.[38] This is an interesting error that no doubt came from seeing Oviedo's pictures and descriptions of houses in New Spain.[39] His statement that they were "large . . . like those in New Spain"[40] is more nearly correct and matches the description given by Juan Rodríguez, who reported seeing one village where fifty Indians lived in one house.[41] Crespí reported seeing lodges big enough to hold sixty people comfortably. They were "round like half oranges," he said, the typical dwelling of the Chumash.[42]

In the middle of each village there was usually "a great plaza," surrounded by a plank fence and a stone curbing three palms high. Inside the enclosures were mastlike posts covered with paintings. The Indians danced around the enclosures in such a way as to lead the Spaniards to conclude they were of great religious significance, though no one could determine their exact meaning.[43]

The captain general was impressed with the abundant food supplies in this semi-agricultural economy. During good years the wooded hillsides, lush grasslands, and coastal marshes furnished rich harvests of seeds and nuts, including acorns (from the *quercus agrifolia*), grass seeds, and cattail (*typha*) seeds used in preparing atole, pinole, and the mush cakes that Juan Rodríguez described as tamales and "good to eat." One of the seeds, probably the acorn, was "as large as maize and white," but maize itself was not grown or eaten there.[44] Herrera saw one account that described hazelnuts as part of the diet, but is not clear what this meant. As would be expected, the Indians ate fish, both cooked and raw, and maguey.[45]

The Channel Indians painted and decorated themselves with beads and daggers of bone and stone and shell. Colorful feathers were stuck here and there in their coiffures, as style and taste dictated, but no detailed descriptions by the men of the expedition survive. Canoe owners and the leading chiefs wore capes of elk hide or bearskin, but most of the people wore nothing at all, a fact that brought no complaints from the men on the ships.[46]

With full stomachs and full water casks, the armada weighed anchor on Monday 6 November, sailing again toward Cabo de Galera and the elusive Rio de Nuestra Señora. Again, the Indians came out in their canoes greeting the Spaniards, and calling off the names of their villages. These included Aguin (El Capitan Beach), Casalic (Cañada del Refugio), Susuquei (Quemada Canyon), and Tucumu (Arroyo Hondo). The armada anchored again at Xexo, waiting for a favorable wind to take them round the cape.[47]

By 11 November they were running along the coast around Point

25. One of the ships in Cabrillo's armada was named after Santa María de la Victoria, an image of the Virgin venerated in the convent of the Minim Friars at Triana, Spain, and a favorite of Spanish seamen in the sixteenth century. The image is now in the Iglesia de Santa Ana at Triana, just across the river from Seville.

Sal in the neighborhood of San Luis Obispo. With a stiff wind from the southwest and no sign of shelter along the coast they dared not attempt to anchor. In any case, they saw no sign of habitation and decided the mountainous area was not so pleasant a place as the channel they had just left. As it was the feast of Saint Martin, they named the range of mountains that runs north from Point Sal the Sierras de San Martín and called the big cape off Piedras Blancas the Cabo de San Martín. They estimated the latitude of the cape to be 38 degrees, about a degree and a half too high.[48]

That night, while they were lying to several miles off the coast, a severe storm struck the fleet and drove the vessels northwest. Running before the wind, with only a small sail on their foremasts, the ships became separated in the rain and wind. Perhaps at the urging of the chaplain, the men on the *San Salvador* said special prayers to the Virgin, calling her Our Lady of the Rosary and the Blessed Mother of Piety. They vowed to make a pilgrimage to her shrine if she would return them home safely. Those on the *Victoria* may have been too busy to pray. Herrera reports that they lost all their deck cargo, and there was doubtless much damage to masts and rigging.[49]

The *San Salvador* had run out to sea, in order to avoid being driven onto the rocky shore, and when the storm abated on the thirteenth, the vessel took advantage of a shift in the wind to make its way back to shore. The sea remained high and the wind strong, shifting a bit more to the west and allowing the flagship to run north. The men sighted Point Reyes, where the pilot measured the sun's position with an astrolobe and called the latitude forty degrees. They named the place Cabo de Pinos because of the great stands of Douglas fir and other evergreens that covered the hillsides.[50]

Still searching for the great river, the lookouts missed the entrance to San Francisco Bay, which everyone else did, too, for the next two centuries and more. Instead, the ship rounded the point and sailed up the coast for another thirty-five or forty miles to the Russian River. This was obviously not the great watercourse they sought, so the commander ordered the pilot to turn back.[51]

South of the Cabo de Pinos the mountains (Santa Cruz) were covered with snow, evidently from a fresh storm the night of the fourteenth. The weather was so cold the seamen could scarcely man the sails. Then, on the morning of the fifteenth, they suddenly came upon the other ships lying at the anchor, one of them leaking badly, with the entire crew exhausted and half frozen.[52]

Continuing south, the fleet rounded the point at Santa Cruz on November 16 and entered the bay they had missed in the storm, now called Monterey Bay. Here again they failed to find the great river. In fact, the surf was so high the boats could not be sent ashore. Instead, the ships cast anchor in forty-five fathoms, while the captain general named the place Baya de los Pinos, computed the latitude at a bit more than thirty-nine degrees, and took formal possession in the name of the king of Spain and the viceroy of Mexico, as he had done at all the other capes and points and bays he discovered and named.[53]

The leaky vessel stayed at anchor for another day, making hasty repairs, while the *San Salvador* beat about the bay looking for the river. The following day, Saturday, 18 October, the fleet sailed on south looking for a safer anchorage. Cypress Point was covered with snow, so the men called it Cabo de Nieve. The northwest wind cleared away the clouds, so they measured the altitude of the sun and computed the latitude at thirty-eight degrees and forty minutes, about two degrees too high.[54]

The mountainous coastline south of Monterey Bay was covered with a blanket of snow, which lay so thick on the trees and cliffs that the men called the mountains the Sierras Nevadas, or the Snowy Moutains.[55] The kind of snowy winter of these years is totally unknown in central and southern California today, but it was the prevailing weather pattern in the sixteenth century. This was the middle part of a cool-moist weather cycle that began about 1370, reached an extreme in 1770, and finally changed to the present warm-dry trend about 1860.[56]

The high, rugged mountains along the coast were an imposing

sight, covered with snow and ice. Sailing close to shore, as the narrative says they did, the shivering sailors thought the cliffs "were about to fall on the ships." Why they clung so close to the cliffs is still something of a mystery, for there was a heavy swell with breakers crashing on offshore reefs, and still no place to anchor. South of Cabo de Martín they again noticed signs of Indian settlements, but the high wind and heavy seas kept them headed for the islands.[57]

The voyage ended on Thursday, 23 November 1542, when the tattered armada arrived "at the Islands of San Lucas, at one of those called Posesión."[58] This was doubtless the one now called San Miguel Island, where there is a good harbor, though a small one with a narrow entrance. The fragata *San Miguel* was by this time leaking so badly that the sailors on board thought it would sink at any time. They quickly hauled the small vessel ashore and began to recaulk the hull and repair the sprung planking.[59] Their refuge, called Cuyler's Harbor, opens to the north, and the heavy swells that accompany the northwest winds make it a treacherous anchorage for much of the year.[60] The other ships probably did not remain there for long, but sought shelter in the other islands.

It is difficult to make much sense of the lists of islands and village names in this part of the narrative. The island called Limu, for example, is said to contain eight towns, though ten names are given. It is said to be a close neighbor of Ciquimuymu (or Posesión) and Nicalque.[61] Linguistic evidence supports the conclusion that Nicalque is the one now called Santa Rosa Island. Another island, mentioned earlier in the narrative as San Lucas, is pretty clearly the one now called Santa Cruz Island.[62] *Limu* and Ciquimuymu are not so easy to identify.

Limu is not even in the same island group. Rather, it is the one now called Santa Catalina Island.[63] The captain general gave this one the name San Salvador, after his flagship, which the crewmen called *Juan Rodríguez* and *La Capitana*. There can scarcely be any doubt that this is the island that sailors Lázaro de Cárdenas and

Francisco de Vargas referred to as *la isla Capitana*, calling it the most important island discovered on the expedition and the headquarters for all the fleet.[64]

Here it was that the fleet wintered, according to Vargas and Cardenas. The Indians who lived there quickly tired of the Spaniards and began a series of running battles with them. Vargas recalled that "all the time the armada was in the Isla Capitana the Indians there never stopped fighting us."[65] On Christmas Eve or thereabouts the captain sent a party ashore for water, and the Indians attacked. The soldiers, outnumbered and sorely pressed, called out to the ship for help. Juan Rodríguez Cabrillo himself determined to rescue them, quickly gathered a relief party and rowed ashore in one of the launches. "As he began to jump out of the boat," said Vargas, "one foot struck a rocky ledge, and he splintered a shinbone." Somehow dragging himself ashore, the captain general refused to leave the island until all of his men were rescued.[66]

There is some conflicting evidence about the nature of the injury. The younger Juan Rodríguez Cabrillo said in 1560 that his father had a broken leg, and Lázaro de Cárdenas verified this.[67] The Urdaneta copy of the narrative says, "He broke an arm close to the shoulder."[68] In a fall such as this, it is certainly possible that he broke both his arm and his leg. Vargas, however, insists that the injury was a shattered shinbone. "The witness knows this," said Vargas, "because he was right there." Juan León, the notary who took the testimony in 1543 also took the testimony in 1560, and he saw no reason to question either account.[69]

Juan Rodríguez Cabrillo was taken back aboard ship, where the surgeon tried to treat the wound. However, the injury could not be helped with the medical knowledge then available. The wound quickly turned morbid and became infested with gangrene. Knowing death was near, Juan Rodríguez called in his chief pilot to hand over command of the armada. He then proceeded to put his papers in the best order possible, though he was not able to summon enough strength to complete that part of his account that recorded the voyage north of the Channel Islands. This section of the narrative remains singularly lacking in detail, having none of the enlightening comments that enliven the earlier pages.[70]

Unable to complete the voyage himself, Juan Rodríguez charged Bartolomé Ferrer with responsibility for doing so and further ordered him to make a complete report to the viceroy. Once this was done, according to Cárdenas, "He called Captain Ferrer and gave him command as captain general of the armada, by the authority of the royal commission that he held."[71] Juan Rodríguez Cabrillo died on 3 January 1543, and was buried on the island Capitana.[72] "Because he died here," said Cardenas, "the island retained the name Capitana."[73]

The fleet remained in the island until 19 January, then headed for the mainland in search of supplies for a renewed journey to the northwest. However, violent winds swept the channel and kept the ships from making their way ashore. The ships were forced to return to San Salvádor, sailing around the islands for several days in the meantime in search of shelter. During this time they sheltered in the lee of Santa Cruz, the island they had called San Lucas, but the stormy seas forced them to cut their anchor cables and make a hasty exit. They returned at the end of the month to retrieve the anchors, took on a few more barrels of water, then tried again to sail to the mainland villages. El Puerto de Sardinas, which had seemed such a rich village in the summer, now had few inhabitants and no extra food. The ships came away with only a small boatload of firewood and nothing else.[74]

Deciding to take advantage of the strong northeast wind, the fleet sailed southwest of the island of San Salvádor. Here the pilots reported finding "six islands, some large and some small."[75] As Henry Wagner says, it is useless to try to guess which islands these might have been.[76] Nor is it easy to guess where or why they went toward the southwest for the next few days.

On Thursday, 22 February, "they made another turn toward land in order to go in search of the Cabo de Pinos, with a south-southwest wind that lasted for three days, each day getting stronger. The following Sunday at daybreak they caught sight of the Cabo de Pinos."[77] This was practically the most northerly point they had reached on the previous voyage. Sailing farther north, they reached Point Arena, which they called Cabo de Fortunas, on 26 February. Then, as the wind continued to build, they sailed on northward until they thought they were in latitude of 43 or 44 degrees, though they were probably some two degrees farther south.[78]

On 28 February, the storm increased in intensity, with huge waves breaking over the ships, so that the two ships without sterncastles were nearly swamped. In these straits, the sailors made new vows to the Virgin—this time to Our Lady of Guadalupe—promising another pilgrimage if they were saved from the storm.[79] Since it was most unlikely that any of the sailors would ever return to Spain for the pilgrimage, their prayer must have been to the Virgin venerated at Guadalupe near Mexico City. This, then, is one of the earliest recorded accounts of veneration of the Mexican Virgin.[80]

As though in answer to their prayers, the wind shifted to the north, and the ships were able to begin running back toward their island haven. The seas remained high, and the waves broke over the bows with crashing blows, "and passed over them as though over a rock." Again they asked the Lord and his Blessed Mother for a miraculous change in weather, and again they thought they received an answer to their prayers.[81]

They had not found the river they sought, "though it seemed to them that there was much evidence of a river," in the form of logs and other debris. The storm had damaged their remaining stores, and the seamen were unable to continue fighting the winds. They turned back once more. For the weakened survivors of many arduous months, the return voyage would tap the last of their resources.[82]

The fleet ran into rough weather again around the Channel Islands, again the ships became separated, and again each ship's crew thought the other ships were lost. However, the *San Salvador* took time to stop at the Pueblo de las Canoas, where four Indians were taken on board, and at San Miguel where two Indian boys were captured, all of whom were to be trained as interpreters for a possible return voyage.[83] If they had failed to comprehend the languages of the Indians, they had at least learned that trained interpreters could be very useful in dealing with the short tempered Indians of California.[84]

One of the ships tried to run into the harbor at San Salvador (Santa Catalina), scraped across the reef, and the ship was very nearly lost. The vow to the Virgin this time was that the men would go to church stripped of all finery, if she would save them. Again the storm passed.[85]

All the ships of the armada were finally reunited off Cedros Island. Several men had died on the journey, from battle wounds or illness or hunger. The ships were battered and leaking. Supplies were nearly exhausted. There was no longer any question of returning north to continue the voyage. Instead, they sailed on to Navidad, where they arrived on Saturday, 14 April 1543, nearly nine months after embarking.[86]

Mendoza's pleasure at their return was tempered by the news that the commander, Juan Rodríguez Cabrillo, had died, and several other men as well.[87] Moreover, the expedition failed to reach the Spice Islands or China, did not locate the Rio de Nuestra Señora, and had no word of the Villalobos expedition. All the money, all the supplies, the ships, the men had been wasted in a fruitless effort to find new riches. The Royal Audiencia demanded to know what had happened. Mendoza sent Juan León to Navidad to question the survivors and to compile a report for these officials and for his own files.[88]

Once the report was finished, Mendoza decided to keep the men together for use in a possible attempt to contact Villalobos, from whom he had heard not a word. For this reason he refitted all three ships or took three others just like them and sent them off to Peru

26. *Antonio de Mendoza, (Huntington Library.)*

with horses and supplies to sell to the Spaniards there.[89] Few of the men and none of the ships ever returned.

A similar fate befell those sent with Villalobos, and that commander also perished before his expedition was completed. Some years later the Dominican scholar Remesal wrote the epitaph for the great armada built by Juan Rodríguez Cabrillo: "The entire fleet perished, some eaten by shipworms, others scattered to different ports in disorder, because the adelantado had died."[90]

27. Following the death of their commander and a vain attempt to resume the voyage, the survivors of the Cabrillo armada returned to the port of Navidad. shown here in an early seventeenth century view. (Nicolás de Cardona, "Descripciones geográphicas," MS, Biblioteca Nacional, Madrid, Spain.)

Chapter 8
Looking for Cabrillo

MUCH OF THE personal fortune amassed by Juan Rodríguez Cabrillo was spent in building the *San Salvador* and in preparations for the expedition to California. As though to add to his problems, Francisco de la Cueva, the acting governor of California, seized some of the explorer's encomiendas while he was off with the armada. The family sued for return of the property, and their cases stayed in the courts for many years, in one form or another.

One suit began in 1541, when Juan Rodríguez gave his wife power of attorney to act for him while he was off exploring the northern coast of the Mar del Sur. News of the explorer's death arrived while the case was in progress, but none of the men who went with him to California came back in time to add their testimony to the documents presented in the case. Nonetheless, these materials furnish a lot of personal information about Juan Rodríguez Cabrillo, his wife, and his children. It is all filed in a single legajo in the Archives of the Indies in Seville, Spain. The file number is *Justicia* 280.

Responding, perhaps, to a suggestion from Friar Andrés de Urdaneta, the Spanish king decided in 1559 to send a new fleet to the East Indies. Urdaneta began looking again into the records of the Cabrillo expedition, and his research played a role in prompting the family to renew its petitions for royal grants and favors. The son of the explorer, also named Juan Rodríguez Cabrillo, summoned witnesses in Santiago, Guatemala, in the early 1560s. Their testimony expands greatly on information available from other sources about the expedition and its leader. The testimony contains two brief but fact-filled contributions from men who were on the voyage to California. Their accounts are supplemented by those of a dozen or so additional witnesses who served with Cabrillo in the conquest of Mexico and Central America. The material is also in the Archivo General de Indias, *Justicia* 290.

Some of the same information is repeated in later presentations of evidence by other Cabrillo descendants. A copy was prepared from the file copy kept in Santiago, Guatemala in 1603. The Santiago original does not now exist, but the copy is filed in the A. G. I. in a legajo numbered *Guatemala* 215. Another copy was made in the same city in 1606. It is now in the Archivo General de Centro America in Santiago, Guatemala, file number A1.29-1, expediente 40132, legajo 4672. A fourth copy, made in 1616 is in the A. G. I., numbered *Patronato* 87. There are textual differences, most of which are unimportant, and each descendant added much information about his own supposed merits. The most dependable copy of the Cabrillo información is in *Justicia* 290, but the paleography is extremely difficult.

One of these documents has been transcribed from its original difficult paleography, printed in Spanish, and recently translated into English. Unfortunately, this is the least reliable of all the copies. The Spanish transcription is full of errors and omissions, and the English translation is somewhat awkward. The transcription was done by Guatemalan archivist Joaquín Pardo, and it was printed in *Anales de la Sociedad de Geografía e Historia de Guatemala* 11 (June 1935): 472-96. More recently, in 1967, the Cabrillo Historical Association published an English translation by Bernice Beagles, "The Merits and Services of Juan Rodríguez Cabrillo," *The Western Explorer: Journal of the Cabrillo Historical Association* 5 (September 1967): 1-19. Most of the defects in this translation are due to errors made in transcribing the original.

Much interesting information about Cabrillo descendants can be found in early genealogical statements they prepared to show their hereditary nobility and the purity of their blood lines. Among these are the *Merecimientos y servicios de los ascendientes de Doña Isabel y de Doña Jerónima de Solórzano y Mazariegos, hijas de don Estevan Medrano y Solórzano, y de Doña Magdalena Mazariegos y Avendano bisnietas de Juan Rodríguez Cabrillo*, Archivo General de Centro America (hereafter AGCA), A3.2, exp. 22.569, leg. 1539, fo. 7-10; and *Libro de los pareceres de la Real Audiencia de Guatemala*, MS in AGCA, A1.29, leg. 2033, exp. 14084, fo 96v-97v. A third copy is in the A.G.I., *Guatemala 215, Ascendientes y desendientes de Esteban de Medrano Solórzano*, June 7, 1664.

The hidalgos in Guatemala were such active litigants and such persistent petitioners for royal favors that many of them testified over and over again in legal proceedings initiated by themselves, their relatives, and their friends. Among the interesting documents of this type are some pages of testimony by Juan Rodríguez Cabrillo, son of the conqueror, calling himself Juan Rodríguez Cabrillo de Medrano. This is found in a 1574 manuscript assembled to show the merits and services of Francisco Díaz del Castillo. In addition to personal information about himself, the younger Rodríguez also gave some interesting bits of information about the manuscript history of the conquest written by Bernal Díaz del Castillo. The manuscript is found in *Patronato 89*, fol. 57-59, A. G. I. It has been published several times, and is most easily available in the Joaquín Ramirez Cabañas edition of Bernal Díaz, *Historia verdadera de la conquista de la Nueva Espana*, 10th ed. (Mexico: Editorial Porrua, S.A., 1974), 646-50.

Several years after the explorer's death his widow married Juan de Aguilar. In asking royal favors for himself, Aguilar gathered information from witnesses who knew his wife's first husband and would testify about him. This information can be found in *Patronato 81*, A. G. I.

Before his marriage to Beatríz Sánchez de Ortega, Juan Rodríguez had several children by one or more Indian women. The names of the children are unknown, but their marriages are recorded in the *Relación de vecinos de Santiago de Guatemala, la mayor parte de ellos conquistadores, en los que se pueden encomendar indios vacos, por sus meritos personales*, 20 July 1548, leg. 2196, exp. 15750, pp. 4, 13, A. G. C. A.

Copies of almost all of these manuscripts are available in the United States. The most complete series is the Reina Collection, University of Pennsylvania Museum, Philadelphia, which consists of typed transcripts prepared by competent paleographers in Guatemala City, Guatemala, and in Seville, Spain. Originals of all these manuscripts are available on microfilm at the American Philosophical Society, Philadelphia. Microfilm copes of most of the documents are also available in the Seaver Western History Library of the Los Angeles County Museum of Natural History and in the Bancroft Library of the University of California, Berkeley. There is a transcript of the 1560 probanza, along with an English translation, in the Wagner Collection of the Honnold Library, Claremont Colleges, Pomona, California. The work was done by Irene Aloha Wright, using *Patronato* 87 at the A. G. I.

There is relatively little dependable information about the Cabrillo expedition. Only two secondary accounts are known. Both are based more or less directly on eyewitness reports, but both are marred by serious errors and omissions. Juan Rodríguez Cabrillo himself completed a *relación* or account of the voyage for Viceroy Mendoza, covering the first four or five months of the expedition. Although the author died on the journey, the account he prepared was taken back to the viceroy. The Real Audiencia asked for an investigation, and the viceroy sent his secretary, Juan León, to take testimony from surviving members of the expedition and to compile some sort of official report. León did this, whereupon the viceroy dispatched most of the men on a voyage to Peru. Few of them came back. Consequently, precious few recollections of the trip have survived.

The results of León's investigation appear in the annoyingly brief "journal" or "log" that has been the source for most of what has been written about the trip to California. This account is only a condensed copy of the original. It combines information from several participants into one not quite coherent story.

What happened to León's original report, no one knows. If Viceroy Mendoza took it to Peru, when he became viceroy there, then it was very likely burned as Mariano Cuevas suggested in his *Monje y marino: La vida y tiempos de Fray Andrés de Urdaneta* (Mexico: Editorial Galatea, 1943), 135. The copy we now have has been attributed to Juan Páez of Santiago, Guatemala and to the royal chronicler Juan Páez de Castro. Neither of them wrote it. Instead, it was copied by Andrés de Urdaneta in 1543 when he went to Navidad on a special mission for the viceroy.

Close analysis of the text shows that it was drawn from at least three and perhaps as many as five original accounts. There appear to be about ten transitions in the text, making it obvious that the compiler skipped back and forth from one source to the other, as most compilers did then and still do today. Adding interpolations and interpretations of his own, the compiler managed to confuse the geography of the California coast so badly that it is nearly impossible to eliminate all the confusion in the text.

In spite of all this it is possible to draw some conclusions about the sources. The first part of the text, about half, is based on the explorer's own report. It includes some of his exact words in the first person. Juan Rodríguez Cabrillo was an experienced navigator, and some of the latitude observations are probably his own work. However, navigation in those days was not the exact science it is now. Because of the several abrupt changes in the accumulated error in navigation, it is possible to conclude that three different instruments were used and therefore that the account is based on the reports of three different navigators, one perhaps the commander himself. Doubtless, the other two were Bartolomé Ferrer and Lorenzo Hernández Barreda, the two pilots on the expedition. Parts of the narrative seem to be the work of the priest who accompanied the expedition, Fray Julián de Lescano. The fifth section was done by another member of the expedition, perhaps Lázaro de Cárdenas, who said he made a report to the viceroy.

Taken to Spain, or sent there, by Andrés de Urdaneta, this "log" of the voyage was later studied by royal cosmographers and chroniclers, including Alonzo de Santa Cruz, Sancho Gutiérrez, Juan Páez de Castro, Juan López de Velasco, Andrés García de Cespedes, and Antonio de Herrera y Tordesillas. Only the last named writer made any significant use of the document.

Working with this document and others—perhaps the originals— Herrera wrote a two-chapter account of the expedition to California. Brief as they are, his two chapters contain some information about the voyage not found in the summary account by León and Urdaneta. Herrera's account was the first to be published. The original edition is extremely rare. It is titled *Historia General de los hechos de los Castellanos en las islas y tierra firme del mar océano* (Madrid: Juan de la Cuesta, 1615), 4:fol. 112-15. Seen more frequently is the edition titled *Descripción de las Indias Occidentales de Antonio Herrera* (Madrid: Nicolas Rodríguez Franco, 1730), vol. 6-7, pp. 89-91. There are no significant differences between the two accounts in these editions.

No one knows what happened to the manuscripts after Herrera used them. The summary prepared by León and copied and condensed by Urdaneta is now in the Archivo General de Indias, *Patronato* 20, no. 5, ramo 13. The other Cabrillo documents he used have disappeared.

Among the other sources used by Herrera were López de Gómara's *Historia de Indias*, first published in 1552. I used the edition of Guillermo de Millis, printed in Medina del Campo in 1553. Gómara's brief account of the voyage to California does not mention the explorer by name, but other sixteenth century works do, some of which Herrera may also have consulted.

One of the most important in this group is that by Bernal Díaz del Castillo, whose *Historia verdadera de la conquista de la Nueva España* was finished before 1579, according to the testimony of the

younger Juan Rodríguez Cabrillo, who said he had read the Díaz manuscript before that date. Seemingly, there are—or were—three separate copies of this manuscript, all compiled at least in part by the original author. One of these exists now only in published form, the one edited by Alonso Remón and published in Madrid: Imprenta del Reyno, 1632. In his *Introducción critica a la "Historia verdadera" de Bernal Diaz del Castillo* (Madrid: Instituto Gonzalo Fernández de Oviedo, 1967,) 30, 40-43, Carmelo Sáenz de Santa María said this version most truly represents what Díaz wanted to say. Another historian, José A. Barbón, *Bernal Díaz del Castillo* (Buenos Aires: Centro Editor de America Latina, S.A., 1968), 21, said the "final and definitive" copy is the Alegría Manuscript, now in the Biblioteca Nacional in Madrid. Both writers agree that a manuscript now preserved in the vault of the Archivo General de Centro America in Guatemala City is a rough copy, but this rough copy contains a brief passage that is of great importance for assessing Cabrillo's part in the conquest of Mexico.

In the center of a page, crossed out with heavy lines, is a remark—almost a throwaway—that Juan Rodríguez Cabrillo had an important role in building the sloops used to recapture the Aztec capital. Genaro García was the first to publish this material in his two volume *Historia Verdadera* (Mexico: Oficina Tipográfica de la Secretaria de Fomento, 1904), 1:475. All three versions were compared in the *Edicion critica*, published at Madrid by the Instituto Gonzalo Fernández de Oviedo in 1940. Only the first volume of this multi-volume work was published. It has recently been superseded by a complete *Edición critica* by Carmelo Sáenz de Santa María, published also at Madrid by the Instituto Gonzalo Fernández de Oviedo, in 1982.

In the early 1570s Juan López de Velasco wrote his *Geografia y descripcion universal de las Indias*, in which he mentioned and briefly described the discoveries by Juan Rodríguez along the coast of Upper California. For various reasons this work lay unpublished until 1894, when it was published by Justo de Zaragoza (Madrid: Establecimiento Tipográfico de Fortanet, 1894), 280-81, calling attention to

Herrera's use of the López manuscript. By this time many original sources had been printed that touched upon the Cabrillo voyage in one way or another.

Two of the earliest, often treated by commentators as independent studies, were based almost entirely on the Herrera *Historia General* and contain little or no independent information. These are Johannes de Laet, *Novus Orbis, seu Descriptionis Indiae Occidentalis* (Lugduni, Batavorum: Ludovicum Elzevirium, 1633), and Johannes Georgius Gemeling, *Disputatio Geographica de vero Californiae* (Marburgi Cattorum: Phil. Casimir Mulleri, 1739). Gemeling copied Laet but added the possibly erroneous information from a letter of the cosmographer Lisle that Juan Rodríguez Cabrillo named Cape Mendocino after Viceroy Mendoza, who sent him on the voyage. This bit of information was repeated by Charles P. Claret Fleurieu (mistakenly citing Laet) in his 1801 introduction to Etienne Marchand, *Voyage autour de monde* (1798-1800), and afterwards the story became accepted as fact in many circles. His source was a letter from the geographer DeLisle in Jean F. Bernard, *Recueil de Voyages au nord contenant divers memoires tres-utiles au Commerce á la navigation* (Rouen: Jean-Baptiste Machuel, 1716), 3:266. One modern author who thinks Juan Rodríguez Cabrillo discovered Cape Mendocino is Maurice G. Holmes, who tells why in his book *From New Spain by Sea to the Californias 1519-1668* (Glendale, Ca.: Arthur H. Clark Co., 1963). In fact, it may be true that the explorer named Cape Mendocino, but the evidence has not appeared to prove the matter one way or the other.

Scholarly interest in early Spanish discoveries took a new turn in the nineteenth century, with the publication of numerous primary documents about these discoveries, largely drawn from the newly established Archivo General de Indias in Seville. First in this distinguished list of titles is Martín Fernández de Navarrete's classic introduction to José Cardero, *Relacion de viage hecho por las goletas Sutil y Mexicana* (Madrid: 1802). Navarrete gave a long and authoritative account of the Cabrillo voyage, citing Fleurieu incidentally as authority for the statement that Juan Rodríguez Cabrillo named Cape Mendocino.

Donald C. Cutter settled the question of the authorship of this important work by locating the original manuscript in Cardero's handwriting. See his "Early Spanish Artists on the Northwest Coast," *Pacific Northwest Quarterly* 54 (October 1963): 153. Hubert Howe Bancroft is authority for the statement that Navarrete wrote the scholarly introduction. See his *History of California*, 7 vols. (San Francisco: The History Company, 1884), 1:509.

By the mid-nineteenth century an entirely new audience became interested in the discovery of California—the English-speaking immigrants from the United States. Foremost among these was Alexander Smith Taylor, who read the summary by Navarrete, plus, as he said, "the works of Humboldt, Venegas, Palou, and all the English, French, amd American authors I could lay hold of." In 1853 Taylor wrote a fairly lengthy account for the San Francisco *Herald*. First published as a single-sheet, undated-broadside *Supplement to the San Francisco Herald* (May 1853), it was then published as a twenty-page pamphlet, *The First Voyage to the Coasts of California; made in the years 1542 and 1543. By Juan Rodriguez Cabrillo and his Pilot Bartolome Ferrelo* (San Francisco: Le Count & Strong, 1853). This enthusiastic summary is not only the first separately printed account of the voyage, it is also one of the first in a long line of more or less scholarly studies in English about this early explorer of the California coast.

Partly as an outgrowth of the work done by Spanish scholars Navarrete, Munoz, and others, additional materials soon began to appear in print, adding vastly to knowledge of the first expedition to the coast of Upper California. In 1857 Buckingham Smith's *Colección de vários documentos para la historia de la Florida y tierras adyacentes* was published in London by Casa de Trubner y Companía, 1857. Smith drew upon copies of original archival documents made by order of Martín Fernández de Navarrete for the Deposito Hidrográfico in Madrid, and documents in the Real Academia de

Historia prepared by Juan Bautista de Muñoz.

Several of these documents cast light on the Cabrillo voyage, most notably a copy of the 1543 report of the expedition made by Navarrete. Within a few years the original copy of this manuscript in the A. G. I. was published by Joaquín F. Pacheco and Francisco de Cárdenas in their monumental *Colección de documentos ineditos relativos al descubrimiento, conquista, y organización de las antiguas posesiones Españolas de America y Oceanía, sacados de los archivos del reino y muy especialmente del de Indias* (Madrid: Imprenta de José María Pérez, 1870), 14:165-91. Unfortunately, this version of the A. G. I. copy was flawed by careless copying errors, including the omission of a line or two of text. Whether for this reason or some other, Richard Stuart Evans chose the Smith edition of Navarrete's copy when he translated the document into English in the 1870s. It was published in 1879, along with introductory notes by H. W. Henshaw, in U.S., Department of the Army, *Report upon United States Geographical Surveys West of the One Hundredth Meridian in Charge of First Lieut. Geo. M. Wheeler*, Vol. VII, *Archaeology* (Washington: Government Printing Office, 1879), 293-314. This was the first full English translation of the 1543 report, just as Buckingham Smith's book was its first publication in Spanish.

Earlier, when Alexander Smith Taylor wrote his account of the voyage, he remarked that the coastal surveys of 1851 and 1852 had given him enormous help in locating some of the places mentioned in the 1543 narrative. Regarding two of the young surveyors who helped make the survey he added: "May God spare them to speedily set right these important questions."

Seemingly, his prayer was answered in 1887 when the superintendent of the U.S. Coast and Geodetic Survey published his *Annual Report for 1886*. No longer young but still fascinated by these questions, Professor George Davidson made a thorough analysis of coastal geography and the historical record, consulting Díaz, Herrera, Smith, Evans and others in a largely successful attempt to identify and describe the places visited by the ships of Juan Rodríguez Cabrillo.

Davidson devised a useful analytical format, setting descriptions of each location in the 1543 account in a column alongside the descriptions of the same places given by Drake, Ulloa, and Vizcaíno. He also analyzed the navigational errors of each explorer, and gave a brief contemporary description of each site along with the modern map coordinates.

In making his study, "An Examination of Some of the Early Voyages of Discovery and Exploration on the Northwest Coast of America, from 1539 to 1603," *Report of the Superintendent of the U.S. Coast and Geodetic Survey, Showing the Progress of the Work during the Fiscal Year Ending with June, 1886*, appendix VII (Washington: Government Printing Office, 1887), pp. 155-253, Davidson consulted with H. H. Bancroft, who had previously provided bibliographical assistance to Evans and Henshaw. In his *History of California* (San Francisco: The History Co., 1884) 1:69-81, Bancroft published his own identifications of the places visited by the expedition, but they do not differ greatly from those given by Davidson. When Henry Wagner published his version of the voyage, *Spanish Voyages to the Northwest Coast of America in the Sixteenth Century* (San Francisco: California Historical Society, 1929), 72-93, 319-37, 450-63, he stated that he followed Bancroft, but his great debt to Davidson is obvious. In fact, Davidson's work with a few minor corrections is the most authoritative geographical analysis of the voyage done to this date.

Citing "numerous inaccuracies and defects in form," in the translations done by Evans and Davidson, Herbert E. Bolton made an entirely new translation of the 1543 narrative for a multivolume compilation of *Original Narratives in Early American History*. Published in 1916, his *Spanish Exploration in the Southwest, 1542-1706*, vol. 17, *Original Narratives of Early American History*, ed. by J. Franklin Jameson (New York: Charles Scribner's Sons, 1916), 1-39, again used the Buckingham Smith text but relied completely on Davidson's site identifications. Said Bolton: "I hereby acknowledge my obligation to this great scholar."

In the years after the First World War knowledge of the Cabrillo expedition expanded greatly. In 1928 Henry R. Wagner published the first in a series of works dealing wholly or partly with Juan Rodríguez Cabrillo, "Spanish Voyages to the Northwest Coast of America; Chapter IV: The Voyage of Juan Rodríguez Cabrillo, *California Historical Quarterly* 7 (March 1928): 20-77. His own encyclopedic command of the printed sources was amplified by the discovery of a number of important manuscripts from the Archivo General de Indias. In addition to documenting much of the early life of Cabrillo, Wagner also published a number of important source materials that had been located and translated for him by Irene Aloha Wright. More important than anything else was his use of the original A. G. I. copy of the 1543 manuscript, to produce an entirely new translation of this account of the expedition. Moreover, his *Spanish Voyages* gave readers for the first time an excellent facsimile copy of this important document.

Notable among Wagner's later works that provide information about the expedition is a chapter entitled "New Cabrillo Information" in his 1937 volume describing *The Cartography of the Northwest Coast of America to the Year 1800*, 2 vols. (Berkeley: University of California Press, 1937), 1:91-96. It is difficult to say how much of this book is the work of Henry R. Wagner, who admitted that "most of the actual writing of this . . . book has been done by my secretary, Mrs. Ruth Frey Axe." (Ibid., I, vii). His final work on the subject was his 1941 book entitled *Juan Rodriguez Cabrillo, Discoverer of the Coast of California* (San Francisco: California Historical Society, 1941), which brought together most of his earlier writings on the subject.

The Muñoz copy of the 1543 report, languishing in archival darkness for nearly two centuries, finally came into print in Spanish in 1943, and an English translation was made in 1963 by James R. Moriarty and Mary Keistman, *A New Translation of the Summary Log of the Cabrillo Voyage in 1542*, San Diego Science Foundation Occasional Paper No. 2 (La Jolla, Ca.: San Diego Science Foundation, 1963).

Only a few additional authors have used original materials to discover more about the expedition and its leader. Notable among those who have are João Antonio de Mascarenhas, Visconde de Lagoa, W. Michael Mathes, and Maurice G. Holmes.

Responding at least in part to the desire of Americans of Portuguese ancestry who wanted to know more about their supposed fellow countryman's exploits, Lagoa combed through archives in Portugal and Spain for material about Cabrillo. Finding nothing in Lisbon, Visconde Lagoa went to Spain, where he discovered numerous lists and accounts that included men with the name Juan Rodríguez Portugues, or something very much like it. His book, *Joao Rodrigues Cabrilho, Achegas para a sua biografia* (Lisboa: Agencia Geral do Ultramar, 1958), is the best of the group of works by Portuguese authors but fatally flawed by his assumption that Juan Rodríguez Cabrillo came from Portugal. Others in the same vein include Euclides Goulart da Costa, *Portugal Descobridor: Apontamentos respeitantes a descoberta da California* (Lisbon: Tip.da Manutencão Militar, 1928); Jaime Cortesão, *Os Portugeses no descobrimiento dos Estados Unidos* (Lisboa: Seara Nova, 1949); and Celestino Soares, *California and the Portuguese: How the Portuguese Helped to Build up California* (Lisbon: Secretariado do Propaganda Nacional, 1939), 9-11, 38-43.

Two American historians gathered information that destroyed all of Lagoa's carefully constructed arguments about Cabrillo's Portuguese birth. Dr. Michael Mathes, writing in 1973 in the *Journal of San Diego History*, used the same and other original documents to show (1) that the name Cabrillo does not now and probably never did exist in Portugal, (2) that the various references to Juan Rodríguez Portugués very likely do not refer to Cabrillo, and (3) that Cabrillo in fact is probably a Spaniard. His study "The Discoveror of Alta California; João Rodrígues Cabrilho or Juan Rodríguez Cabrillo?" *Journal of San Diego History* 19 (Summer 1973): 1-8, is thorough and dependable.

Dr. Holmes, noting the weakness of the case presented by Portuguese historians, decided the nationality question was not terribly important anyway, and concentrated instead on adding to the fund of knowledge about the man and his expedition. Again using the rich resources of the A. G. I., Dr. Holmes found and quoted testimony by Juan Rodríguez Cabrillo himself and later testimony from his wife and son to show that the discoverer of Upper California was a rich and influential soldier and landowner in Guatemala. See his book *From New Spain by Sea to the Californias*, 41-47, 61-73, 102-12, 269-84.

In addition to the *Historia General* compiled by Antonio de Herrera, there are a few other early secondary works that deserve attention because of what they say about Juan Rodríguez Cabrillo, his family, and his friends. Writing about the same time as Herrera but an ocean apart, Fray Antonio de Remesal composed an extended and authoritative history of Guatemala and other parts of Central America, drawing his information from documents that he found in archival collections in Santiago. For various religious and political reasons his *Historia General de las Indias Occidentales* was not published in the seventeenth century, but the Sociedad de Geografía e Historia de Guatemala brought out a complete edition in 1932 (Guatemala, C.A.: Tipografía Nacional), and in 1964 the work was republished by the Biblioteca de Autores Españoles in Madríd: Ediciones Átlas, 1964.

The same holds true for the somewhat later work of Francisco Antonio de Fuentes y Guzmán, *Recordación Florida: discurso historial y demonstración natural, material, militar y politica del reyno de Guatemala*, 3 vols. (Guatemala, C.A.: Tipografía Nacional, 1932-33). Another edition was published by the Biblioteca de Autores Españoles in Madríd: Ediciones Átlas, 1969. J. Antonio Villacorte's edition of the *Libro viejo de la fundacion de Guatemala* (Guatemala, C.A.: Tipografía Nacional, 1934), contains the first volume of the city records of colonial Santiago, with a number of interesting references to Juan Rodríguez Cabrillo.

One other sixteenth century publication has relevance for a study of Juan Rodríguez Cabrillo. This is the *Relacion del espantable terremoto*, a pamphlet first published in Mexico in 1541. José Luis Reyes reprinted the pamphlet from a sixteenth-century Spanish edition in the *Anales de la Sociedad de Geografia e Historia de Guatemala* 23 (March-June 1948) 92-97. Reyes identified the work as that of Juan Rodríguez Cabrillo, and there is good reason to think his identification is correct.

The original Mexican edition is now unknown. At least, no one has reported seeing a copy since 1886, when Joaquín García Icazbalceta described the first edition in his *Bibliografia Mexicana del siglo XVI*, 1st ed. (México: Librería de Andrade y Morales, 1886), 6; 2nd ed. (México: Fondo de Cultura Económica, 1954), 62. Oviedo apparently saw a copy soon after it was printed, for he included a description of the earthquake in his *Historia General y Natural de Las Indias*, ed. by José Amador de los Ríos (Madríd: Imprenta de la Real Académia de la Historia, 1855), 4:32, that was very much like that in the Rodríguez pamphlet.

There were other variant editions. One with a slightly different title was reported by Antonio Paláu y Dulcet, *Manual del librero hispano-americano*, 2nd ed., (Barcelona: A. Paláu, 1948), XX. A copy of this printing of the *Relacion* is listed in the general catalogue at U. C. L. A., but no one on the library staff can now recall having seen it.

Two manuscripts in *Patronato* 181 at the A. G. I. also contain much the same information as is found in the Spanish editions of this pamphlet and in Oviedo. There are significant differences, however, and these are important enough to suggest the existence of one or more additional sources, perhaps the two missing Mexican and Spanish editions. Bernal Díaz wrote an account in his *Historia verdadera* (Madríd: Imprenta del reyno, [1632]), fo. 255v, that is based on other sources. The description is found in a chapter erroneously numbered CCXXII (actually CCXI), a chapter omitted from the first printing of the book. Antonio de Remesal included a good deal of folklore in his account, which nonetheless bears a striking resemblance to the Rodríguez pamphlet (B.A.E. edition, I, 274-77).

In any case, the *Relación* is quite likely the work of Juan Rodríguez Cabrillo. It is also the first known secular publication in the New World.

An English translation has been made by Bernice Beagles (trans.), "Record of What Happened in Guatemala," *The Western Explorer: Journal of the Cabrillo Historical Association* 5 (September 1967): 20-23. A French translation of one of the A. G. I. manuscripts was published in Henri Ternaux-Compans, *Voyages, Relations et memoires originaux pour servir a l'histoire de la decouverte de l'Amerique, publies pour la première fois en Francais* (Paris: Arthus Bertrand, 1838), 269-85. However, this is not the Rodríquez manuscript, but one generally attributed to Bishop Marroquín. Actually, the only real reason to consider this to be the bishop's work is a paragraph added at the end in the bishop's hand and bearing his signature. The rest of the manuscript is written in an entirely different hand.

One modern author has published extensive excerpts and summaries from the more important Cabrillo legajos in the A. G. I., Andre Saint-Lu, *La Vera Paz: Esprit Evangélique et Colonisation* (Paris: Centre de Recherches Hispaniques, 1968), 93-105, 519-36. Strangely enough, he was totally unaware of Cabrillo's identity and historical significance. Admittedly, the focus of his study was Las Casas and the Dominican efforts to evangelize the Vera Paz. If Las Casas could write as much as he did without mentioning Cabrillo, it is perhaps forgivable for Saint-Lu to write about Cabrillo without mentioning his significance. In the grand scheme of Spanish settlement in the New World, Juan Rodriguez Cabrillo played only a supporting role.

Notes
Chapter 1

1. Philip Mills Jones, "Archaeological Investigations on Santa Rosa Island," *University of California Anthropological Records* 17 (1956): 204, 206, 233. Jones did not say exactly where the stone was found, simply that it was "from the surface of an eroded camp site near the Rancho Viejo." His journal for Monday, 4 March, gives general information about collecting in this area. On 17 March his helper, Guillermo "Billy" Guivara, collected a "fine mortar on the surface in this area." If he also found the broken metate at that time, he neglected to say so.

2. Robert F. Heizer, the anthropologist in question, believes the grave was on San Miguel Island, and that Indians moved the stone to Santa Rosa. See his "A Probable Relic of Juan Rodríguez Cabrillo," *The Masterkey* 47 (April-June 1973): 62-67; and Heizer, *California's Oldest Historical Relic?* (Berkeley: University of California, Robert W. Lowie Museum of Anthropology, 1974), 6-8. My own opinion about the burial site is found in chapter VII.

3. A facsimile copy of the original report may be found in Henry R. Wagner, *Spanish Voyages to the Northwest Coast of America in the Sixteenth Century* (San Francisco: California Historical Society, 1929), 450-63. Wagner's translation of this "log" appears on pages 72-93 of the same work. A copy of this document was made by Martín Fernández de Navarrete and later published by Buckingham Smith in *Colección de varios documentos para la historia de la Florida y tierras adyacentes* (London: Casa de Trubner & Co., 1857), 173-89. The original was published for the first time in *Colección de documentos inéditos, relativos al descubrimiento, conquista y organización de las antiguas posesiones Españolas de América y Oceanía* (Madrid: Imprenta de José María Pérez, 1870), 14:165-91. This is a very careless copy, with many errors, including the omission of an entire line on page 188. The copy made by Martín Fernández de Navarrete and published by Buckingham Smith was first translated into English by Richard Stuart Evans, and published as "Translation from the Spanish of the Account by the Pilot Ferrel of the Voyage of Cabrillo along the

West Coast of North America in 1542." in *Report of United States Geographical Surveys West of the One Hundredth Meridian*, vol. 7, *Archaeology* (Washington: G. P. O., 1879), 293-314. This was edited and republished by George C. Davidson as "Voyages of Discovery and Exploration," in U. S. Coast and Geodetic Survey *Annual Report for 1886*, Appendix Number 7 (Washington: G. P. O., 1887) 222-34. The same text was translated and published anew by Herbert E. Bolton in *Spanish Exploration in the Southwest, 1542-1706* (New York: Charles Scribner's Sons, 1916), 13-39. Two recent authors used Navarrete's original manuscript copy, and their text differs in many respects from the one printed by Buckingham Smith. See James R. Moriarty and Mary Keistman trans. and eds., "Cabrillo's Log, 1542-43, a Voyage of Discovery: A Summary by Juan Páez, *The Western Explorer* 17 (September 1968): 5-42. Henry R. Wagner's translation of the original manuscript was first published in the *California Historical Society Quarterly* 7 (March 1928): 20-54, along with a facsimile of the original manuscript. It was published again without the facsimile in his *Juan Rodríguez Cabrillo* (San Francisco: California Historical Society, 1941), 35-61. Wagner's facsimile reproductions of the original document did not include the title or cover page, which was first seen reproduced in Richard E. Pourade, *The History of San Diego: The Explorers* (San Diego, CA: The Union Tribune Publ. Co., 1960), 44.

4.   The main sources in the Archivo General de Indias (hereafter A. G. I.) are: *Patronato* 87, "*Información de los servicios del general Juan Rodríguez Cabrillo*"; *Patronato* 182, "*Escritura de renuncia otorgada a favor de S. M. por Juan Rodríguez Cabrillo*"; *Justicia* 280, "*Beatríz Sánchez de Ortega, vecina de Guatemala, con Don Francisco de la Cueba, vecino de dicha ciudad sobre ciertos indios*"; *Justicia* 286, "*Juan Rodríguez Cabrillo, vecino de la provincia de Guatemala con Don Francisco de la Cueba y otros consortes sobre los pueblos de los yndios de Jumaytepeque y Tacuba*"; *Justicia* 290, "*Juan Rodríguez Cabrillo, vecino de la ciudad de Santiago de Guatemala, con el fiscal de S. M. sobre los yndios de los pueblos de Cobán y Acatenango.*" These and other Guatemalan manuscripts (a total of seventy thousand pages) were micro-filmed in 1967 and succeeding years by Dr. Rubén E. Reina of the University of Pennsylvania and the staff of his Hispanic-Latin American Research Project. His staff also prepared a file of twenty-seven thousand pages of typed extracts and transcripts of this material, which he very graciously made available for my use. The microfilm is in the permanent custody of the American Philosophical Society in Philadelphia, where it is available for scholarly use under certain restrictions. There is a much smaller collection of similarly pertinent manuscripts in the Archivo General de Centro America (hereafter A. G. C. A.), the most useful of which are *signatura* A1.29, *legajo* 4672, *expediente* 401312, "*Meritos y servicios de Juan Rodríguez Cabrillo*"; and sig. A3.2, leg. 1539, exp. 22569, "*Merecimientos y servicios de los ascendientes de doña Isabel y de doña Jerónima de Solórzano y Mazariegos . . . bisnietos de Juan Rodríguez Cabrillo.*"

5.   Pilar Sanchíz Ochoa, *Los hidalgos de Guatemala: realidad y apariencia en un sistema de valores*, vol. 13 of *Publicaciones del Seminario de Antropología Americana* (Seville: Universidad de Sevilla, 1976), 37-50.

6.   Ibid.

7. A. G. C. A., sig. A1.29, leg. 2033, exp. 14084, fol. 96v-97v, *"Libro de los pareceres de la Real Audiencia de Guatemala,"* and A. G. C. A., sig. A3.2, leg. 1539, exp. 22569, fol. 7ff.

8. Antonio de Herrera y Tordesillas, *Descripción de las Indias Ocidentales* (Madrid: Nicolás Rodríguez Franco, 1730), decada 7, libro 5, capitulo 3, p. 89, Huntington Library rare book 48448.

9. Correa made no secret of his Portuguese origins. His statement is summarized in Francisco A. de Icaza, *Diccionario autobiográfico de conquistadores y pobladores de Nueva España* (Madrid: Imprenta de "El Adelantado de Segovia," 1923), 2: 342-43. See also the testimony of Lázaro de Cárdenas, 26 April 1560, in A. G. I., *Justicia* 290.

10. *João Rodrigues Cabrilho, achegas para a sua biografia* (Lisbon: Agencia Geral do Ultramar, 1958), 32-33.

11. See note 4. Lagoa and his Portuguese compatriots follow a long tradition in translating this name. One of the earliest to do so was Joannes Laet, a seventeenth-century writer who wrote in Latin and called the explorer Joannes Rodericus Cabrillus. *Novis orbis seu descriptionis Indiae occidentalis* (Leyden: Ludovicus Elgevirus, 1633), 306-07, Huntington Library rare book 139796.

12. Celestino Soares, *California and the Portuguese* (Lisbon: SPN Books, 1939), 39. Apparently the name exists—or nearly so—among Portuguese in the United States. A "Portuguese fisherman" named Juan Cabrill took the part of Juan Rodríguez Cabrillo in San Diego's Cabrillo Celebration in 1894. *Los Angeles Evening Express,* 26 September 1894, 3.

13. Maurice Holmes, *From New Spain by Sea to the Californias,* vol. 9 of the Spain in the West series (Glendale, CA: Arthur H. Clark Co., 1963), 269-71.

14. Lagoa, *João Rodrigues Cabrilho,* 33. Joan M. Jensen, "Notes from a Western Explorer," *The Western Explorer: Journal of the Cabrillo Historical Association,* 4 (March 1967): 3-5. Euclides Goulart da Costa, *Portugal Descubridor: Apontamentos respeitantes á descoberta de California* (Lisbon: Tipografia de Manutencão Militar, 1928), 28. Peter Boyd-Bowman, *Patterns of Spanish Immigration to the New World (1493-1580)* (Buffalo: State University of New York, Special Studies, 1973), 15.

15. *Enciclopedia universal ilustrada Europeo-Americana* (Barcelona: Hijos de J. Espasa, 1905-1930), 10:218-19.

16. Jensen, "Notes," 3-5.

17. W. Michael Mathes, "The Discoverer of Alta California: João Rodrigues Cabrilho or Juan Rodríguez Cabrillo," *Journal of San Diego History* 19 (Summer 1973):1

18. Ibid., 7.

19. D. R. Luis Mendoca Albuquerque, "An Aspect of the Political Application of the Tordesillas Treaty," *Cabrillo and His Era,* Sixth Annual Cabrillo Festival Historic Seminar 1 (September 1978): 1-7. A. Teixeira da Mota, "The Teaching of Navigation in Spain and Portugal in the Time of Cabrillo," ibid., 9-18.

20. U. S., Department of the Interior, National Park Service, *Cabrillo National Monument, California,* leaflet (Washington: G. P. O., 1974). California, Senate Concurrent Resolution No. 15, *Statutes of 1935,* 2409., contains the text of a resolution declaring in part that "John Rodriguez Cabrillo, a native of Portugal, discovered

California on Thursday, September 28, 1542, while in the service of Spain by enter-ing the harbor of San Diego." The original resolution, as introduced by Senator Walter McGovern of San Francisco, used the form "John Rodríguez Cabrillo." See California Senate *Journal*, 51st sess., 21 January 1935, 142. Senate Concur-rent Resolution No. 44, *Statutes of 1935*, 2693-94, had the name spelled as "John Rodriquez Cabrillo," which says something about the then-prevailing Anglo at-titudes toward Hispanic names.

21. João Goncalves da Costa, *Montalegre e terras de Barroso, notas historicas sobre Montalegre freguesias de concelho e região de Barroso* (Braga, Portugal: Edição da Cámara Municipal de Montalegre, 1968).

22. Cámara Municipal de Montalegre, unanimous resolution of 2 September 1978, addressed to the City Council of San Diego, California.

23. Ibid.

24. The identification of the ports is covered at length in chapter 5 below.

25. Cámara Municipal de Montalegre to City Council of San Diego, 2 September 1978.

26. A. G. I., *Patronato* 87, fol. 36v.

27. Cleve Hallenbeck, *Alvar Núñez Cabeza de Vaca: The Journey and Route of the First European to Cross the Continent of North America, 1534-1536* (Glendale, CA: Arthur H. Clark Co., 1940), 15.

28. Gonzalo Fernández de Oviedo y Valdés, *Historia general y natural de las In-dias, islas, y Tierra-Firme del Mar Océano* (Madrid: Imprenta de la Real Academia de la Historia, 1853), 3:580. He described Alvarado the same way: ibid., 4:25.

29. Las Casas, *Historia de las Indias*, ed. by Agustín Millares Carlo, intro. by Lewis Hanke (Mexico: Fondo de Cultura Economica, 1951), tomo 4, libro 3, cap. 26, pp. 524-25.

30. Herrera, *Descripción de las Indias occidentales*, tomo 1, decada 1, libro 9, pp. 242-43.

31. Las Casas, *Historia de las Indias*, tomo 4, libro 3, cap. 26, pp. 524-25.

32. Herrera, *Historia general de los hechos de los Castellanos*, intro. and notes by Antonio Ballesteros-Beretta (Madrid: n. n., 1934-1955), 1:33. Enriqueta Vila Vilar, *Gran Enciclopedia Rialp* (Madrid: Ediciones Rialp, 1973), 6:580.

33. A. G. I., *Justicia* 286, fol. 196v, 311v-312.

34. Herrera, *Descripción de las Indias occidentales*, tomo 4, libro 3, cap. 26, p. 5.

35. A. G. I. *Audiencia de Guatemala* 110, fol.2, "*Probanza e petición de Diego Sánchez de Ortega*," 28 July 1531. A. G. I., *Justicia* 290, testimony of Diego López de Villanueva, fol. 113v, and testimony of Bernal Díaz del Castillo, fol. 114v, 29 May 1564. A. G. I., *Patronato* 87, fol. 34, testimony of Bernal Díaz del Castillo, 30 January 1561.

36. Beatríz Sánchez de Ortega said in a power of attorney dated 9 December 1545 that her father lived in Seville. A. G. I., *Justicia* 280, fol. 9v. A certain Juan Rodríguez, native of Valladolid, went to the Indies in 1513, but there is no evidence he was our man. Peter Boyd-Bowman, *Indice geobiográfico de cuarenta mil pobladores Españoles de America en el siglo XVI*, vol. 1, *1493-1519* (Bogotá: Instituto Caro y Cuervo, 1964), 154.

37. Boyd-Bowman, *Patterns of Spanish Immigration*, 5.

38. Mary Elizabeth Perry, *Crime and Society in Early Modern Seville* (Hanover, NH: University Press of New England, 1980), 13, 197-202, 210. See also John E. Boswell, "*Expositio* and *Oblatio*: The Abandonment of Children and the Ancient and Medieval Family," *American Historical Review* 89 (February 1984): 10-33.

39. A. G. I., *Justicia* 280, fol. 9v.

40. Baltasar Dorantes Carranza, *Sumaria relación de las cosas de la Nueva España*, ed. by José Mariano Agreda y Sánchez (Mexico: Imprenta del Museo Nacional, 1902), 410-11, Huntington Library rare book 269940. The Huntington Library copy contains a marginal note by Henry Raup Wagner identifying one of the men as Juan Rodríguez Cabrillo. The basis for Wagner's identification is not known.

41. Soares, *California and the Portuguese*, 39.

42. Helen Nader, *The Mendoza Family in the Spanish Renaissance, 1350-1550* (New Brunswick, NJ: Rutgers University Press, 1979), xi-xii.

43. See the legal document they signed on 1 July 1551 in A. G. I., *Justicia* 286, fol. 193v-94.

44. A. G. I., *Patronato* 87, fol. 36v-38.

45. Sanchíz Ochoa, *Los hidalgos de Guatemala*, 53-54.

46. Fernando Benítez, *The Century after Cortés*, trans. by Joan MacLean (Chicago: University of Chicago Press, 1965), 140-42. These nicknames are given a considerably different meaning in other translations. For example, see Genaro García ed., *The True History of the Conquest of New Spain*, trans. by Alfred Percival Maudslay, Hakluyt Society Works, ser. 2, vol. 40 (London: Hakluyt Society, 1916), 5:19, 228, 233, 237.

47. A sixteenth-century resident of Huelva, Spain, called himself Juan Rodríguez Cabrito. See the testimony of Gonzalo Quintero, 30 June 1554, A. G. I., *Justicia* 839, fols. unnumbered.

48. A. G. I., *Patronato* 20, *Repartimiento de la ciudad de Gracias a Dios*, 20 July 1536. There is a transcript of this manuscript in *Colección de documentos*, 15:5-18.

49. A. G. I. *Justicia* 280, power of attorney dated 29 August 1541, fol. 4v.

50. *Relación del espantable terremoto que agora nuevamente ha acontecido en las Yndias en una ciudad llamada Guatimala*, 2nd ed. (Madrid: n.n., 1543), facsimile reprint in *Colección de incunables Americanos siglo XVI* (Madrid: Ediciones Cultura Hispanica, 1944), 1: pages unnumbered.

51. A. G. I., *Justicia* 280, fol. 24v.

52. A. G. I., *Justicia* 286, fol. 228, testimony of Francisco López, 20 May 1552.

53. A. G. I., *Justicia* 290, testimony of Lázaro de Cárdenas, 26 April 1560, fol. 68; testimony of Francisco de Vargas, 26 April 1560, fol. 73v.

54. Diego García de Palacio, *Instrucción náutica para navegar* (Mexico: Casa de Pedro Ocharte, 1587), fol. 111-13v.

55. Ralph V. Turner has shown that reading and writing in medieval times were separate skills and that many literate people were unable to master the art of writing. "The *Miles Literatus* in Twelfth- and Thirteenth-Century England: How Rare a Phenomenon?" *American Historical Review* 83 (October 1978): 928-45.

56. *Documentos Americanos del Archivo de Protocolos de Sevilla, siglo XVI* (Madrid:

Tipografía de Archivos, 1935), 13.

57. Ibid. 22, 29, 100; Boyd-Bowman, *Indice geobiográfico,* 1:132.

58. James Lockhart and Enrique Otte trans. and eds., *Letters and People of the Spanish Indies, Sixteenth Century,* Cambridge Latin American Studies, vol. 22 (Cambridge: Cambridge University Press, 1976), p. ix.

59. Ibid. 3.

60. Hernando de Castro to Alonso de Nebreda, 31 August 1520, translated in ibid., 30.

61. Bernal Díaz del Castillo, *Historia verdadera de la conquista de la Nueva España,* intro. and notes by Joaquín Ramírez Cabañas, 10th ed. (Mexico: Editorial Porrúa, 1974), chap. 1, pp. 2-4; chap. 20, p. 33.

62. Juan de Herrera to Juan de Rios, 1 May 1520, translated in Lockhart and Otte, *Letters and People of the Spanish Indies,* 32.

63. Samuel Eliot Morison, *The European Discovery of America,* vol. 2, *The Southern Voyages, A. D. 1492-1616* (New York: Oxford University Press, 1974), 66-70, 123-24.

64. Irene A. Wright, *The Early History of Cuba, 1492-1586* (New York: Macmillan Co., 1916), 17-22. José M. Pérez Cabrera, "The Circumnavigation of Cuba by Ocampo: When Did It Take Place?" *Hispanic American Historical Review* 18 (February 1938): 101-108.

65. Wright, *Early History of Cuba,* 17-22. There is no agreement about the way the men were armed. Some authors say the men carried crossbows. Francisco Calcagno, *Diccionario biográfico Cubano* (New York: Imprenta de N. Ponce de León, 1878), 447-48. Wright, *Early History of Cuba,* 27. Las Casas, who was there, says they were armed with bows and arrows. See his *Historia de las Indias,* tomo 2, libro 3, cap. 26, p. 525. This is puzzling, especially in view of his remark that the Spanish bowmen were more deadly marksmen than the Indians who were armed with bows and arrows. No one disputes the fact that crossbows were the preferred armament for Spanish soldiers in the Indies. See Alberto María Salas, *Las Armas de la Conquista* (Buenos Aires: Emecé Editores, 1950), 204, 222, and passim.

66. Ramiro Guerra y Sánchez, *Historia de Cuba* (Havana: Sociedad Editorial Cuba Contemporanea, 1921), 1: 181-82. Calcagno, *Diccionario Biográfico Cubano,* 447-48. Wright, *Early History of Cuba,* 27.

67. Las Casas, *Historia de las Indias,* tomo 2, libro 3, cap. 29, pp. 535-38. Henry R. Wagner insists there was "only one massacre," even though Las Casas seems to imply a continuing slaughter of the Indians. See his work, *"The Life and Writings of Bartolomé de las Casas,* in collaboration with Helen Rand Parish (Albuquerque: University of New Mexico Press, 1967), 6.

68. Las Casas, *Historia de las Indias,* tomo 2, libro 3, cap. 29, pp. 536-38.

69. Ibid. 535-36.

70. Herma Brissault, trans., *The Devastation of the Indies: A Brief Account* (New York: Seabury Press, 1974), 56.

71. Las Casas, *Historia de las Indias,* tomo 2, libro 3, cap. 29, p. 536.

72. Ibid. 538-39.

73. Wagner, *Life and Writings of las Casas,* 7,15-16.

74. Robert S. Chamberlain, *Castilian Backgrounds of the Repartimiento-Encomienda,*

Carnegie Institution of Washington Publication No. 509, Contributions to American Anthropology and History No. 25 (Washington: Carnegie Institution of Washington, 1939), 45-53.

75. Wagner, *Life and Writings of las Casas*, 7, 11.

76. Las Casas, *Historia de las Indias*, tomo 2, libro 3, cap. 58, p. 91; cap. 74, p. 110.

77. Las Casas, *Devastation of the Indies*, 57.

78. Oviedo describes the process in his *Sumario de la natural historia de las Indias*, ed. José Miranda (Mexico: Fondo de Cultura Economica, 1950), 247-54. The original manuscript at the Huntington Library includes a poignant drawing of exhausted Indians working the placers. *"Natural y general historia de las indias, yslas, & tr̄ra firme dl mar Oceano,"* fol. 18v, MS HM 177, Huntington Library.

79. Oviedo, *Historia general y natural de las Indias*, 1:496. Wright, *Early History of Cuba*, 65.

80. Las Casas, *Historia de las Indias*, tomo 2, libro 2, cap. 32, p. 545.

81. Boyd-Bowman, *Indice geobiográfico*, 1:32. A. G. I., *justicia* 286, fol. 201.

82. Díaz, *Historia verdadera*, chap. 1, p. 3.

83. Ibid. chap. 6, p. 13. Las Casas, *Historia de las Indias*, tomo 2, libro 2, cap. 41, p. 340; libro 3, cap. 22, p. 511.

84. Díaz, *Historia Verdadera*, chap. 1, p. 4.

85. Robert Lewis Scheina, "Mass Labor: The Key to Spanish Maritime Construction in the Americas during the Sixteenth Century," *The Mariner's Mirror* 58 (May 1972): 197. Wright, *Early History of Cuba*, 79.

86. Francisco López de Gómara, *Cortés: The Life of the Conqueror by his Secretary, Francisco López de Gómara*, trans. Lesley Byrd Simpson (Berkeley: University of California Press, 1964), 190.

87. C. Harvey Gardiner, *Naval Power in the Conquest of Mexico* (Austin: University of Texas Press, 1956), 15-17.

88. Díaz, *Historia verdadera*, chap. 2, pp. 5-6; chap. 3, pp. 7-8.

89. Ibid. chap. 8, pp. 15-16.

90. There has been a good bit of speculation about the birth date of Bernal Díaz del Castillo. Most of this arises from an apparently erroneous interpretation of two passages in his *Historia verdadera*. Genaro García compiled an edition based on his reading of the original manuscript draft in the Archivo General de Centro America, Guatemala City. This edition was published in Mexico in 1904. García's work was later translated by Alfred Percival Maudslay, and this translation has become the standard English version. García's rendering of the manuscript has Bernal Díaz say that he was twenty-four years old in 1516, when Díaz meant to say that was his age when he was in Mexico with Cortés. For the original García edition see *Historia verdadera de la conquista de la Nueva España* (Mexico: Secretaría de Fomento, 1904), chap. 7. This question and a number of related matters are discussed in Ramón Iglesia, "Introduction to the Study of Bernal Díaz and His True History," in *Columbus, Cortés, and Other Essays*, trans. and ed. Lesley Byrd Simpson (Berkeley: University of California Press, 1964), 66-68. Bernal Díaz gave sworn testimony about his age on many occasions, though not always with faithful consistency. In 1563, for example, he said he was sixty-seven years old;

The same figure was used in his testimony given a year later; A. G. I. *Justicia* 290, fol. 114v. In 1552 he said he was fifty-four years old; A. G. I., *Justicia* 286, fol. 213.

91. A. G. I., *Justicia* 286, fol. 202; age 60 in 1552.
92. Ibid., fol. 226v; age 50 in 1552.
93. Ibid., fol. 227v-28.
94. Díaz, *Historia verdadera*, chap. 136, p. 283. A. G. I., *Justicia* 290, fol. 114v.
95. Díaz, *Historia verdadera*, chap. 136, p. 283. A. G. I. *Justicia* 290, fol. 114v.
96. A. G. I., *Justicia* 290, fol. 67-75. A. G. C. A., *"Relación de vecinos de Santiago de Guatemala,"* 20 July 1548, typed transcript in the Rebén Reina Collection, University of Pennsylvania Museum, Department of Anthropology, Philadelphia.
97. A. G. I., *Justicia* 295, fol. cxxxv.

Notes
Chapter 2

1. Wright, *Early History of Cuba*, 68-75.
2. Ibid.
3. Díaz, *Historia verdadera*, chap. 8, p. 157.
4. Ibid., chap. 8, p. 15; chap. 19, p. 31.
5. Ibid., chap. 26, p. 42; chap. 28, p. 45. Francisco López de Gómara, *La historia general de las Indias*, intro. and notes by Joaquín Ramírez Cabañas, 2 vols., (Mexico: Editorial Pedro Robredo, 1943), I, chap. 8, p. 62. There is an English translation by Lesley Byrd Simpson, *Cortés: The Life of the Conqueror by his Secretary, Francisco López de Gómara* (Los Angeles: University of California Press, 1964).
6. Gómara, *Historia general*, chap. 30, pp. 115-17.
7. Ibid. chap. 31, pp. 117-119. Díaz, *Historia verdadera*, chap. 54, p. 91.
8. Ibid., chap. 88, p. 162.
9. Hernan Cortés, *Carta de relaciō enbiada a su S.* Majestad del ēperador nro senor por el capitá general de la nueva spaña: llamado fernādo cortes (Sevilla: Jacobo Cromberger Aleman, 1522), fo. 14v, Huntington Library rare book 108651. English translations are not very satisfactory. It was long thought that the best versions were those based on the Vienna Codex, but that manuscript seems to be a copy of the earliest printed editions of the letters. Ralph H. Vigil, "A Reappraisal of the Expedition of Pánfilo de Narváez to Mexico in 1520," copy of undated, unpublished MS received from the author in January, 1979, p. 11. A new translation may be found in A. R. Pagden (trans. and ed.), *Hernan Cortés: Letters from Mexico* (New York: Grossman Publishers, 1971). One of the older good translations is J. Bayard Morris (trans. & ed.), *Hernando Cortés: Five Letters, 1519-1526* (London: George Routledge & Sons, Ltd., 1928). A less dependable version is that of Francis A. MacNutt, *Fernando Cortés: His Five Letters of Relation to the Emperor, Charles V.*, 2 vols., (New York: G.P. Putnam's Sons, 1908; reprint Glorieta, New Mexico, Rio Grande Press, 1977). Díaz, *Historia verdadera*, chap. 93, p. 178.

10. Díaz, *Historia verdadera*, chap. 58, p. 98.
11. Cortés, *Cartas de relacion*, intro. by Manuel Alcalá, Sepan Cuantos, Num. 7, 5th ed. (Mexico: Editorial Porrua, 1970), p. 117.
12. Gardiner, *Naval Power*, 62, 68, 104. Holmes, *New Spain*, 33.
13. Díaz, *Historia verdadera*, chap. 28, p. 45.
14. "*Quattuor construxit in falsa lacuna parvas biremes, dictos bergantinos, ut ingruente aliqua necessitate posset una viginti comites, in terram cum equis demittere*". Petrus Martyris Angleria, *De Orbe Novo Petri Martyris ab Anglería* (Alcalá: Míchael de Equia, 1530), dec. V., cap. 4, fol. lxxi verso, Huntington Library rare book 11392. It is not clear how the author fit *equis* into the sentence. There were scarcely twenty horses in the whole army at that time.
15. Gardiner, *Naval Power*, 68, 104. Holmes, *New Spain*, 33-34. Both authors quote MacNutt's translation of the Cortés letters, p. 257.
16. Cortés, *Carta de relacion*, fol. 14v.
17. Hernando de Castro to Alonso de Nebreda, August, 1520, text printed in Enrique Otte, "Mercaderes burgaleses en los inicios del comercio con México," *Historia Mexicana* 18 (July-September 1968): 120-21, 125, 129. This and other letters printed by Otte have been translated with a commentary in Lockhart and Otte, *Letters and People*, 28, 33.
18. Díaz, *Historia verdadera*, chap. 109, p. 211. Cortés, *Cartas de relación*, Alcalá ed., 69-70. Gómara, *Historia general*, I, chap. 96, p. 278.
19. A. G. I., *Justicia* 286, fol. 196v.
20. Díaz, *Historia verdadera*, chap. 109, p. 211.
21. See the account of Francisco de Aguilar in Patricia de Fuentes, trans. and ed., *The Conquistadors: First-person Accounts of the Conquest of Mexico* (New York: Orion Press, 1963), p. 162.
22. Hernando de Castro to Alonso de Nebreda, August, 1520, trans. in Lockhart and Otte, *Letters and People*, 29.
23. Díaz *Historia verdadera*, chap. 113, p. 218, chap. 124, p. 242.
24. Testimony of Diego Holguín, 2 May 1552, A. G. I., *Justicia* 286, fol. 201v, 203. Boyd-Bowman, *Índice Geobiográfico*, 1:32.
25. Testimony of Juan de Espinar, 2 May 1552 (?), A. G. I., *Justicia* 286, fol. 205-07; 28 April 1560 (?), A. G. I., *Justicia* 290, fol. 76. Díaz, *Historia verdadera*, chap. 136, p. 284.
26. Testimony of Pedro de Ovide, 20 April 1560, A. G. I., *Justicia* 290, fol. 52-54v, ibid., 29 May 1564, fol. 116.
27. Testimony of Francisco López, 20 May 1552, A. G. I., *Justicia* 286, fol. 226-28. Díaz, *Historia verdadera*, chap. 131, p. 271.
28. *Probanza a petición de Diego Sánchez de Ortega*, 28 July 1531, A. G. I., *Guatemala* 1109, fol. 1v, typescript in the Reina Collection, University of Pennsylvania Museum, Philadelphia; microfilm copy, American Philosophical Society Library, Philadelphia.
29. Hubert Howe Bancroft, *History of Mexico*, vol. 1, *1516-1521* (San Francisco: A. L. Bancroft & Co., 1883), 362, 378.
30. Ibid., 393-98.

31. See the account of Andrés de Tapía in Fuentes, *The Conquistadors*, 47.
32. Ibid.
33. Bancroft, *History of Mexico*, 1:406-07.
34. Díaz, *Historia verdadera*, chap. 113, p. 218; chap. 124, p. 242.
35. Ibid., chap. 125, p. 245.
36. Ibid., chap. 128, p. 255.
37. Ibid., 255, 260.
38. Ibid., 255-56.
39. Ibid., 257. In a document dated 19 April 1560, the son of Juan Rodríguez said that his father was present in Mexico City "when the Indians killed more than six hundred Spaniards." A. G. I., *Justicia* 290, fol. 42v, 47.
40. Díaz, *Historia verdadera*, 260-61. There are many conflicting estimates of the number of men lost in the campaign. For a good summary of the evidence see Bancroft, *History of Mexico*, 1:488.
41. Díaz, *Historia verdadera*, chap. 131, pp. 270-71.
42. Ibid., chap. 133, pp. 275-76; chap. 134, p. 276; chap. 136, p. 284.
43. Ibid., chap. 130, p. 269; chap. 135, p. 279; chap. 136, p. 283.
44. Ibid., chap. 136, pp. 283-84.
45. Ibid., 283.
46. Ibid. The information about Juan Rodríguez appears as a footnote in the printed edition with the notation that it was "scratched out in the original." The question is, which is the original manuscript? That sentence has certainly been "scratched out" of the middle of the page in the Guatemala manuscript, which many scholars consider to be the original. However, Carmelo Sáenz de Santa María, thinks the 1632 edition of Alonso Remón is based on a missing "original" and most truly represents what Díaz wished to say. The Guatemala manuscript is a "rough draft," with changes made by Bernal Díaz and others. See Sáenz, *Introducción crítica a la "Historia verdadera" de Bernal Díaz del Castillo* (Madrid: Instituto Gonzalo Fernández de Oviedo, 1967), 30, 42-43. José A. Barbón says the Guatemala copy "can be called both the 'original manuscript' and the 'rough copy'." *Bernal Díaz del Castillo* (Buenos Aires: Centro Editor América Latina S.A., 1968), p. 21. Barbón says that the Alegría manuscript from the Biblioteca Nacional de Madrid, is an early seventeenth century "clean copy, final and definitive." Barbón, *Díaz*, 25. Sáenz says it contains many changes made by Bernal's son. *Introducción crítica*, p. 31. In any case, the Remón edition does not include the reference to Juan Rodríguez Cabrillo. *Historia verdadera de la conquista de la Nueva España* (Madrid: Emprenta del Reyno, 1632), chap. 136, fol. 118v, Huntington Library rare book 45888.
47. A. G. I., *Justicia* 290, fol. 114v.
48. Gómara, *Historia general*, vol. 1, chap. 118, p. 332. Cortés, *Cartas de relación*, Alcalá ed., 105-106.
49. One of the best descriptions of the process is found in Thomas Bent, "The Way of Making Pitch, Tarr, Rosin and Turpentine near Marseilles," Royal Society of London *Philosophical Transactions* 20 (August 1698): 291, Huntington Library rare book 98681. There is also useful information in the following reference works:

Abraham Rees, *The Cyclopedia or Universal Dictionary of Art, Sciences and Literature* London: Longman, Hurat, Rees, Orme, & Brown, 1819), vol. 27, "Pitch," and vol. 25, "Tar" (the pages are not numbered in these volumes). *Encyclopedia Britannica* 23 (1895): 57-59. *Enciclopedia Universal Ilustrada, Europeo-Americano* (Madrid: Espasa-Calpe, 1921), 44:333-35. For information about the use of bonfires to make the sap run freely, see the letter from Diego García de Palacio to the king, March 8, 1576, in E. G. Squier, *Collection of Rare and Original Documents and Relations concerning the Discovery and Conquest of America* (New York, Charles B. Norton, 1860), 52; there is a somewhat abbreviated translation of the passage on page 55.

50. Díaz, *Historia verdadera*, chap. 136.

51. For conflicting views of the relationship between Aztec human sacrifices and the lack of domestic cattle herds see Michael Harner, "The Emergence of Aztec Sacrifice," *Natural History*, 86 (April 1977): 46-51; and Bernard R. Ortiz de Montellano, "Aztec Cannibalism: An Ecological Necessity?" *Science* 200 (May 1978): 611-17.

52. Oviedo *Historia general*, 3: 423-24.

53. Gómara, *Historia general*, vol. 2, cap. 130, p. 28. The translation here is by Lesley Byrd Simpson, *Cortés*, 262.

54. Thomas Gage, *Travels in the New World*, ed. and intro. by J. Eric S. Thompson (Norman: University of Oklahoma Press, 1958), 54.

55. Ibid., intro., xxvi-xxvii, xliv-xlix.

56. A. G. I., *Justicia* 290, fol. 227-28.

57. Gardiner, *Naval Power*, 117-28.

58. Ibid.

59. Ibid.

60. Díaz, *Historia verdadera*, chaps. 148-49, pp. 328-30, chap. 156, p. 370.

61. Ibid., chap. 150, pp. 331-32.

62. A. G. I., *Justicia* 290, fol. 43.

63. Díaz, *Historia verdadera*, chap. 151, p. 340, chap. 152, pp. 350-52.

64. Ibid., chap. 156, pp. 367-69.

65. Ibid., chap. 157, pp. 373-78.

66. Bancroft, *History of Mexico* 2:38-39.

67. Testimony of Juan de Aragón, 13 September 1542, A. G. I., *Justicia* 286, fol. 133v. Díaz, *Historia verdadera*, chap. 157, p. 378, chap. 162, p. 397.

68. A. G. I., *Justicia* 290, fol. 59v.

69. A. G. I., *Patronato* 87, fol. 17. A. G. C. A., A1. 29, leg. 4672, exp. 40132, fol. 17v.

70. Díaz, *Historia verdadera*, chap. 23, p. 39.

71. Juan de Aragón, 13 September 1542, A. G. I., *Justicia* 286, fol. 133v. Pedro de Ovide, 20 April 1560, and Cristóbal de Salvatierra, 20 April 1560, A. G. I., *Justicia* 290, fol. 52v-53, 56v.

72. Bancroft, *History of Mexico* 2:38-39.

73. Ibid., 39.

74. A. G. I., *Justicia* 290, fol. 43v.

75. Testimony of Cristóbal Rodríguez Picón, 29 August 1542, A. G. I., *Justicia*

280, fol. 34.

76. Bancroft, History of Mexico 2:39-40, Díaz, Historia verdadera, chap. 161, p. 396.

77. Díaz, Historia verdadera, chap. 161, p. 397.

78. Ibid., chap. 161, pp. 397-98.

79. Bancroft, History of Mexico 2:41. A. G. I., Justicia 290, fol. 43v.

80. Bancroft, History of Mexico 2:93-101, 105.

81. A. G. I., Justicia 290, fol. 44. See, in the same manuscript, the testimony of Pedro de Ovide, 20 April 1560, fol. 52v-53; Francisco Sánchez, 20 April 1560, fol. 59v-60; Cristóbal de Salvatierra, 20 April 1560, fol. 56v. Diego López de Villanueva, 9 May 1564, fol. 113v. See also the testimony of Bernal Díaz del Castillo, 30 January 1561, A. G. I., Patronato 87, fol. 34. Testimony of Juan de Valladolid, 6 February 1561, A. G. I., Guatemala 52, fol. 15.

82. Testimony of Bernal Díaz del Castillo, A. G. I., Patronato 87, fol. 33v.

83. A. G. I., Justicia 290, fol. 44.

84. Ibid., fol. 44-44v.

85. Probanza a petición de Diego Sánchez de Ortega, A. G. I., Guatemala 110, fol. 1v, 2.

86. Christopher H. Lutz, "Santiago de Guatemala, 1541-1773: The Socio-Demographic History of a Spanish American Colonial City," unpublished Ph.D. dissertation, University of Wisconsin, 1976, 1:50-55, 57-58; referred to hereafter as Lutz, "Santiago."

87. Murdo J. McLeod, Spanish Central America: A Socioeconomic History, 1520-1720 (Berkeley and Los Angeles: University of California Press, 1973), 40. Hubert Howe Bancroft, History of Central America, 3 vols. (San Francisco: The History Co., 1886-87), 1:619, 622-23.

88. McLeod, Spanish Central America, 41. Bancroft, Central America, 1:621, 623-24.

89. Lutz, "Santiago," 1:55, 132, 168. See also the testimony of the various Indios Mexicanos, Alonso Rodríguez, Juan Xúarez, and Juan Indio, in A. G. I., Justicia 290, fol. 16v-17, 20-21.

90. Bancroft, Central America, 1:625-26.

91. A. G. I., Justicia 290, fol. 43v-44.

92. Bancroft, Central America, 1:632-51.

93. Adrián Recinos, Pedro de Alvarado, Conquistador de México y Guatemala (Mexico: Fondo de Cultura Económica, 1952), 68-71.

94. Bancroft, Central America, 1:656-60. Alvarado to Cortés, 28 July 1524, translated in John E. Kelley, Pedro de Alvarado, Conquistador (Princeton: Princeton University Press, 1932), 141-42.

95. Bancroft, Central America, 1:660-62.

96. Relación de vecinos de Santiago de Guatemala, la mayor parte de ellos con-quistadores, en los que se pueden encomendar indios vacos, por sus meritos personales, 20 July 1548, A. G. C. A., leg. 2196, exp. 15750, pp. 4, 13, typescript in Reina Collection, University of Pennsylvania Museum, Philadelphia.

97. Bancroft, Central America, 1:663-77.

98. Alvarado to Cortés, 28 July 1524, in Kelley, Pedro de Alvarado, 145-46. Francis Gall, "Conquista de El Salvador y fundación del primigenio San Salvador, 1524" Antropolgía e Historia de Guatemala, 18 (January 1966): 27-29, quoting Alvarado's account of the march from the Codex Vindobonensis in the Osterreichische Nationalbibliothek, Vienna.

99. Alvarado to Cortés, 28 July 1524, in Kelley, *Pedro de Alvarado*, 149. Bancroft, Central America, 1:678.

100. *Libro viejo de la fundación de Guatemala y papeles relativos a D. Pedro de Alvarado*, prologue by Jorge García Granados, Biblioteca "Goathemala," vol. 12 (Guatemala: Sociedad de Geografía e Historia de Guatemala, 1934), 7.

Notes
Chapter 3

1. Alvarado to Cortés, 28 July 1524, in Kelley, *Pedro de Alvarado*, 141, 149-50.
2. Antonio de Remesal, *Historia general de las Indias Occidentales y particular de la gobernación de Chiapa y Guatemala*, edited by Carmelo Sáenz de Santa María, Biblioteca de Autores Españoles, vols. 175 and 189 (Madrid: Ediciones Atlas, 1964), 1:82.
3. Christopher H. Lutz, "Santiago de Guatemala, 1541-1773: the Socio-Demographic History of a Spanish American Colonial City," 2 vols., unpublished Ph.D. dissertation, University of Wisconsin, 1976, 1:57-59, 77.
4. Gall, "Conquista de El Salvador," 23-41.
5. Lutz, "Santiago," 59, 77.
6. Bartolomé de Las Casas, *Brevíssima relación de la destruyción de las Indias* (Seville: Sebastian Trugillo, 1522), pages unnumbered; Huntington Library rare book 1552. Facsimile reprint in *Biblioteca argentina de libros raros* Buenos Aires: Instituto de Filosofía y Letras, 1924), 3:43-46. For an English translation see Brissault, trans., *The Devastation of the Indies*, 78-84.
7. Bancroft, *Central America*, 2:74 ff.
8. A. G. I., *Justicia* 290, fol. 43v.
9. Bancroft, *Central America*, 2:101.
10. Lutz, "Santiago," 2:60.
11. *Libro viejo de la fundación de Guatemala y papeles relativos a D. Pedro de Alvarado*, prologue by Jorge García Granados, Biblioteca "Goathemala," vol. 12 (Guatemala: Sociedad de Geografía e Historia de Guatemala, 1934), 21, 23.
12. *Libro viejo*, 20-21, 24.
13. Don Stanislawski, "Early Spanish Town Planning in the New World," *Geographical Review*, 37 (January 1947): 94-105. Spain, Ministerio de Trabajo y Previsión, *Selección de las Leyes de Indias* (Madrid: Imprenta Artistica 1929), 48-57. Bancroft, *Central America*, 1:496-98.

14. *Libro viejo*, 23.
15. Ibid., 25.
16. Ibid., 25.
17. Ibid., 24-25.
18. Ibid., 29. This first permanent capital was located at the place now known as San Miguel de Escobar, rather than in Ciudad Vieja or even Antigua as is sometimes stated. See Janos de Szecsy, *Santiago de los Caballeros de Goathemala en Almolonga: investigaciones del año 1950*, trans. from the original English by Yolanda de Oreamuno (Guatemala: Editorial del Ministerio de Educación Publica, 1953), passim, especially 149-54. See also Stephen F. de Borhegyi, "Estudio arqueológico en la falda norte del Volcán de Agua," *Antropología e Historia de Guatemala*, 2 (Enero 1950): 3-4, 14-20. The details are summarized in Lutz, "Santiago," 61-63, 78.
19. *Libro viejo*, 30.
20. Ibid., 31-32.
21. The original cabildo records appear to have been lost, and those published in the *Libro viejo* seem to be based on copies of the originals. The first records were kept on loose sheets, many of which did not survive. The extant records were not bound into book form until 1530. See Remesal, *Historia general*, p. 111. These were in such bad condition in 1590 that they were recopied. Guatemalan officials now maintain that the 1590 copy was lost while the original was preserved. See *Libro viejo*, 3, note. This seems unlikely in view of the fact that volumes two and three, covering the years after 1530, when Juan Rodríguez and his family lived in Santiago, are themselves lost. Lutz, "Santiago," p. 165, note 3. Bancroft, *Central America*, 2:106-107.
22. *Libro viejo*, 66.
23. Juan Rodríguez, *Relación del espantable terremoto que agora nuevamente ha acontescido en las yndias en una ciudad llamada Guatemala; es cosa de gräde admiración y de grande exemplo para que todos enmēdemos de nuestros peccados y estemos aprescibiados para quando dios fuerre servido de nos llamar*, 2nd ed. (Madrid [?] : n.n., 1543 [?]), pages unnumbered.
24. Verle L. Annis, *La Arquitectura de la Antigua Guatemala, 1543-1773*, Bilingual Edition (Guatemala: University of San Carlos, 1968), 22, citing A. G. C. A., A1.2.4-2196-138 (1538), *Dispónese que en la construcción de las casas, solamente sea empleada la piedra y el ladrillo y que los techos sean de teja; las salas amplias y los patios con sol.*
25. Remesal, *Historia general*, 119. *Libro viejo*, 37. Lutz summarizes other measurements of the *caballería* and *peonía*. See his "Santiago," pp. 124, 165, note 5.
26. *Libro viejo*, 43, 47.
27. Herrera, *Historia general*, decada 4, libro 7, capitulo 5, tomo IX, p. 34.
28. Bancroft, *Central America*, 2:121. Testimony of Francisco Marroquín, 19 April 1560, A. G. I., *Patronato* 87, fol. 12. One author argues that Cobán was never under the effective control of Rodríguez, Sánchez, and Barahona. See André Saint-Lu, *La Vera Paz: Espirit Evangélique et Colonisation* (Paris: Centre de Recherches Hispaniques, 1968), 93-99, 529-36. See also Arden R. King, *Coban and the Vera Paz: History and Cultural Process in Northern Guatemala*, (New Orleans: Tulane University,

1974), 13-19. King seems to be unaware of the conquest in 1530; he calls Rodríguez Juan Fernández.

29. *Probanza a petición de Diego Sánchez Ortega*, 28 July 1531, A. G. I., *Guatemala* 110, fol. 1v.

30. Remesal, *Historia general*, 130-31. Francisco Ximénez, *Historia de la provincia de San Vicente de Chiapa y Guatemala de la órden de predicadores*, Biblioteca "Goathemala," vols. 1-3 (Guatemala Sociedad de Geografía e Historia, 1929), 1:171-73. Agustín Estrada Monroy, *Datos para la historia de la iglesia en Guatemala*, Biblioteca "Goathemala," vol. 26 (Guatemala: Sociedad de Geografía e Historia de Guatemala, 1973), 81-82.

31. Testimony given on 19 April 1560, *Patronato* 87, fol. 12.

32. Testimony of Gonzalo Ortíz, 24 April 1560, *Patronato* 87, fol. 21.

33. *Libro viejo*, 73, 86, 96, 101-102.

34. Ibid, 72. Testimony of Gonzalo Ortíz, 9 January 1564, A. G. I., *Justicia* 290, fol. 15-15v.

35. Lutz, "Santiago," p. 165, note 3.

36. Díaz *Historia verdadera*, chap. 113, p. 128, chap. 124, p. 242.

37. Testimony given on 9 January 1564, A. G. I., *Justicia* 290, fol. 16v-17.

38. Oviedo, *Sumario de la historia natural de las Indias*, 251. Various other reports mention cuadrillas that ranged from sixty to a hundred and fifty Indians. William L. Sherman, *Forced Native Labor in Sixteenth Century Central America* (Lincoln: University of Nebraska Press, 1979), 99-100.

39. Testimony of Gonzalo Ortíz, 9 January 1564, A. G. I., *Justicia* 290, fol. 15.

40. Testimony given on 13 June 1564, *Justicia* 290, fol. 19v-20.

41. Ibid., fol. 20-20v.

42. Testimony given on 28 June 1564, *Justicia* 290, fol. 20v-21.

43. Díaz, *Historia verdadera*, chap. 108, p. 210.

44. Marroquín to the king, 17 August 1545, in *The Americas*, 5 (January 1949): 344-45, paleography by Lázaro Lamadrid.

45. Testimony of Francisco de Torres, 22 December 1564, A. G. I., *Justicia* 290, fol. 23v-24.

46. *Libro viejo*, 282-83.

47. Ibid.

48. Alvarado to the king, 12 May 1536, in ibid., 305-06.

49. Alvarado to the king, 1 September 1532, in ibid., 282-83.

50. Interrogatory, 1 September 1541, A. G. I., *Justicia* 280, fol. 24v-25v.

51. See her power of attorney, 9 December 1545, A. G. I., *Justicia* 280, fol. 9v.

52. MS dated 6 December 1543, A. G. I., *Justicia* 280, fol. 1.

53. Rodríguez, *Relación*.

54. El Inca Garcilaso de la Vega, *Historia general del Peru* (Cordova: Viuda de Andrés Barrera, 1617), libro II, cap. I, fol. 34v (numbered in error 33); Huntington Library rare book 183418. for an English translation see Harold L. Livermore, ed., *Royal Commentaries of the Incas and General History of Peru*, 2 vols. (Austin: University of Texas Press, 1965), 2:733-34.

55. Alvarado to the king, 28 July 1524, translated in Kelley, *Pedro de Alvarado*,

145, 150, and 155 note 50.

56. A. G. I., *Justicia* 286, fol. 201, 221v-222.

57. Ibid., 215v-216, 218-218v.

58. On 15 December 1563 Paz said he had arrived in Santiago about thirty years earlier. A. G. I., *Justicia* 290, fol. 79v-80v. On 24 January 1559 Paz said he had arrived in Santiago about twenty-five years earlier. These statements seem to establish his date of arrival between December 1533 and January 1534. See his *probanza* in A. G. I. *Patronato* 62, fol. 2v.

59. Pilar Sanchíz Ochoa, *Los hidalgos de Guatemala: realidad y apariencia en un sistema de valores*, Publicaciones del Seminario de Antropolgía Americana, vol. 13 (Seville: Universidad de Sevilla, 1976), 67-68.

60. *Libro viejo*, 21.

61. Sanchíz, *Los hidalgos de Guatemala*, 68-69.

62. Testimony given 29 August 1542, A. G. I., *Justicia* 280, fol. 32, 35, 38.

63. Testimony given on 19 April 1560, A. G. I., *Patronato* 87, fol. 16. This testimony also appears (as does much of the other testimony) in *Justicia* 290, fol. 58. *Patronato* 87 is written in a much better hand and is easier to read.

64. Testimony given on 29 May 1564, A. G. I., *Justicia* 290, fol. 117v.

65. Ibid., fol. 116.

66. Ibid., fol. 115.

67. Ibid., fol. 113.

68. George Kubler, *Mexican Architecture of the Sixteenth Century*, 2 vols. (New Haven: Yale University Press, 1948), 2:188-207 and illustrations facing p. 185. Annis, *Arquitectura*, 22ff. Remesal, *Historia general*, 1:385. Sidney David Markman, *Colonial Architecture of Antigua Guatemala*, Memoirs of the American Philosophical Society, vol. 64 (Philadelphia: American Philosophical Society, 1966), 22-27.

69. Testimony of Francisco de Torres, 4 May 1560, A. G. I., *Patronato* 87, fol. 28-28v.

70. *Tasaciones de los pueblos de los terminos y jurisdicción de la ciudad de Santiago de la provincia de Guatemala*, 26 April 1549, A. G. I. *Guatemala* 128, fol. 100.

71. Ibid., 23 May 1549, fol. 128. Testimony of Francisco de Torres, 4 May 1560, A. G. I. *Patronato* 87, fol. 28. See also the description given for Comitlán in *Tasaciones de quince pueblos de los terminos y jurisdicción de la ciudad de Santiago de Guatemala*, in Francisco del Paso y Troncoso, *Espistolario de Nueva España, 1505-1818*, series 2, *Biblioteca Historica Mexicana de Obras Ineditas*, 16 vols. (Mexico: Antigua Librería Robredo de José Porrua e Hijos, 1940), 5:211-12.

72. *Tasaciones*, 1549, A. G. I., *Guatemala* 128, fol. 116. Paso y Troncoso, *Epistolario*, 5:213.

73. Lutz, "Santiago," 166. Adrián Recinos and Delia Goetz, *The Annals of the Cakchiquels* (Norman: University of Oklahoma Press, 1953), 129-131. On page 61 of the original manuscript is a marginal note, perhaps made by Francisco Vásquez in the late seventeenth century, affirming the use of 1,600 Indian laborers in these two projects in 1529. Francisco Hernández Arana, Francisco Díaz, et al., "Manuscrito Cakchiquel, o sea memorial de Tecpán-Atitlán," Brinton Collection, Rare Book Room, University of Pennsylvania Library, Philadelphia.

74. Testimony of Luis Pérez, 26 August 1542, A. G. I., *Justicia* 280, fol. 43; Pero Hernández, fol. 49; and Pedro de Paredes, fol. 51.
75. Testimony of Juan de Argujo, 24 September 1563, A. G. I., *Justicia* 290, fol. 7v-8.
76. Cédula, 23 December 1540, A. G. I., *Justicia* 280, fol. 7v-8. See also Salvador Rodríguez Becerra, *Encomienda y conquista: los inicios de la colonización en Guatemala*, Publicaciones del Seminario de Antropología Americana, vol. 14 (Seville: Universidad de Sevilla, 1977), 115.
77. Cédula, 31 March 1540, A. G. I., *Justicia* 290, fol. 7. This is the document issued after the death of Diego Sánchez de Ortega, granting full title to Juan Rodríguez Cabrillo.
78. Testimony of Maese Pedro, A. G. I., *Justicia* 286, fol. 62v-63. Reply of Francisco de la Cueva, A. G. I., *Justicia* 280, fol. 67.
79. Interrogatory prepared by Juan Rodríguez Cabrillo in the summer of 1541, A. G. I., *Justicia* 280, fol. 25, 29; cited hereafter as Rodríguez, 1541, A. G. I., *Justicia* 280. The name of the ship is given as *San Antonio* by Maurice G. Holmes in his book *New Spain*, 66. I repeated his error in "The California Armada of Juan Rodriguez Cabrillo," *Southern California Quarterly* 41 (Winter 1979): 314.
80. Alvarado to the *Ayuntamiento de Guatemala*, 23 March (1534), in *Libro viejo*, 289.
81. Agreement dated 26 August 1534 in *Libro viejo*, 293-94; letter to Real Consejo, 20 November 1536, *Libro viejo*, 314.
82. Rodríguez, 1541, A. G. I., *Justicia* 280, fol. 25. For a good summary of the early years of the Peruvian trade see Woodrow Borah, *Early Colonial Trade and Navigation Between Mexico and Peru*, Ibero-Americana, vol. 38 (Berkeley: University of California Press, 1954), chap. 2.
83. Testimony of Domingo del Castillo, 2 September 1541, *Justicia* 280, fol. 28.
84. Ibid.
85. Ibid., fol. 25-26.
86. *Repartimiento de la ciudad de Gracias á Dios*, 1536, A. G. I. Patronato 20 no. 4, ramo 6. There is a printed copy of the document in *Colección de documentos*, ser. 1, 15:5-18.
87. Ibid.
88. Robert S. Chamberlain, *The Conquest and Colonization of Honduras, 1502-1550* Carnegie Institution of Washington Publication No. 58 (Washington, D.C.: Carnegie Institution, 1953), 48-65.
89. A. G. I., *Justicia* 290, fol. 45v.
90. Rodríguez, 1541, A. G. I., *Justicia* 280, fol. 25v.
91. A. G. I., *Justicia* 286, fol. 193v.
92. Testimony given in May 1552, A. G. I., *Justicia* 286, fol. 222.
93. *Justicia* 290, fol. 14. The witnesses were sworn on 9 January 1564, and testimony continued until 28 December 1564. Ibid., fol. 4v, 16v, 19, 19v, 23v.
94. *Probanza de Francisco Díaz del Castillo*, 12 February 1579, printed in Díaz, *Historia verdadera*, 647, 650.
95. Poder de la tutora, 9 August 1543, A. G. I., *Justicia* 280, fol. 6.

96.   In any case the notary was wildly mistaken about their age, saying "by their appearance they seem to be about fourteen years old." Ibid. This was doubtless a lazy man's way of saying they were under legal age, while refusing to take the trouble to find out their exact age.

Notes
Chapter 4

1. Letter from Diego García de Palacio to the king, 8 March 1576, in E.G. Squier, *Collection of Rare and Original Documents and Relations concerning the Discovery and Conquest of America* (New York: Charles B. Norton, 1860), 32, 107.
2. Ibid.
3. Letter from Alvarado to the king, 7 January 1534 in *Libro viejo*, 288.
4. *Autos e información secreta de la ciudad de Santiago de los caballeros de la provincia de Guatemala sobre que el rey nuestro senor le haga merced para poder abio el puerto de Iztapa*, 2 May 1589, A. G. I., *Guatemala* 41, fol. 9, 11, 16v, 17v; referred to hereafter as *Autos*, 1589, A. G. I., *Guatemala* 41.
5. Squier, *Rare Documents*, 32.
6. *Autos*, 1589, A. G. I., *Guatemala* 41, fol. 16v.
7. Squier, *Rare Documents*, 38-40, 108.
8. Juan Rodríguez, statement made c. August 1541, A. G. I., *Justicia* 280, fol. 25.
9. There has been some uncertainty about the location of Girabaltique (also Jirabaltique and Xirabaltique). Henry Raup Wagner thought it was another name for the port of Acajutla. See his *Spanish Voyages*, 571. He apparently based his conclusion on a statement by Francisco de Vargas that "he saw Juan Rodríguez Cabrillo in Ystapa overseeing the construction of the armada, and he went with the armada when it was careened in the shipyard at Girabaltique." See his testimony of 26 April 1560 in A. G. I. *Justicia* 290, fol. 70v, where the name is spelled Guevaltiq and A. G. I. *Patronato* 87, fol. 23v, where it is spelled Girabaltique. Adrián Recinos, apparently following Wagner, said there was a shipyard at Iztapa and another at "Jeravaltique, located on the coast of San Miguel" some distance from Acajutla. See his *Pedro de Alvarado: Conquistador de Mexico y Guatemala* (Mexico: Fondo de Cultura Economica, 1952), 188. In 1536 Alvarado reported that he had "discovered a very good port, with a good anchorage at the mouth of the river Lempa." Here he founded the Villa of San Miguel, were ships "can be careened

and loaded." Pedro de Alvarado to the Real Consejo de Indias, 20 November 1535, in *Colección de Documentos*, 24:246-47. See Recinos, *Pedro de Alvarado*, 157, for information about the date of the letter. In spite of this it seems pretty clear that Girabaltique was at or near Iztapa and that Acajutla was simply a place to assemble the ships and take on supplies. See A. G. I., *Patronato* 87, fol. 8, 23v, 30v. When Alvarado took the fleet to Mexico in 1540, two ships were still under construction in his shipyard at Girabaltique. See the agreement between Alvarado and Antonio de Mendoza, 29 November 1540, A. G. I., *Patronato* 21, There are two nearly identical versions printed in *Colección de documentos*, ser. 1, vol. 3, pp. 351-62; vol. 16, pp. 342-55; Diego García de Palacio described both Iztapa and Acajutla in his report to the king in 1576, but the only shipyard he mentioned was at Iztapa, where he said Alvarado's entire fleet was built. See his letter in *Rare Documents*, 32, 38, 40, 107, 108. See also *Autos*, 1589, A. G. I., *Guatemala* 41, fol. 9, 11, 16v, 17v, which identifies Iztapa as the location of Alvarado's shipyard.
10.   García de Valverde to the king, 8 September 1579, quoted in Manuel Rubio Sánchez, *Historia del puerto de la Santísima Trinidad de Sonsonate ó Acajutla* (San Salvador: Editorial Universitaria, 1977), 34, 36. Francisco Antonio de Fuentes y Guzmán, *Recordación Florida: discurso historial y demonstración natural, material, militar, y política del reyno de Guatemala*, Biblioteca "Goathemala," vols. 6, 7, 8 (Guatemala: Tipografía Nacional, 1933), 1:359-60; 2:105. Remesal, *Historia general* 1:201-202.
11.   Alvarado to the king, 12 May 1535, in *Colección de documentos*, ser. 1, vol. 24, pp. 229-30. Also reprinted in *Libro viejo*, 305. Both these sources give the date as 1536, but Adrián Recinos dates it as 1535 and says he has seen the original. See his *Pedro de Alvarado*, 154-57, especially fn.105.
12.   *Contrato de compra-venta de la armada del Adelantado Don Pedro de Alvarado*, 26 August 1534, reprinted in *Libro viejo*, 293. Alvarado to Real Consejo de Indias in *Colección de documentos*, ser. 1, vol. 24, pp. 229-30.
13.   Alvarado to the king, 12 May 1535, in *Colección de documentos*, ser. 1, vol. 24, p. 229. *Libro viejo*, 305.
14.   Juan Escalante de Mendoza, *"Itenerario de navegación de los mares y tierras occidentales,"* MS in the Biblioteca Nacional, Madrid, fol. 36. The author lived in Guatemala and Honduras, serving "with a special appointment from the Real Audiencia" (fol. 7). His manuscript was written in 1575, apparently as a result of these experiences in Guatemala.
15.   Alvarado to the king, 1 September 1532, reprinted in *Libro viejo*, 282-83. There is some question about his use of *tonel*, which he seems to interchange with *tonelada.* A *tonel* is equivalent to 2 *pipas* or casks, each holding about 125 gallons. See Diego García de Palacio, *Instrucción Náutica*, fol. 90, 155v, Huntington Library rare book 106304. The meanings of the terms are nearly identical, in any case, or near enough for most estimates of ship size. There is a nice explanation of this point in O. H. K. Spate, *The Spanish Lake*, vol. 1 of *The Pacific since Magellan*, 2 vols. (Minneapolis: University of Minnesota Press, 1979, xxii-xxiv. The matter of ship size is also covered in Celsus Kelly, *La Australia del Espíritu Santo*, 2 vols. (Cambridge: Cambridge University Press, 1966), 1:28-29.
16.   García de Palacio, *Instrucción Náutica*, fol. 91v.

17. Alvarado to Real Consejo de Indias, 20 November 1535, in *Colección de documentos*, ser. 1, vol. 24, p. 240-41. See Recinos, *Pedro de Alvarado*, 157 for information about the date of the letter.

18. It is not clear exactly when the work was started. In August 1541, Juan Rodríguez said he had started work on the fleet "about six years ago." *Justicia* 280, fol. 25. The fire of the 1536 is mentioned in Remesal, *Historia general*, 1:271-72.

19. See the testimony of one of the sailors, Diego Hernández, in *Autos*, 1589, A. G. I. *Guatemala* 41, fol. 17v. Another witness is cited by Oviedo in his *Historia general*, 4:23.

20. Remesal, *Historia general*, 1:201, 245-46. Fuentes y Guzmán, *Recordación Florida*, 359-60. Alvarado to the Real Consejo, 20 November 1535, in *Colección de documentos*, ser. 1, vol. 24, p. 241. Antón de Morales, 11 January 1538, A. G. I., *Justicia* 295, fol. 510-11v.

21. Alvaro de Paz, testimony given 15 December 1563, A. G. I., *Justicia* 290, fol. 81v; 20 May 1559, A. G. I., *Patronato* 62. fol. 3-3v.

22. Letter from the Indians to the king, 15 March 1547, A. G. I., *Guatemala* 52.

23. Torres, testimony given 22 December 1564, A. G. I., *Justicia* 290, fol. 24.

24. Las Casas, *Brevíssima relación*, pages unnumbered.

25. Marroquín to the king, 20 November 1539, A. G. I., *Guatemala* 156.

26. Testimony given in August 1541, A. G. I., *Justicia* 280, fol. 25v.

27. Remesal, *Historia general*, 267-70, quoting the Alvarado testament prepared by Bishop Marroquín.

28. Alvarado-Mendoza agreement, 29 November 1540, *Colección de documentos*, ser. 1, vol. 16, 342-43.

29. A. G. I., *Justicia* 259 testimony of Alvar Nuñez, c. July 1542, fol. 260.

30. An anonymous oil commemorating the battle of Lepanto (National Maritime Museum, Greenwich, England) shows the flagship with the name of the *capitán general*, Andrea Doria, painted on the bow. Christian vessels in the picture fly the royal ensign and other banners as well.

31. Díaz, *Historia verdadera*, chap. 149, p. 330; Bernal says one of the boats was called *Busca Ruido*, or *Looking for a Fight*. Cf. ibid, chap. 151, p. 334.

32. Testimony of Luis González, 28 April 1560, A. G. I., *Justicia* 290, fol. 63v.

33. For the rules about the use of banners see *Las Siete Partidas*, trans. and notes by Samuel Parsons Scott (Chicago and New York: American Bar Association, 1931), part 2, title 23, pp. 477-78. About 1600 Jan van der Straet printed copperplate engravings showing Columbus and Magellan on their respective ships. The banner on Magellan's ship carried the royal arms, while Columbus' banner carried a crucifix. Undated copies of the engravings from *America Retectio* are in the Shearman Collection, Los Angeles County Museum of Natural History; see also copies in the Huntington Library, rare book 322072.

34. Alvarado to the *ayuntamiento* of Guatemala, 4 April 1539, *Libro viejo*, 328-29. Remesal, *Historia general*, 1:223.

35. Las Casas, *Brevíssima relación*.

36. Alvarado to Real Consejo, 20 November 1535, in *Colección de documentos*, ser. 1, vol. 24, p. 240. Alvaro de Paz, statement of 11 January 1538, A. G. I. *Justicia*

295, fol. 510-11v, quoted in William L. Sherman, "A Conqueror's Wealth: Notes on the Estate of Don Pedro de Alvarado," *The Americas*, 26 (July 1969): 209.

37. Louis-Andre Vigneras, *The Discovery of South America and the Andalusian Voyage* (Chicago: published for the Newberry Library by the University of Chicago Press, 1976), 38-39. See also Remesal, *Historia General*, 1:234, who referred to the three small vessels in the Alvarado fleet as *fustas de remo* or row-galleys. In a letter to Ruy López de Villalobos, 18 September 1542, Mendoza referred to one of the ships as a *fusta* in one sentence and as a *bergantín* in another. *Colección de documentos*, ser. 2, vol. 2, p. 30. John Minsheu, after consulting with Pedro de Valdés, captain general of the Andalusia Squadron of the Great Armada, decided that *fragata*, *galeota*, *fusta*, and *bergantín* were terms that could be interchanged freely. See his *Dictionaire, in Spanish and English, First Published into the English Tongue by Ric. Percivale* London: Edm. Bollifant, 1599), p. 198, Huntington Library rare book 62921-22. The words doubtless had special meanings, but men who were familiar with the sea interchanged them at will.

38. A. G. I., *Justicia* 280, fol. 25v.

39. The *teredo navalis* could riddle the hull of a ship with holes in only a few months, and removing the vessel from salt water was the only real defense. Remesal reported that most of Alvarado's fleet later fell victim to shipworms. See his *Historia general*, 1:288. For an account of the *teredo navalis* of Central America see A. Myra Keen and James H. McLean, *Sea Shells of Tropical West America: Marine Mollusks from Baja California to Peru*, 2nd ed. (Stanford, CA: Stanford University Press, 1971), 280-84.

40. Alvaro de Paz, 11 January 1538, quoted in Sherman, "A Conqueror's Wealth," 209. Diego Hernández said only that seven or eight ships were build *de novo*. A. G. I., *Guatemala* 41, fol. 17v. See also the testimony of Francisco de Vargas, 26 April 1560, A. G. I., *Justicia* 290, fol. 70, which refers to the careening of the older vessels.

41. Oviedo, *Historia general*, 4:23.

42. Fuentes y Guzmán, *Recordación Florida*, p. 95. Díaz, *Historia verdadera*, chap. 136, pp. 283-84. Juan Fernández de Ladrillero, who saw the fleet, confirmed the number. His testimony is quoted in Wagner, *Spanish Voyages*, 70. The ships are listed in the Mendoza-Alvarado *asiento* of 29 November 1540, *Colección de documentos*, ser. 1, vol. 16, 342-55. There is another copy of the asiento in vol. 3 of the same series, but that copy lacks some of the ship names that appear in the copy cited above. The fleet is also described by Oviedo in his *Historia general*, 4:20, 23, and by Alvarado in his letter to the king, 28 March 1541, *Colección de documentos*, ser. 2, vol. 2, pp. 1-3. Alvaro de Paz, mayordomo for Alvarado, also confirmed the number. See his testimony of 20 May 1559, A. G. I., *Patronato* 62 fol. 3v.

43. Alvarado to the king, 12 May 1535, *Colección de documentos*, ser. 1, vol. 24, p. 230.

44. Oviedo, *Historia general*, 3:245.

45. A. G. I., *Guatemala* 41, fol. 17v.

46. Marroquín to the king, 10 May 1537, in *Cartas de Indias* (Madrid: Imprenta de Manuel G. Hernández, 1877), 421.

47. Remesal, *Historia general*, 288.
48. See his letter to the king, 8 March 1576, in Squier, *Rare Documents*, 32.
49. Testimony of Diego Hernández, 19 April 1589, A. G. I., *Guatemala* 41, fol. 17v.
50. Testimony of Alvaro de Paz, 5 May 1569, *Patronato* 86, fol. 210-210v. Even in his earlier testimony Paz did not always distinguish carefully between galleons and ordinary ships. See his testimony of 14 May 1559, A. G. I., *Patronato* 62.
51. Testimony of Juan de León, 6 February 1561, A. G. I., *Guatemala* 52, fol. 22-22v. Testimony of Lázaro de Cárdenas, April 26, 1560, A. G. I., *Justicia* 290 fol. 69; testimony of Francisco de Vargas, 26 April 1560, ibid., fol. 72 there is a facsimile copy of the manuscript account of the voyage in Wagner, *Spanish Voyages*, 450-63; Wagner's translation appears in the same book on 79-93. The original manuscript is now in the A. G. I., *Patronato* 20. no. 5, ramo 13. The "de Juan Páez" written at the head of the manuscript, has given rise to much speculation. Henry R. Wagner thought the man was Juan Páez de Castro (*Spanish Voyages*, 319), but Maurice G. Holmes thought this unlikely; see his *New Spain* 115-27. The same phase, *de Juan Páez*, appears at the head of the *Relación hecha por el capitán Juan Jaramillo, 1537*, A. G. I., *Patronato* 20, no. 5, ramo 8, and elsewhere. The same notation also appears on numerous MSS in the library of El Escorial, where many Páez de Castro manuscripts were deposited. See the description of this material in Fernando Rubio, "Las noticias referentes a America, contenidas en el manuscrito V-II-4 de la Biblioteca de el Escorial." *Revista de Indias*, 11 (January-June 1951): 111-21. Moreover, the Juan Páez to whom Holmes made reference was dead by the winter of 1541, well before Juan Rodríguez made his voyage to California. See the letter written by Bishop Marroquín to the king, October 1541, A. G. I., *Patronato* 181, fol. 2. All this is discussed at length in Chapter V below.
52. *Las Siete Partidas*, part 3, title 16, law 26, pp. 675-76, and part 3, title 17, p. 689. Testimony of Juan León, 30 January 1561, A. G. I., *Patronato* 87, fol. 35-35v; *Justicia* 290, passim.
53. *Relación*, in Wagner, *Spanish Voyages*, 459.
54. Ibid., *461*.
55. Evans, "Translation from the Spanish of the Account by the Pilot Ferrel of the Voyage of Cabrillo along the West Coast of North America in 1542," in *Report of the United States Geographical Surveys West of the One Hundredth Meridian*, vol. 7, *Archaeology* (Washington: G.P.O., 1879), 310, 313. Alexander Smith Taylor, *Discovery of California and Northwest America: The First Voyage to the Coast of California, Made in the Years 1542 and 1543 by Juan Rodríguez Cabrillo and His Pilot Bartolomé Ferrelo* (San Francisco: Le Count and Strong, 1853), 9-18; Huntington Library rare book 455. George C. Davidson, "Voyages of Discovery and Exploration," 222-34. Davidson, "The Discovery of San Francisco Bay," *Geographical Society of the Pacific, Transactions and Proceedings*, ser. 2, vol. 4 (1907): 13. Herbert E. Bolton, *Spanish Explorations in the Southwest, 1542-1706* (New York: Charles Scribner's Sons, 1916), 5, 39. Wagner, in one place, insisted that Juan Rodríguez made his trip "in two small vessels, neither of which had decks." But later in the same book he explained that *puente* meant "a deck over a compart-

ment; it is no doubt used in that sense here." See his *Juan Rodríguez Cabrillo, Discoverer of the Coast of California* San Francisco: California Historical Society, 1941), 29, 90. The most recent translation makes *no tener puentes* mean that the vessels lacked bridges and "were not completely decked." Moriarty and Keistman, trans. and eds., "Cabrillo's Log," 13.

56. Antonio de Herrera, *Historia general de los hechos de los Castellanos en las islas y Tierra Firme del mar océano*, 4 vols. (Madrid: Juan de la Cuesta, 1615), 4:90, Wagner Collection, Honnold Library, Pomona, CA.

57. Ibid.

58. García de Palacio, *Instrucción náutica*, fol. 90, 92, 93v, 130, 140, 149, 151. Richard Percyvall, who had much of his information on Spanish naval terms from two captured officers of the Great Armada, defined *puente* as "a halfe deck," which was the compartment on the main deck running from the mainmast to the stern. See Minsheu, *A Dictionarie in Spanish and English*, 198.

59. *Relación* in Wagner, *Spanish Voyages*, 461.

60. Ibid., 462.

61. Herrera, *Historia general*, 4:91.

62. Testimony of Luis González, 20 April 1560, A. G. I., Justicia 290, fol. 63v.

63. I am indebted to Roger Hatheway for advising me about the rigging of sailing ships. The best illustrated book on ship construction during this period is Bjorn Landstrom, *The Ship: An Illustrated History* (Garden City, N.Y.: Doubleday & Co., 1961), especially the reconstructed view of a Spanish galleon of 1540 on pages 112-13.

64. Oviedo, *Historia general*, 4:20-23.

65. Ibid. 20.

66. Testimony of many witnesses, including Luis González, 20 April 1560, A. G. I., Justicia 290, fol. 63v.

67. Statement by Juan Rodríguez Cabrillo, about August 1541, A. G. I., Justicia 280, fol. 25-26.

68. Herrera, *Historia general*, 4:91.

69. Remesal, *Historia general*, 1:270.

70. Letters from Antonio de Mendoza to Ruy López de Villalobos, 18 September 1542, and 22 October 1542, *Colección de documentos*, ser. 2, vol. 2, pp. 29-30, 47. See also the testimony of Luis González, 19 April 1560, A. G. I., Justicia 290, fol. 63v; and the Alvarado-Mendoza asiento, 29 November 1540, *Colección de documentos*, ser. 1, vol. 16, p. 343. In the first document González says he is pilot on the *San Miguel*, which had to be left in Acapulco for repairs; in the second, Alvarado says his bergantín is beached for repairs in Acapulco, but the other twelve vessels are in port in Navidad; *San Miguel* is the bergantín.

71. Alvarado to the king, 18 November 1539, ibid., ser. 1, vol. 24, p. 340, and 28 March 1541, ibid., ser. 2, vol. 1, p. 3.

72. Ibid., ser. 2, vol. 1, pp. 29-30, 54. Herrera, *Historia general* 98.

73. A. G. I., Justicia 259, fol. 260-60v.

74. García de Palacio, *Instrucción náutica*, fol. 93-97; Landstrom, *The Ship*, 112-13.

75. Alvarado to the king, 18 November 1539, *Colección de documentos*, ser. 1, vol. 24, p. 340.

76. Oviedo, *Historia general*, 4:20.

77. Alvarado to the king, 18 November 1539, *Colección de documentos*, ser. 1, vol. 24, p. 340. The context implies that another twenty-oared *galeota* and perhaps other small vessels were included in the dozen or so ships Alvarado described.

78. Testimony in Ginovés de Mafra, 2 September 1540, A. G. I., *Justicia* 280, fol. 29.

79. Questions by García Piñeda "en nombre de Juan Rodríguez Cabrillo," 5 September 1542, A. G. I., *Justicia* 286, fol. 38-39, 41. Testimony of Juan Rodríguez Cabrillo, August 1540; testimony of Juan Cansino, Martín Sánchez, Domingo del Castillo, and Ginovés de Mafra, 2 September 1540, A. G. I., *Justicia* 280, fol. 25-30.

80. Testimony of Juan Rodríguez Cabrillo, August 1540, A. G. I., *Justicia* 280, fol. 25v-26.

81. Testimony of Alonso de Torres, 1553, quoted in Recinos, *Pedro de Alvarado*, 191.

82. According to Bernaldo de Molina the fleet sailed in August 1540. He gave this report to Oviedo when stopping in Santo Domingo on his way to Spain, and Oviedo added it immediately to his manuscript history. See Oviedo, *Historia general*, 4:20, 23. This does not seem to agree with the 1533 testimony of Alonso de Torres, who said the fleet sailed in September (quoted in Recinos, *Pedro de Alvarado*, 191), or the 14 October 1541, letter of Francisco de Castellanos, who said the fleet sailed 1 September 1540 (ibid.). Perhaps the fleet sailed from Iztapa in August and from Acajutla in September.

83. Marroquín to the king, 25 November 1541, in *Cartas de Indias*, 433. Testimony of Francisco de Girón, 15 September 1549, A. G. I., *Patronato* 59, fol. 4.

84. Probanza de los méritos y servicios de Don Antonio de Figueroa, 17 April 1559, sig. A1.29-1, exp. 40129, leg. 4671, folios unnumbered.

85. Testimony of Francisco Marroquín, 19 April 1560, A. G. I., *Justicia* 290, fol. 51.

86. The document with additions, is printed as *Asientos y capitulaciones hechas por S.M. con el adelantado D. Pedro de Alvarado*, April 15, 1538, October 3, 1539, and July 26, 1541, *Colección de documentos*, ser. 2, vol. 2, p. 9. Hereafter *Asientos y capitalaciones*.

87. Testimony given 2 September 1541, A. G. I., *Justicia* 280, fol. 27v.

88. Testimony of Nicolás López de Yzarraga, 30 January 1561, A. G. I., *Patronato* 87, fol. 33. Testimony of Lázaro de Cárdenas, 26 April 1560, fol. 68, and Francisco de Vargas, 26 April 1560, A. G. I., *Justicia* 290, fol. 72v.

89. Testimony of Diego de Robledo, 30 January 1561, A. G. I., *Patronato* 87, fol. 34v, 35; and 20 December 1569, *Patronato* 86, fol. 255v-257.

90. Testimony of Nicolás López de Yzárraga (also Yrázaga in Recinos, *Pedro de Alvarado*, 164. and Ynárraga in A. G. I., *Patronato* 87), 15 September 1549, A. G. I., *Patronato* 59, fol. 29v; 11 December 1553, *Guatemala* 52; 30 January 1561, *Patronato* 87, fol. 32v.

91. Testimony of Diego de Abuenza, 17 April 1559, sig. A1.29-1, exp. 40129, leg. 4671, A. G. C. A. Testimony of Andrés Dubón, 14 May 1559, A. G. I., *Patronato* 62.

92.   Testimony of Antonio de Castellanos, 17 April 1559, sig. A1.29-1, exp. 40129, leg. 4671, A. G. C. A.

93.   Testimony of Alonso Torres, 1553, quoted in Recinos, *Pedro de Alvarado*, 191.

94.   Testimony given 26 April 1560, A. G. I., *Justicia* 290, fol. 68.

95.   Testimony given 26 April 1560, A. G. I., *Justicia* 290, fol. 73.

96.   Testimony given 20 April 1560, A. G. I., *290, fol. 63v.*

97.   Testimony of Diego Hernández, 19 April 1589, A. G. I., *Guatemala* 41, fol. 17v.

98.   Tomás de la Torre, *Desde Salamanca, España, hasta Ciudad Real, Chiapas, diario de viaje, 1544-45*, intro. and notes by Franz Blom (Mexico: Editora Central, 1945), 71-73.

99.   Ibid.

100.   Ibid., 73.

101.   Evidence for horses on board the ships is in A. G. I., *Justicia* 290, fol. 44v-45, 50v, 54, 57v, 61, 63v, 64, 67v, 70v, 77, 79, 81.

102.   According to Fray Tomás, Bishop Las Casas took, among other things, chickens for the friars to eat. After landing at Santo Domingo, the friars restocked for the remainder of the journey. In addition to salted beef, they took three calves, six sheep, and thirty chickens on board. Torre, *Diario,* ·72, 103.

103.   *Asientos y capitulaciones*, 1538, 1539, 1541, *Colección de documentos*, ser. 2, vol. 2:19, 25.

104.   Wagner, *Spanish Voyages*, 53-54, 313 note 13.

105.   Ibid., 56, 314 note 14. See also the petition of 16 July 1543, by Hernando Cortés in P. Mariano Cuevas, *Cartas y otros documentos de Hernan Cortés* (Seville: Imprenta de F. Díaz, 1915), 208-09. Cuevas gives the date of this document as 1542, but Wagner, who saw the original, dates it 6 July 1543.

106.   Cuevas, *Cartas*, 208.

107.   Alvarado-Mendoza asiento, 29 November 1540, *Colección de documentos*, ser. 1, vol. 16, 343. Testimony of Luis González, 20 April 1560, A. G. I., *Justicia* 290, fol. 63v. It is apparently the vessel *que se hace de nuevo* in Alvarado to the king, 28 March 1541, ibid., ser. 2, vol. 2, p. 3.

108.   Alvarado-Mendoza asiento, 29 November 1540, ibid., ser. 1, vol. 16, p. 343. Wagner, *Spanish Voyages*, 56.

109.   The agreement is printed in its entirety in ibid., ser. 1, vol. 16, pp. 342-55 and vol. 3, pp. 351-62, in which latter copy the names of the ships are omitted. The original is in A. G. I., *Patronato* 21. At least one man, Alarcón, thought Alvarado might take matters into his own hands. When Alarcón returned from his trip to the Colorado River in November 1540, he stopped for supplies at Santiago. Seeing Alvarado's ships in port and fearing for the safety of his own vessels, Alarcón and his smaller fleet slipped out of the port in the dead of night and sailed quietly for Acapulco. See Arthur S. Aiton, *Antonio de Mendoza, First Viceroy of New Spain* (Durham, NC: Duke University Press, 1927), 130.

110.   Cortés, petition of 6 July 1543, in Cuevas, *Cartas*, 208.

111.   Alvarado-Mendoza asiento, 29 November 1540, *Colección de documentos*, ser. 1, vol. 16, p. 348.

112.   Ibid. The royal cedula required Alvarado to have such a shipyard. *Asien-*

tos y capitulaciones, 1538, 1539, 1541, *Colección de documentos,* ser. 2, vol. 2, p. 10.
113. Statement of Francisco Marroquín, 19 April 1560, A. G. I., *Justicia* 290, fol. 51.
114. *Cedula de encomienda del Adelantado en Cabrillo: pueblos de Xumaytepeque y Tacuba,* 20 December 1540, A. G. I., *Justicia* 280, fol. 7v-9v.
115. Aiton, *Antonio de Mendoza,* 146, note 19. Whether Mendoza named the place or not is still uncertain Bishop Marroquín was there with Alvarado, Rodríguez Cabrillo, and Mendoza, so the bishop may have done the naming. See his testimony of 19 April 1560, A. G. I., *Justicia* 290, fol. 51.
116. *Cedula de encomienda,* 20 December 1540, A. G. I., *Justicia* 280, fol. 7v-9v. Testimony of Francisco de Marroquín, 19 May 1552, A. G. I., *Justicia* 286, fol. 201, 223.
117. Questions presented by Alonso de Aguilar, 26 April 1552, A. G. I. *Justicia* 286, fol. 198.
118. The cover page on the legal records reads as follows: "This litigation began on 6 June 1542, and ended on 19 December 1568," A. G. I., *Justicia* 286.
119. Letter from Alvarado to the king, 18 March 1541, *Colección de documentos,* ser. 2, vol. 2, p. 3.
120. Ibid., 5.
121. Herrera, *Historia general,* vol. 4, dec. 6, lib. 7, cap. 8, p. 159 and dec. 7, lib. 2, cap. 10, p. 39.
122. Testimony of Francisco de Vargas, 26 April 1560, A. G. I., *Justicia* 290, fol. 71v; testimony of Lázaro de Cárdenas, 26 April 1560, A. G. I., *Justicia* 290, fol. 68.
123. Alvarado and Mendoza to Zuñiga, 29 April 1541, translated in Wagner, *Spanish Voyages,* 418-25. The original is in the Real Biblioteca de San Lorenzo de El Escorial. See Manuel Fraile Miguélez, *Catálogo de los códices españoles de la Biblioteca del Escorial* (Madrid: Imprenta Helénica, 1917), 1:240. Juan Rodríguez Cabrillo, c. August 1541, and Domingo del Castillo, 2 September 1541, A. G. I., *Justicia,* 280, fol. 26, 28v.
124. Mendoza, *descargo* xxxvi., 1546, A. G. I., *Justicia* 259, fol. liii. This document is printed in part in Ciriaco Pérez Bustamante, *Don Antonio de Mendoza, Primer virrey de la Nueva España (1535-1550),* vol. 3 of *Anales de la Universidad de Santiago* (Santiago: Tipografía de "El Eco Franciscano," 1928), p. 159. Mendoza to Alarcón, 31 May 1541, in Thomas Buckingham Smith, ed., *Colección de varios documentos,* 3.
125. Mendoza, *descargo* xxxvi, 1546, in Pérez Bustamante, *Don Antonio de Mendoza,* 158-59; A. G. I., *Justicia* 259, fol. lii.
126. Mendoza, *descargo* xxxvii, 1546, in Pérez Bustamante, *Don Antonio de Mendoza,* 160.
127. Díaz, *Historia verdadera,* chap. 202. Juan de Aldaz, 3 February 1570, A. G. I., *Patronato* 69, no. 3, ramo 1.
128. Autlán was a journey of no more than a day or so from Navidad. From a comparison of Mendoza's statements on the matter it appears that the thirty horsemen taken by Alarcón to Autlán were shortly reassigned to Francisco de

Godoy and sent to Compostela. See his testimony of 1546 in Pérez Bustamante *Don Antonio de Mendoza*, 159, and his *descargos*, 30 October 1546 in Joaquín García Icazabalceta, *Colección de documentos para la historia de Mexico* (Mexico: Antigua Libreria, 1866), 110. The date of the descargos is given in Aiton, *Antonio de Mendoza*, 167-68 and fn. 69.

129. Wagner, *Spanish Voyages*, 63. Holmes, *New Spain*, 98-99. Wagner later changed his mind about Alarcón. See his *Cartography of the Northwest Coast of America to the year 1800* (Berkeley: University of California Press, 1937), 1:30ff.

130. Testimony of Francisco de Vargas, 26 April 1560, A. G. I., *Justicia* 290, fol. 70v-71.

131. Smith, *Colección de varios documentos*. 3.

132. Vargas, 26 April 1560, A. G. I., *Justicia* 290, fol. 71. See also the testimony of Juan Fernández de Ladrillero, 20 December 1574, in Wagner, *Spanish Voyages*, 63-71.

133. Mendoza to Juan de Aguilar, undated but obviously written after the early part of 1543, in Smith, *Colección de varios documentos*, 8-9. Aiton says the letter was written "as early at 1544." See his *Antonio de Mendoza*, p. 164, fn. 60.

134. See the records of the case in A. G. I., *Justicia* 280, especially fol. 7-9v, 61-63.

135. Ibid., fol. 16-20, 61-63, 71-72. *Justicia* 286, fol. 3-30. For a good summary of some of the arguments see Holmes, *New Spain*, 275-80.

136. A. G. I., *Justicia* 280, fol. 24v.

137. A. G. I., *Justicia* 280, fol. 24v-26v.

138. *Poder de Cabrillo*, 29 August 1541, ibid., fol. 4v-7.

139. Marroquín to the king, 10 August 1541, *Cartas de Indias*, 427-29.

140. Ibid. Remesal, *Historia general*, 258-59.

141. Remesal, *Historia general*, 258-59, 279. Marroquín to the king, 10 August 1541, *Cartas de Indias*, 427-29. Marroquín et al. to the king, 25 November 1541, *Cartas de Indias*, 432-33.

142. The letter is reproduced in *Libro viejo*, 385.

143. Marroquín to the king, 6 October 1541, A. G. I., *Guatemala* 156.

144. A. G. I., *Justicia* 280, fol. 4v-7. *Libro viejo*, 385.

145. Remesal, *Historia general*, 263-65.

146. *Libro viejo*, 385. Remesal, *Historia general*, 263.

147. Holmes, *New Spain*, 54, 70-71.

148. Marroquín et al. to the king, 25 November 1541, *Cartas de Indias*, 432-33. Marroquín to the king, 20 February 1542, A. G. I., *Patronato* 180, quoted in Sherman, *Forced Native Labor*, 394, n. 42. Remesal, *Historia general*, 264-65.

149. Ibid., 265-66.

150. Ibid., 266.

151. Ibid., 274-75. Historians today tend to say there was no earthquake, but people who were there thought there was. See, for example, the testimony of Alvaro de Paz, 4 January 1559, A. G. I., *Patronato* 62, fol. 2, who referred to the year 1541 as the time of "the earthquake and storm in this city of Guatemala." For a summary of evidence pro and con see Lutz, "Santiago de Guatemala," 1:82, note 55. The best contemporary description is in Marroquín to the king, c. October

1541, in A. G. I., *Patronato* 181, fol. 2v. This is probably one of the reports mentioned in the letter of 15 November 1541 as having been written *en este mes passado*. *Cartas de Indias*, 432.

152. Juan Rodríguez, *Relación*, facsimile reprint in Ramón Menéndez Pidal, ed., *Colección de incunables Americanos*, 1: no page numbers; cited hereafter as Rodríguez, *Relación*. The original Mexican edition seemingly does not now exist in a public collection, though it was reported in Joaquín García Icazbalceta, *Bibliografía Mexicana del siglo XVI* (Mexico: Libreria de Andrade y Morales, 1886), 6, which recorded this colophon from the last sheet of the original: *Fue impresa en la grã cibdad d Mexico en casa de Iuã Cromberger año de mill y quinietos y cuarẽta y uno*. Henry R. Wagner tried to locate the original Mexican edition mentioned by Icazbalceta, but without success. See Wagner, *Nueva bibliografía Mexicana del siglo XVI* (Mexico: Editorial Polis, 1940), 66-67. There are modern transcriptions of the purported Madrid text in various places. José Luis Reyes M. in *Anales de la Sociedad de Geografía é Historia de Guatemala*, 23 (March-June 1948): 92-97, is the first historian to attribute authorship to Juan Rodríguez Cabrillo. There is another edition of the *Relación* bound with manuscripts of the years 1541 and 1542 in the library of the Real Monasterio de San Lorenzo de El Escorial, Spain; *Relaciones historicas*, sig. V. II. 4., no. LVI, fol. 167-70. It appears to have been printed at about the same time as the purported Madrid edition and is described by Manuel Fraile Miguélez in his *Catálogo de los códices españoles de la Biblioteca del Escorial* (Madrid: Imprenta Helenica, 1917), 92-93.

153. Carlos Alfredo Chamier, *De como el periodismo en América se originó en Guatemala en 1541* (Mexico, Costa-Amic, (1968), 7-13. See also Ramon Menéndez Pidal, "Los incunables Americanos," *Colección de incunables Americanos siglo XVI* (Madrid: Ediciones Cultura Hispánica, 1944), 1:xvii. Alberto María Carreño, "Don Fray Juan de Zumárraga Pioneer of European Culture in America," *The Americas*, 4 (July 1949): 70.

154. José Luis Reyes M., "Relacion del espantable terremoto," *Anales de la Sociedad de Geografia e Historia de Guatemala*, 23 (March-June 1948): 92-97. Bernice Beagles, "Record of What Happened in Guatemala," *Western Explorer: Journal of the Cabrillo Historical Association*, 5 (September 1967): 20-23.

155. Rodríguez, *Relación*.

156. Marroquín to the king, c. October 1541, A. G. I., *Patronato* 181, fol. 2v.

157. Rodríguez, *Relación*.

158. Chamier, *El periodismo en América*, 15-16.

159. A. G. I., *Patronato* 181, fol. 2v.

160. Ibid., fol. 2.

161. Rodríguez, *Relación*.

162. Marroquín to the king, 25 November 1541, *Cartas de Indias*, 432.

163. Díaz, *Historia verdadera*, edition of Alonso Remón (Madrid: Imprenta del Reyno, (1632)), 237, Huntington Library rare book 45888.

164. Oviedo, *Historia general*, 4:32.

165. Agustín Estrada Monroy, *Datos para la historia de la iglesia en Guatemala*, Sociedad de Geografía e Historia de Guatemala, vol. 26 (Guatemala: Tipografía

Nacional, 1972), 91-98.

166.   Díaz, *Historia verdadera*, Remón edition, 237. Juan de Alvarado may have become a Franciscan. See the testimony of Juan de Alvarado, given in 1547, A. G. I., *Justicia* 265, fol. 214, 217v-218, 220-220v, 226.

167.   Rodríguez, *Relación*.

168.   A. G. I., *Justicia* 290, fol. 46v. Mendoza to Marqués de Saviotte, 10 March 1542, *Cartas de Indias*, 253.

Notes
Chapter 5

1. Antonio de Mendoza to the Marques de Saviotte, 10 March 1542, in *Cartas de Indias* (Madrid: Ministerio de Fomento, 1877), 255. Arthur S. Aiton, *Antonio de Mendoza, First Viceroy of New Spain* (Durham, N. C.: Duke University Press, 1927), 151-57.
2. Mendoza to Saviotte, 10 March 1542, *Cartas de Indias*, 255. Testimony of Juan de Salazar, 10 January 1547, A. G. I., *Justicia* 266, fol. 707. Antonio de Mendoza to Juan de Aguilar, c. 1543, in Buckingham Smith, *Colección de varios documentos*, 8.
3. Antonio de Remesal, *Historia general de las Indias occidentales y particular de la gobernación de Chiapa y Guatemala*, 2nd ed. (Guatemala: Sociedad de Geografía e Historia, 1932), 1:235-36.
4. *Las Siete Partidas*, pt. 4, title 6, pp. 1217-21.
5. Mendoza to Aguilar, c. 1543, in Smith, *Colección de varios documentos*, 8-9.
6. A. G. I., *Justicia* 280, fol. 24v.
7. Remesal, *Historia general*, 267-71.
8. Las Casas, *Brevíssima relación*, no page numbers.
9. A. G. I., *Justicia* 290, fol. 44v-45.
10. A. G. I., *Justicia* 290, fol. 46.
11. A. G. I., *Justicia* 290, fol. 68v, 73v.
12. A. G. I., *Justicia* 290, fol. 68-68v.
13. A. G. I., *Patronado* 87, fol. 33.
14. A. G. I, *Guatemala* 52, fol. 15.
15. A. G. I., *Justicia* 286, fol. 307.
16. The text reads *"tres navíos e un bergantín,"* but the sense of the document is "three ships, one a bergantin." A. G. I., *Justicia* 290, fol. 71v.
17. *Los bienes secuestrados del adelantado*, 19 August 1538, A. G. I., *Justicia* 296, fol. 42v.
18. Testimony given 29 December 1546, A. G. I., *Justicia* 266, fol. 464.

19. *Probanza del Virrey de la Nueva España Don Antonio de Mendoza hecha en la villa de Colima*, 21 February 1547, A. G. I., *Justicia* 263, fol. 26.

20. Testimony of Juan Bautista, 21 February 1547, A. G. I., *Justicia* 263, fol. 107.

21. Testimony of Maestre Jácome Ginovés, 21 February 1547, A. G. I., *Justicia* 263 fol. 78.

22. Herrera, *Historia general* (Madrid: Juan de la Cuesta, 1615), 4: fol. 112, Wagner Collection, Honnold Library, Pomona, CA.

23. A. G. I., *Justicia* 280, fol. 24v.

24. A. G. I., *Justicia* 290, fol. 68.

25. Mendoza to Saviotte, 10 March 1542, *Cartas de Indias*, 255.

26. A. G. I., *Justicia* 290, fol. 46.

27. Wagner, *Juan Rodríguez Cabrillo*, 27.

28. A. G. I., *Justicia* 290, fol. 71v.

29. A. G. I., *Justicia* 290, fol. 71v.

30. Consuelo Varela, ed., intro., and notes, *El viage de Don Ruy López de Villalobos a las Islas del Poniente, 1542-1548* (Milan: Instituto Editoriale Cisalpino-LaGoliardica, 1983), 39-44. The original MS is in the British Library (Add. 9944). Sra. Varela's edition is based on the briefer version in the Biblioteca Nacional, Madrid (Res. 18), which was seemingly compiled for publication by its anonymous sixteenth century author.

31. Herrera and other chroniclers simply say Puerto de Juan Gallego, but all the modern historians say the Puerto de Juan Gallego is Navidad. Herrera, *Historia general* (Madrid: Juan de la Cuesta, 1615), 4: fol. 115.

32. One of the most important is the Cavendish map, an original sailing chart of the 1580s. The original is in the Algemeen Rijksarchief, The Hague, Netherlands. A good copy can be seen in Frederick Caspar Weider, *Monumenta Cartographica: Reproductions of Unique and Rare Maps, Plans, and Views in the Actual Size of the Originals, Accompanied by Cartographical Monographs*, 5 vols. in 1 (The Hague: Martinus Nijhoff, 1925-1933), 1: 6-7; fol. 1, plate 5. The various ports are shown in some detail in the *Derrotero genl del Mar del Sur desde las Californias hasta los estrechos de Magellanes y San Vicente*, HM 918, Huntington Library, San Marino. Seventeenth-century maps and descriptions can be found in J. Francisco V. Silva, "Itinerario Marítimo de California al Río de la Plata," Segundo Congreso de Historia y Geografía Hispano-Americanas, Sevilla, 1921, *Actas y Memorias* (Madrid: Establecimiento Tipográfico de Jaime Rates, 1921), 484.

33. Alonso de Santa Cruz, *Crónica del Emperador Carlos V*, 5 vols. (Madrid: Imprenta del Patronato de Huérfanos de Intendencia e Intervención Militares, 1923), 5: 481. This section was written before 1551; see the introduction by F. de Laiglesia in 1:vi.

34. Varela, *Viage de Villalobos*, 39-44.

35. Andrés de Urdaneta, "Memoria de las cosas qué me parece qué será bien que el rei nro señor tenga noticia," undated MS, c. 1560, A. G. I., *Patronato* 23, ramo 15, fol. 1.

36. A. G. I., *Justicia* 290, fol. 70, 72v.

37. The Huntington Library has three manuscript atlases by Agnese that illustrate

this point. They are HM 27 (Venice, 1553), fol. 4v-5; HM10 (c. 1550), fol. 4v-5; and HM 25 (c. 1550), fol. 3v-4. See also the Agnese atlases in the Newberry Library, Ayer MS Map 12, fol. 3v-4; and Ayer MS Map 13, which has several unfinished sheets.

38. Giacomo de Gastaldi, *Cosmographia universalis et exactissima iuxta postremam neotericorum traditionem* (Venice: n.n. 1562?) The map is undated, but it is apparently the one described in his brief work, *La universale descrittione del mondo* (Venice: Matthio Pagano, 1561), no page numbers. There is a Xerox copy of this work in the Newberry Library, and the existence of several other copies is noted in Román Rainero, "Observations sur l'activité cartographique de Giacomo Gastaldi (Venice, XVe siècle)" Paper read at VIII Congres International Sur L'Histoire de la Cartographie, Berlin, 17-20 September 1979; unpublished typescript in Rijksarchief map room, The Hague. 1562 is the date tentatively assigned at the British Library. I would guess that 1560 or 1561 would be more likely.

39. Giuseppe Caraci, "Map of the Pacific Ocean by G. Tatton," *Tabulae geographicae vetustiores in Italia adservatae*, 2 vols. (Florence, Otto Lange, 1926), 1:12-15; 2: pl. XV-XVII. A number of other interesting and pertinent sixteenth-century maps are reproduced in Alvaro del Portillo, *Descubrimientos y exploraciones en las costas de California*, 1532-1650 2nd ed. (Madrid: Ediciones Rialp, 1982), 29, 33, 37, 43, and 47.

40. Francisco Antonio Lorenzana, *Historia de Nueva España escrita por su esclarecido conquistador Hernán Cortés* (Mexico: Imprenta del Superior Gobierno, 1770), 328.

41. Testimony given 29 December 1546, A. G. I., *Justicia* 266, fol. 307.

42. Mendoza to Hernando de Alarcón, 31 May 1541, fol. 6, Spanish Manuscript Collection, Thomas Gilcrease Institute of American History and Art, Tulsa, Oklahoma.

43. Wagner remained convinced that the Diego Gutierrez map of 1552, in which the name appears about midway on the peninsula, was the earliest map of California. See his *Juan Rodríguez Cabrillo*, p. 73, n. 1. This repeats his earlier opinion given in *Spanish Voyages*, p. 331, n. 21.

44. For information about Humboldt see Ernest J. Burrus, *Kino and the Cartography of Northwestern New Spain* (Tucson: Arizona Pioneers Historical Society, 1965), p. 30, n. 3. Humboldt saw the Castillo map in the "archives of the Cortés family." As Burrus notes, Humboldt discussed both the manuscript and the printed version as though there were no appreciable differences between them. See Humboldt, *Ensayo politico sobre el reino de la Nueva España*, edición crítica por Vito Alessio Robles, 5 vols. (Mexico: D. F. Robredo, 1941), 1:162 185.

45. Cortés to Diego Hurtado de Mendoza, 1532, in Martín Fernández de Navarrete, Miguel Salvá, and Pedro Sainz de Baranda, *Colección de documentos ineditos para la historia de España* (Madrid: Imprenta de la Viuda de Calero, 1844), 4: 167-75. Cortés and Alvarado to Zuñiga, 29 April 1541, translated in Wagner, *Spanish Voyages*, 418-25. The original orders to Zuñiga are in the Real Biblioteca de San Lorenzo de El Escorial, Relaciones Historicas, sig. V-II-4, no. LXIV, fol. 382-86v.

46. The instructions to Alarcón are in Mendoza to Alarcón, 31 May 1541, in Smith, *Colección de varios documentos*, 1-6.

47. A. G. I., *Indiferente General* 417, fol. 17-18.

48. See the discussion of the size of the vessels in chapter 4. See also García de Palacio, *Instrucción náutica*, fol. 91, Huntington Library rare book 106304. The matter is also discussed in Harry Kelsey, "The California Armada of Juan Rodríguez Cabrillo," *Southern California Quarterly*, 41 (Winter 1979): 313-36.

49. Pedro de Alvarado to the king, 18 November 1539, in *Colección de documentos*, 24: 340. The original letter is in A. G. I., *Guatemala* 9.

50. Magellan set the tone for Spanish seamen by naming his own flagship after this image of the Virgin and naming the shrine in his will. Quoted in Navarrete, *Colección de los viages y descubrimientos que hicieron por mar los españoles* (Madrid: Imprenta Nacional, 1837), 4:LXXX.

51. Testimony of Alvar Nuñez, 20 July 1542, A. G. I., *Justicia* 259, fol. 260-60v.

52. García de Palacio, *Instrucción náutica*, fol. 108. Hernando de Alarcón mentioned a sail on his batel when he sailed up the Colorado River. See the translation of his report in George P. Hammond and Agapito Rey, *Narratives of the Coronado Expedition, 1540-1542* (Albuquerque: University of New Mexico Press, 1940), 129.

53. "*Asiento e capitulación de compañia que celebraron Don Antonio de Mendoza virrey de Nueva España y el adelantado Don Pedro de Alvarado,*" 29 November 1540, in *Colección de documentos*, 16-343. The original document is in A. G. I., *Patronato* 21; there is a second copy in *Patronato* 28. See also Herrera, *Historia general*, 4: fol. 114.

54. Estimates of crew size are based on García de Palacio, *Instrucción náutica*, fol. 111-21.

55. Celsus Kelly estimated that the three-ship armada of Quirós had a crew of 250. See his *La Australia del Espiritu Santo*, 2 vols., Hakluyt Society Works, ser. 2, vol. 126-27. (Cambridge: Cambridge University Press, 1966), 1:26-29. Carla Rahn Phillips has compiled figures on average crew size during this era. See her "Spanish Ships and Shipbuilding during the Renaissance," *Boat and Shipbuilding in San Diego* (San Diego: Cabrillo Historical Association, 1983), 8-9.

56. A. G. I., *Justicia* 266, fol. 544v.

57. A. G. I., *Justicia* 263, fol. 78.

58. A. G. I., *Justicia* 266, fol. 424v-25.

59. García de Palacio, *Instrucción náutica*, fol. 120v-24v. Inventory of the ship *Trinidad*, 1539, Spanish Manuscript Collection, Gilcrease Institute, fol. 2-4. Mendoza to Zúñiga, 29 April 1541, Biblioteca de El Escorial, Relaciones Historicas, sig. V-II-4, no. LXIV, fol. 382.

60. Zúñiga orders, *Relaciones historicas*, fol. 382.

61. Zúñiga orders, *Relaciones historicas*, fol. 382-82v.

62. *Colección de documentos*, 2:37, 57.

63. Tomás de la Torre, *Desde Salamanca, España, hasta Ciudad Real, Chiapas: diario de viaje, 1544-45*, intro. and notes by Franz Blom (Mexico: Editora Central, (1945)), 71-73.

64. Las Casas, *Brevíssima relación*, pages not numbered.

65. "*Proceso de la justicia eclesiástica contra Juan Fernández Ladrillero, vecino de*

la villa de Colima, por blasfemo, 17 October, 1556, Mexico, Archivo General de la Nacion, sec. *Inquisición, Colima,* tomo 8, fol. 82-85.

66. *"Relación de las derrotas y navegación qué hizo el Capital Francisco Cortés Ogea,* Colección Navarrete, vol. 20, fol. 52v, Museo Naval, Madrid.

67. Zúñiga orders, *Relaciones historicas,* fol. 384v-85.

68. Zúñiga orders, *Relaciones historicas,* fol. 384-84v.

69. Zúñiga orders, *Relaciones historicas,* fol. 385-85v.

70. Zúñiga orders, *Relaciones historicas,* fol. 386.

71. Testimony of Francisco de Vargas, 26 April, 1560, A. G. I., *Justicia* 290, fol. 73v. Vargas said there were sufficient supplies to last "for more than three years," but this seems excessive. The expedition had to return after nine months, partly because of a lack of supplies. A good part of the supplies was destroyed or lost in storms, but three years still seems an excessive number.

72. García de Palacio, *Instrucción náutica,* fol. 109-16.

73. Antonio de Guevara, *Arte de Marear,* ed. by R. O. Jones, Exeter Hispanic Texts, vol. 2 (Exeter: University of Exeter, 1972), 33.

74. García de Palacio, *Instrucción náutica,* fol. 115v-116v.

75. García de Palacio, *Instrucción náutica,* fol. 117v. Guevara, *Arte de Marear,* 33.

76. A. G. I., *Justicia* 290, fol. 45.

77. Testimony given 10 January 1547, A. G. I., *Justicia* 266, *fol. 707.*

78. A. G. I., *Justicia* 266, fol. 707.

79. Testimony of Nicolás López, 31 January 1561, A. G. I., *Patronato* 87, fol. 33. Herrera gives the name as S. Remo in his *Historia general,* 4: fol. 113. The name San Remo appears as one of the mariners in Juan Castellón's ship *Trinidad,* which sailed to California in 1539. See the inventory in the Spanish Manuscript Collection, Gilcrease Institute, fol. 1.

80. The men who knew him called him Ferrer. See the testimony of Francisco Gutierrez, A. G. I., *Justicia* 263, fol. 59v, and similar testimony by Francisco de Cifonte in the same manuscript, fol. 38v. See also the testimony of Lázaro de Cárdenas in A. G. I., *Justicia* 290, fol. 68v. Herrera lists the same name in his *Historia general* fol. 113, but the narrative of the expedition in the A. G. I. gives the name as "Ferrelo." *Patronato* 20, fol. 5v.

81. Nicolás López called him Lorenzo Fernández Barreda in his testimony in A. G. I., *Patronato* 87, fol. 33. Francisco de Vargas called him Lorenzo Hernández in A. G. I., *Justicia* 290, fol. 72v. Herrera called him Bartolomé Fernández in his *Historia general,* fol. 113.

82. Testimony of Antonio Correa, 21 February 1547, A. G. I., *Justicia* 263, fol. 68. Herrera calls him Carrera in his *Historia general,* fol. 113.

83. This is the testimony of Lázaro de Cárdenas in A. G. I., *Justicia* 290, fol. 68. The same information is contained in Francisco A. de Icaza's summaries of probanzas prepared by some of the early settlers. See his *Diccionario autobiográfico de conquistadores y pobladores de Nueva España* (Madrid: Imprenta de "El Adelantado de Segovia," 1923), 2:342-43.

84. *Patronato* 20, no. 5, ramo 13, fol. 5v.

85. A. G. I., *Justicia* 266, fol. 474, 477.

86. Testimony given 3 January 1565, A. G. I., *Patronato* 87, fol. 35v.

87. *Relación del descubrimiento que hizo Juan Rodríguez navegando por la contra costa del mar del Sur al Norte,* A. G. I., *Patronato* 20, no. 5, ramo 13.

88. See his "Introductory Notes" to the translation by Richard Stuart Evans entitled "Translation from the Spanish of the Account by the Pilot Ferrel of the Voyage of Cabrillo along the West Coast of North America in 1542," in *Report of United States Geographical Surveys West of the One Hundredth Meridian,* vol. 7, *Archaelogy* (Washington: G. P. O., 1879), 293 ff.

89. *The First Voyage to the Coasts of California: Made in the Years 1542 and 1543. By Juan Rodríguez Cabrillo and His Pilot Bartolome Ferrelo* (San Francisco: Le Count & Strong, 1853), 13 ff.

90. Santiago de Guatemala, *cabildo* records, 21 May 1529, in J. Antonio Villacorte C., ed., *Libro viejo de la fundación de Guatemala y papeles relativos a D. Pedro de Alvarado,* vol. 12 of Biblioteca "Goathemala" de la Sociedad de Geografía e Historia (Guatemala: Tipografía Nacional, 1934), 66.

91. The manuscript in question is actually a letter signed by Bishop Francisco Marroquín and concluding with a paragraph in his hand. *"Relación de lo sucedido en la ciudad de Sanctiago de Guatemala sabado diez dias de Setiembre, año de 41,"* c. October 1541, A. G. I., *Patronato* 181, fol. 2v.

92. "Anotaciones curiosas," in *Relaciones historicas,* sig. iii.V.lo, fol. 1, Real Biblioteca San Lorenzo de El Escorial. See also the manuscripts listed in Manuel Fráile Miguélez, *Catálogo de los códices españolas de la Biblioteca del Escorial* (Madrid: Imprenta Helenica 1917), 1: 92-93.

93. For a good comparison see Andrés de Urdaneta, *"Memoria de las cosas qué me parece qué será bien qué el rei nro señor tenga noticia,"* undated MS, c. 1560, A. G. I., *Patronato* 23, ramo 15. Photostats of this and other documents are in the Wagner Collection, Honnold Library, Pomona, See also *Patronato* 20, no. 5, ramo 8, which has the same Juan Páez notations as the report of the Cabrillo expedition.

94. The best biography of Urdaneta is Marin Mitchell, *Friar Andrés de Urdaneta,* O. S. A. (London: Macdonald & Evans, 1964). There is also much useful information in Mariano Cuevas, *Monje y marino: la vida y los tiempos de Fray Andrés de Urdaneta* (Mexico: Editorial Galatea, 1943).

95. The document is dated 18 April 1543, four days after the armada of Juan Rodríguez Cabrillo returned to Navidad. The manuscript is part of a collection called *Mercedes,* vol. 2, exp. 167, fol. 60v-61. Archivo General de la Nación, Mexico.

96. Henry Wagner, "A Map of Sancho Gutierrez of 1551," *Imago Mundi,* 8 (1951): 47-49. David O. True, "Cabot Explorations in North America," *Imago Mundi,* 13 (1956): 17.

97. This is fully described in France, Bibliothèque Nationale, *Catalogue des cartes nautiques nes velin conservees au Département des Cartes et Plans* (Paris: Bibliothèque Nationale, 1963), 69-74. For a discussion of the California portion of this document see Henry R. Wagner, "A Map of Cabrillo's Discoveries," *California Historical Society Quarterly* 11 (March 1932): 44-46.

98. Several Mexican scholars have shown that Urdaneta was deeply involved in discussions of another Pacific voyage at least as early as 1557. The basic documents are in J. Ignacio Rubio Mañé, "La expedición de Miguel López de Legazpi a Filipinas," *Boletín del Archivo General de la Nación*, ser. 2, vol. 5, nos. 3-4 (1964), 429-798. See also Enrique Cárdenas de la Peña, *Urdaneta y "El Tornaviaje"* (Mexico: Secretaría de Marina, 1965), 78; and Luis Muro, *La expedición Legazpi-Urdaneta a las Filipinas (1557-1564)*, 2nd ed. revised (Mexico: Secretaría de Educación Pública, 1975), 7-13.

99. See footnote 37.

100. Francisco López de Gómara, *Primera y Segunda parte de la historia general de las Indias cō todo el descubrimiento y cosas notables que han acaescido dende que se ganaron hasta el año de 1551. Con la conquista de Mexico y de la Nueva España* (Medina del Campo: Guillermo de Millis, 1553), part 1, fol. IX verso and CXV verso. Huntington Library rare book 55847.

101. Alonso de Santa Cruz, *Crónica del emperador Carlos V*, 5 vols. (Madrid: Imprenta del Patronato de Huérfanos de Intendencia e Intervención Militares, 1923), 5: 133, 481-86.

102. For information about the frequent letters exchanged by Santa Cruz and Mendoza see Alonso de Santa Cruz, *Libro de las Longitudines*, ed. and intr. by D. Antonio Blázquez y Delgado Aguilera, El Centro de Estudios Americanistas de Sevilla, Biblioteca Colonial Americana, vol. 5 (Sevilla: Tipografía Zarzuela, 1921), 30, 47.

103. Their reports are in A. G. I., *Patronato* 49, ramo 12.

104. A. G. I., *Patronato* 20, no. 13.

105. A. G. I., *Patronato* 46, ramo 4, fol. 1; *Indiferente General* 1528.

106. For an example see *"Relación de lo qué descubrió Ruy López de Villalobos,"* A. G. I., *Patronato* 46, ramo 4, fol. 1. The inventory of the Santa Cruz papers is in Cristóbal Pérez Pastor, *Bibliografía Madrileña, ò descripción de las obras impressas en Madrid* (Madrid: Tipografía de la "Revista de Archivos, Bibliotecas y Museos," 1907), 3: 478.

107. See the marginal notes on A. G. I., *Patronato* 20 no. 5, ramos 4 and 7. See also Pérez Pastor, *Bibliografía Madrileña*, 478.

108. Rómulo D. Carbia, *La Crónica oficial de las Indias Occidentales: Estudio histórico y crítico acerca de la historiografía mayor de Hispano-America en los siglos XVI a XVIII*, Biblioteca Humanidades, Universidad de la Plata, vol. 14 (La Plata: Universidad de la Plata, 1921), 62.

109. Juan López de Velasco, *Geografía y descripción universal de las Indias recopilada por el cosmógrafo-cronista Juan López de Velasco desde el año de 1571 al de 1574*, ed. by Justo Zaragoza (Madrid: Establecimiento Tipográfico de Fortanet, 1894), 281.

110. Carbia, *Crónica oficial*, 152-53. José Pulido Rubio, *El piloto mayor de la (Casa de) Contratación de Sevilla: Pilotos mayores del siglo XVI (datos biográficos)*, Biblioteca Colonial Americana, Centro Oficial de Estudios Americanistas, vol. 10 (Seville: Tipografía Zarzuela, 1925), 278-81.

111. Antonio de Herrera, *Historia general* (Madrid: Juan de la Cuesta, 1615), 4: fol. 103; here Herrera discusses the various royal officials who delivered papers to him.

Notes
Chapter 6

1. A. G. I., *Patronato* 20, no. 5, ramo 13, fol. 1. All information about the voyage is from this source, unless otherwise noted.

2. Herrera, *Historia general*, (Madrid: Juan de la Cuesta, 1615), 4: fol. 112.

3. This point is made in Francisco López de Gómara, *Historia general*, (Medina del Campo: Guillermo de Millis, 1553), part I, fol. *CXV verso*.

4. Manuel Carrera Stampa, "The Evolution of Weights and Measures in New Spain," *Hispanic American Historical Review* 29 (February 1949): 10, gives a good summary of measurements in New Spain. In the sixteenth century the Spanish league varied greatly, depending on who did the measuring. See Florian de Ocampo, *Los Quatro libros primeros de la cronica general de España* (Zamora: Juan Picardo, 1543), fo. vii. Huntington Library rare book 139792.

5. A. G. I, *Patronato* 20, no. 5, ramo 13, fol. 1.

6. Cited by Henry R. Wagner in "Francisco Ulloa Returned," *California Historical Society Quarterly*, 19 (September 1940): 242.

7. Discussed in Chapter V. See also Armando Cortesão, "Antonio Pereira and his Map of Circa 1545," *The Geographical Review* 29 (April 1939): 214.

8. A. G. I., *Patronato* 20, no. 5, ramo 13, fol. 1.

9. Herrera, *Historia general*, 4:113.

10. A. G. I., *Justicia* 263, fol. 77.

11. Wagner, "Francisco Ulloa," 242.

12. Donald C. Cutter, "Sources of the Name 'California,'" *Arizona and the West* 3, (Autumn 1961): 234-35.

13. One early reference calling it an island is in A. G. I., *Patronato* 78, no. 2, ramo 8, *Meritos y Servicios de Alvaro de Ceballos*, 21 August 1561, question 5,

14. A. G. I., *Mapas y planos, Mexico* 518, Portillo dates this map in 1587. See his *Descubrimientos y exploraciones en las costas de California*, 131. For a similar copy from the Archivo General de la Nacion, Mexico, dated 1588, see W. Michael

Mathes, *The Capture of the Santa Ana, Cabo San Lucas, November 1587* (Los Angeles: Dawson's Book Shop, 1969), opp. 54.

15. Herrera, *Historia general*, 4:113.

16. George C. Davidson, "Voyages of Discovery and Exploration," 160.

17. Davidson, "Voyages of Discovery and Exploration," 160.

18. These instruments are all listed in the inventory of the ship *Trinidad* made at Tehuantepec in 1539. See the copy in the Spanish Manuscript Collection, Gilcrease Institute, Tulsa, Oklahoma. Ulloa's pilots used the astrolabe for computing their latitudes, as Ulloa noted in his report to Cortés, May 29, 1540, A. G. I., *Patronato* 20, No. 5, ramo 11, fol. 1.

19. Ursula Lamb, "Science by Litigation: A Cosmographic Feud," *Terra Incognita, the Annals of the Society for the History of Discoveries* 1 (1969): 41.

20. This is his opinion about the location of the Moluccas and the Philippines, c. October 8, 1566, A. G. I., *Patronato* 49, ramo 12, parecer no. 2, fol. 3.

21. Alonso de Santa Cruz, *Libro de las longitudines*, ed. and intro. Antonio Blázquez and Delgado Aguilera, vol. 5 of Biblioteca Colonial Americana, Centro de Estudios Americanistas de Sevilla (Sevilla: Tipografía Zarzuela, 1921), 30.

22. This conclusion is based on an extrapolation of the declination charts in Willem Van Bemmelen, *De Isogonen in de XVI^{de} en XVII^{de} Eeuw*. (Utrecht: J. Van Douten, 1893), foldout sheet.

23. Santa Cruz, *Libro de las longitudines*, 30.

24. Lamb, "Science by Litigation," 41-43.

25. Wagner, *Spanish Voyages*, 305, n. 21.

26. A. G. I., *Patronato* 20, no. 5, ramo 11, fol. 1. We need not give much credence to Ulloa's opinion about Castellón, who was originally slated to be commander of the expedition. See Castellón's inventory of the Trinidad in the Spanish Manuscript Collection, Gilcrease Institute, Tulsa. Castellón's suit for damages is described in Wagner, "Francisco Ulloa," 240-44.

27. A. G. I., *Patronato* 20, no. 5, ramo 13, fol. 1.

28. The manuscript account of the voyage says five leagues, an obvious error for fifty leagues. A. G. I., *Patronato* 20, no. 5, ramo 13, fol. 1. Davidson, "Voyages of Discovery," 162. Wagner, *Spanish Voyages*, 331, n. 24.

29. U. S. Department of the Navy, *Sailing Directions for the West Coast of Mexico and Central America*, Hydrographic Office Publication No. 26, 9th edition (Washington: G.P.O., 1951), sec. 3-114, 56. Hereafter referred to as *Sailing Directions*.

30. *Sailing Directions*, sec. 3-120, 58.

31. A. G. I., *Patronato* 20, no. 5, ramo 13, fol. 1.

32. Compasses produced in Seville were "corrected" five degrees east. Lamb, "Science by Litigation," 45. The Cortés map of the tip of the California peninsula shows north about eight or ten degrees west of its proper position. Assuming his pilots were using a "corrected" compass, his map shows the declination at that time to be about thirteen to fifteen degrees east. This corresponds with the compass variations computed by Van Bemmelen, *De Isogonen*, foldout chart. The compass readings of Juan Rodríguez Cabrillo and his pilots were always ten or fifteen degrees too far to the west, an indication that they used the "corrected" compasses from Seville. They were either unaware of the real variations or convinced that it made no difference as long as everybody used the same compass.

33. There is a good reproduction of such a compass in Alonso de Santa Cruz, *Islario general*, 51. The work was completed just prior to 1540 and so the compass is doubtless a good representation of the ones in use at the time.

34. A. G. I., *Patronato* 20, no. 5, ramo 13, fol. 1. *Sailing Directions*, sec. 3-114, 56. Wagner, *Spanish Voyages*, 331, n. 27.

35. Davidson, "Voyages of Discovery," 164.

36. Davidson, "Voyages of Discovery," 167. *Sailing Directions*, sec. 3-100, 52.

37. Wagner, *Spanish Voyages*, 64, 67, 318, n. 16, 33, n. 35. A. G. I., *Patronato* 20, no. 5, ramo 13, fol. 1.

38. Juan Fernández de Ladrillero, "Apreciable declaración," in Spain, Museo Naval, *Colección de documentos y manuscritos compilados por Fernández de Navarrete* (Neudeln, Liechtenstein: Kraus-Thompson Organization, 1971), facsimile reproductions, vol. 15, 176v-77.

39. Ladrillero, "Declaración," 176v-77. Daniel M. Cohen, "Names of the Hakes," *Marine Fisheries Review* 42 (January, 1980): 2-3. Giles W. Mead and Daniel M. Cohen, "Comments on Common Names of Fishes," *Copeia*, 30 (No. 4, 1960): 378-80. Donald A. Thompson and Noni McKibbin, *Gulf of California Fishwatchers Guide* (Tucson: Golden Puffer Press, 1976), 16, 26. The names given by Ladrillero are those used in Spain, for which see Conseil général des pêches pour la Méditerranée, *Catalogue des poissons ayant une importance comercial en Méditerranée* (Rome: Food and Agricultural Organization of the United Nations, 1960), 14, 189.

40. A. G. I., *Patronato* 20, no. 5, ramo 13, fol. 1.

41. A. G. I., *Patronato* 20, no. 5, ramo 13, fol. 1. Juan Rodríguez, *Relación del Espantable Terremoto* (Madrid(?): n. n., 1543 (?)), fol. 1.

42. Burney J. Le Boeuf, "Report of an expedition to the Gulf of California, Mexico, on Scripps Institution of Oceanography R/V *Ellen B. Scripps*, 12 June to 8 July 1984" (Department of Biology, University of California, Santa Cruz, mimeographed), table 1.

43. A. G. I., *Patronato* 20, no. 5, ramo 13, fol. 1v. *Sailing Directions*, sec. 3-84, 48.

44. A. G. I., *Patronato* 20, no. 4, ramo 13, fol. 1v.

45. Wagner, *Spanish Voyages*, 45.

46. A. G. I., *Patronato* 20, no. 5, ramo 13, fol. 1v. Both Davidson and Wagner misread the manuscript, seeing *"pelada"* (barren) where the author had written *"peludo"* (hairy). See *Spanish Voyages*, 81, and "Voyages of Discovery," 172.

47. A. G. I., *Patronato* 20, no. 5, ramo 13, fol. 1v.

48. A. G. I., *Sailing Directions*, sec. 3-64, 43.

49. A. G. I., *Patronato* 20, no. 5, ramo 13, fol. 1v.

50. A. G. I., *Patronato* 20, no. 5, ramo 13, fol. 1v.

51. A. G. I., *Patronato* 20, no. 5, ramo 13, fol. 2.

52. A. G. I., *Patronato* 20, no. 5, ramo 13, fol. 2. Davidson, "Voyages of Discovery," 184. *Sailing Directions*, sec. 3-27, 35.

53. Wagner thought it possible that Ulloa went much farther north, but there is little or no evidence to support this view. See *Spanish Voyages*, 14, 283.

54. The coast runs true north here for more than twenty miles. Davidson, "Voyages of Discovery," 184.

55. A. G. I., *Patronato* 20, no. 5, ramo 13, fol. 2.

56. This is from Ulloa's own report in A. G. I., *Patronato* 20, no. 5, ramo 11. There is another translation by Irene A. Wright in Wagner, *Spanish Voyages*, 46.

57. A. G. I., *Patronato* 20, no. 5, ramo 13, fol. 2. Davidson, "Voyages of Discovery," 184.

58. A. G. I., *Patronato* 20, no. 5, ramo 13, fol. 2. *Sailing Directions* sec. 3-32, 36. Herrera describes similar repairs to the fragata in his *Historia general*, 4:fol. 113.

59. There is a blank space in the manuscript here. Wagner thought there were three "arms" in the lagoon. Three "villages" seems to fit the context better. A. G. I., *Patronato* 20, no. 5, ramo 13, fol. 2.

60. A. G. I., *Patronato* 20, no. 5, ramo 13, fol. 23.

61. A. G. I., *Patronato* 20, no. 5, ramo 13, fol. 2. G. H. von Langsdorff, *Voyage and Travels in Various Parts of the World during the years 1803, 1804, 1805, 1806 and 1807*. (London: Henry Colburn, 1814), 2:193-95.

62. Wagner, *Spanish Voyages*, 226.

63. A. G. I., *Patronato* 20, no. 5, ramo 13, fol. 2-2v.

64. A. G. I., *Patronato* 20, no 5, ramo 13, fol. 2v. Davidson, "Voyages of Discovery," 186. *Sailing Directions*, sec. 3-27, 35.

65. A. G. I., *Patronato* 20, no. 5, ramo 13, fol. 2v.

66. A. G. I., *Patronato* 20, no. 5, ramo 13, fol. 2v. Wagner, *Spanish Voyages*, 333, nn. 62-65.

67. A. G. I., *Patronato* 20, no. 5, ramo 13, fol. 2v.

68. A. G. I., *Patronato* 201, no. 5, ramo 13, fol. 2v. Wagner, *Spanish Voyages*, 333, n. 62. Wagner, *The Cartography of the Northwest Coast of America to the Year 1800*, 2 vols. (Berkeley: University of California Press, 1937), 1:290.

69. A. G. I., *Patronato* 20, no 5, ramo 13, fol. 2v.

70. A. G. I., *Patronato* 20, no. 5, ramo 13, fol. 2v.

71. A. G. I., *Patronato* 20, no. 5, ramo 13, fol. 2v. See the illustrations in Woodes Rogers, *A Cruising Voyage Round the World, First to the South Seas, thence to the East-Indies and Home-wards* (London: A. Bell and B. Lintot, 1712).

72. A. G. I., *Patronato* 20, no. 5, ramo 13, fol. 2v. *Sailing Directions*, sec. 3-19, 33.

73. A. G. I., *Patronato* 20, no. 5, ramo 13, fol. 3.

74. A. G. I., *Patronato* 20, no. 5, ramo 13, fol. 3. Davidson, "Voyages of Discovery," 190.

75. A. G. I., *Patronato* 20, no. 5, ramo 13, fol. 3.

76. A. G. I., *Patronato* 20, no. 5, ramo 13, fol. 3.

77. A. G. I., *Patronato* 20, no. 5, ramo 13, fol. 3.

78. Henry T. Lewis, *Patterns of Indian Burning in California: Ecology and Ethnohistory*, Ballena Press, Anthropological Papers, no. 1 (Ramona, CA: Ballena Press, 1973), 25-31, 41-59.

Notes
Chapter 7

1. A. G. I., *Patronato* 20, no. 5, ramo 13, fol. 3-3v.
2. A. G. I., *Patronato* 20, no. 5, ramo 13, fol. 3.
3. A. G. I., *Patronato* 20, no. 5, ramo 13, fol. 3.
4. A. G. I., *Patronato* 20, no. 5, ramo 13, fol. 3-3v.
5. A. G. I., *Patronato* 20, no. 5, ramo 13, fol. 3v.
6. A. G. I., *Patronato* 20, no. 5, ramo 13, fol. 3v.
7. Henry Wagner first thought that both names, San Salvador and Victoria, were originally applied to Santa Catalina Island, which has a sort of figure-eight appearance and could perhaps be mistaken for two islands. *Spanish Voyages*, 333-34, n. 72. He changed his mind about this after seeing Homem's map, which shows them as two distinct islands at some distance from each other. See his *Juan Rodriguez Cabrillo, Discoverer of the Coast of California* (San Francisco: California Historical Society, 1941), 17.
8. A. G. I., *Patronato* 20, no. 5, ramo 13, fol. 3v.
9. A. G. I., *Patronato* 20, no. 5, ramo 13, fol. 3v.
10. A. G. I., *Patronato* 20, no. 5, ramo 13, fol. 3v. Davidson, "Voyages of Discovery," 196, says the bay was Santa Monica, rather than San Pedro.
11. A. G. I., *Patronato* 20, no. 5, ramo 13, fol. 3v. Davidson, "Voyages of Discovery," 196, identifies the place as Laguna Mugu.
12. A. G. I., *Patronato* 20, no. 5, ramo 13, fol. 3v. Davidson, "Voyages of Discovery," 198, identifies the site as Ventura.
13. A. G. I., *Patronato* 20, no. 5, ramo 13, fol. 4.
14. Herrera, *Historia general*, 4:fol. 113.
15. A. G. I., *Patronato* 20, no. 5, ramo 13, fol. 3v-4.
16. A. G. I., *Patronato* 20, no. 5, ramo 13, fol. 3v.
17. A. G. I., *Patronato* 20, no. 5, ramo 13, fol. 4, 6.

18. A. G. I., *Patronato* 20, no. 5, ramo 13, fol. 4. Chester King and Thomas Blackburn, "The Names and Locations of Historic Chumash Villages," *Journal of California Anthropology* 2 (Winter 1975): 176. Alan K. Brown, "The Aboriginal Population of the Santa Barbara Channel," *University of California Archaeological Survey Reports*, no. 69 (January 1967): 42-44.

19. A. G. I., *Patronato* 20, no. 5, ramo 13, fol. 4. Brown, "Aboriginal Population," 39-41.

20. Herrera, *Historia general*, 4:fol. 113.

21. A. G. I., *Patronato* 20, no. 5, ramo 13, fol. 4. King and Blackburn, "Chumash Villages," 176. Brown, "Aboriginal Population," 36-37.

22. A. G. I., *Patronato* 20, no. 5, ramo 13, fol. 4. King and Blackburn, "Chumash Villages," 176. Brown, "Aboriginal Population," 24-28. Campbell Grant, "Eastern Coastal Chumash," *Handbook of North American Indians*, edited by William C. Sturtevant, vol. VIII, *California*, edited by Robert F. Heizer (Washington: Smithsonian Institution, 1978), 510.

23. A. G. I., *Patronato* 20, no. 5, ramo 13, fol. 4. Testimony of Lázaro de Cárdenas, 26 April 1560, *Justicia* 290, fol. 68v.

24. A. G. I., *Patronato* 20, no. 5, ramo 13, fol. 4. H. W. Henshaw thought these "cattle" might be bison. See his notes to the translation by Richard Stuart Evans, "Translation from the Spanish of the account of the Pilot Ferrel of the Voyage of Cabrillo along the West Coast of North America in 1542," 307.

25. A. G. I., *Patronato* 20, no. 5, ramo 13, fol. 4.

26. A. G. I., *Justicia* 290, fol. 68-68v.

27. "On Thursday the 23rd day of the month they neared the end of their voyage in the Islands of San Lucas *at one of those* called Posesión." Italics mine. The phrase is *"a una dellas llamada la posesión."* A. G. I., *Patronato* 20, no. 5, ramo 13, fol. 5v.

28. Urdaneta, *Memoria de las cosas que me paresce que sera bien que el Rey Nr° señor tenga noticia*, undated MS, c.1559, A. G. I., *Patronato* 23, ramo 15.

29. There is a reasonably good reproduction of the Homem map in Armando Cortesão and Avelino Teixeira Da Mota, *Portugaliae Monumenta Cartographica*, 5 vols. (Lisbon: n.n., 1960), 2: 67-71, and plates 187-91.

30. Urdaneta thought San Salvador was in latitude 33° 50'. "Relación de Fray Andrés de Ardaneta [sic] del descubrimiento de las yslas del Maluco nuevamente descubiertas," fol. 7, Biblioteca de Francisco Zabálburu, Madrid, Spain. This section of his report is quoted in Fermín de Uncilla y Arroita-Jáuregui, *Urdaneta y la conquista de Filipinas* (San Sebastián: Imprenta de la Provinica, 1907), 261. Both Esteban Rodríguez and Rodrigo de Espinosa had it as 33° 45'. "Derrotero de Esteban Rodríguez piloto mayor del armada de las yslas del poniente," A. G. I., *Patronato* 23, ramo 16, fol. 62, 65, 65v. See also Wagner, *Spanish Voyages*, 114, 473.

31. A.G.I., *Patronato* 20, no. 5, ramo 13, fol. 4v.

32. Herrera, *Historia general*, fol. 114.

33. Smith, *Varios documentos*, p.4. In 1574 Juan Fernández de Lladrillero spoke of the search for a passage to the North Sea along these coasts, but it is wrong to interpret his testimony as evidence that Juan Rodríguez Cabrillo was looking for such a strait. Lladrillero, "Declaracion," 15:fol. 179-179v. More likely, the

testimony was prompted by Gastaldi's recent map and pamphlet suggesting that there was a Strait of Anian connecting the Mar del Sur to the Mar del Norte.

34. A. G. I., *Patronato* 20, no. 5, ramo 13, fol. 4v-5.

35. Herrera, *Historia general*, 4:fol. 113. A. G. I., *Patronato* 20, no. 5, ramo 13, fol. 4v-5.

36. Herbert E. Bolton (ed.), *Fray Juan Crespi, Missionary Explorer on the Pacific Coast, 1769-1774* (Berkeley: Univ. of California Press, 1927), 168.

37. A. G. I., *Patronato* 20, no. 5, ramo 13, fol. 5.

38. Herrera, *Historia general*, 4:fol. 113.

39. Oviedo, *Primera parte de la general y natural historia de las Indias* (Seville: Imprenta de Juan Cromberger, 1535), fol. viii verso and lix.

40. Herrera, *Historia general*, 4:fol. 113.

41. A. G. I., *Patronato* 20, no. 5 ramo 13, fol. 6.

42. Quoted in Brown, "Aboriginal Population," 4.

43. A. G. I., *Patronato* 20, no. 5, ramo 13, fol. 5.

44. A. G. I., *Patronato* 20, no. 5, ramo 13, fol. 5. Grant, "Eastern Coastal Chumash", 516-17. Lowell John Bean and Harry W. Lawton, "Some Explanations for the Rise of Cultural Complexity in Native California with Comments on Proto-Agriculture and Agriculture," *Native Californians: A Theoretical Retrospective*, edited by Lowell John Bean and Thomas C. Blackburn (Socorro, N.M.: Ballena Press, 1976), 35-38.

45. Herrera, *Historia general*, 4:fol. 113. A. G. I., *Patronato* 20, no. 5, ramo 13, fol. 3v.

46. A. G. I., *Patronato* 20, no. 5, ramo 13, fol. 5. Grant, "Eastern Coastal Chumash," 510, 514-16.

47. Herrera, *Historia general*, 4:fol. 114. A. G. I., *Patronato* 20, no. 5, ramo 13, fol. 5. King and Blackburn, "Chumash Villages," 176-77, Brown "Aboriginal Population," 16-24.

48. A. G. I., *Patronato* 20, no. 5, ramo 13, fol. 5.

49. A. G. I., *Patronato* 20, no. 5, ramo 13, fol. 5. Herrera *Historia general*, 4:fol. 114.

50. Herrera, *Historia general*, 4:fol. 114 A. G. I., *Patronato* 20, no. 5, ramo 13, fol. 5-5v. John Thomas Howell, *Marin Flora: Manual of the Flowering Plants and Ferns of Marin County, California*, 2nd edition (Berkeley: Univ. of California Press, 1970), 7-10.

51. A. G. I., *Patronato* 20, no. 5, ramo 13, fol. 5v.

52. A. G. I., *Patronato* 20, no. 5, ramo 13, fol. 5v. Herrera, *Historia general*, 4:fol. 114.

53. A. G. I., *Patronato* 20, no. 5, ramo 13, fol. 5v. Herrera, *Historia general*, 4:fol. 114.

54. A.G.I., *Patronato* 20, no. 5, ramo 13, fol. 5v. Herrera, *Historia General*, 4:fol. 114.

55. A. G. I., *Patronato* 20, no. 5, ramo 13, fol. 5v.

56. Michael J. Moratto, Thomas F. King, and Wallace B. Woolfenden, "Archaeology and California's Climate," *Journal of California Anthropology* 5 (Winter 1978): 151.

57. A. G. I., *Patronato* 20, no. 5, ramo 13, fol. 5v.
58. A. G. I., *Patronato* 20, no. 5, ramo 13, fol. 5v.
59. Herrera, *Historia general*, 4:fol. 114.
60. Davidson, "Voyages of Discovery," 226.
61. A. G. I., *Patronato* 20, no. 5, ramo 13, fol. 6.
62. King and Blackburn, "Chumash Villages," 177-78.
63. King and Blackburn, "Chumash Villages," 178. A.L. Kroeber, *Handbook of the Indians of California*, Bureau of American Ethnology Bulletin 78 (Washington: Smithsonian Institution, 1925), 554-55. For identification of some of the village names on Limu-Catalina see C. Hart Merriam, "Village Names in Twelve California Mission Records," edited by Robert F. Heizer, University of California Archaeological Survey Reports, No. 74 (July 1968): 97, 128-37. See also Henry Wagner, "The Names of the Channel Islands," Historical Society of Southern California *Annual Publication*, 15 (1933): 16-18.
64. A. G. I., *Justicia* 290, fol. 69, 72v.
65. A. G. I., *Justicia* 290, fol. 72v-73.
66. A. G. I., *Justicia* 290, fol. 73.
67. A. G. I., *Justicia* 290, fol. 68v.
68. A. G. I., *Patronato* 20, no. 5, ramo 13, fol. 6.
69. A. G. I., *Justicia* 290, fol. 73.
70. Testimony of Francisco de Vargas, A. G. I., *Justicia* 290, fol. 72-73v. A. G. I.
71. A. G. I., *Justicia* 290, fol. 68v.
72. A. G. I., *Patronato* 20, no. 5, ramo 13, fol. 6.
73. A. G. I., *Justicia* 290, fol. 69. See also the family tradition recounted in the questions in fol. 46v.
74. There is much confusion in the narrative about the names of the specific islands. Wagner, *Spanish Voyages*, 336-37, n. 115, thinks the abbreviations "S.S." in the narrative MS, fol. 6-6v, should be understood as meaning San Sebastian, whose feast was celebrated on January 20. But the narrative also says S.S. is the island called Limun. Limun is Catalina, the one Cabrillo named San Salvador. My own opinion is that *"la isla de S.S."* is intended to mean *"la isla de San Salvador,"* as it clearly does in fol. 7. Wagner's argument only adds to the confusion, and I do not think he is correct. Later in his own account Herrera referred to an island called San Sebastian, but it does not seem to be the one Wagner had reference to. Herrera, *Historia general*, 4: fol. 115.
75. A. G. I., *Patronato* 20, no. 5, ramo 13, fol. 6v.
76. Wagner, *Spanish Voyages*, 337, n.117.
77. A. G. I., *Patronato* 20, no. 5, ramo 13, fol. 6v.
78. Herrera, *Historia general*, 4:fol. 114-15.
79. A. G. I., *Patronato* 20, no. 5, ramo 13, fol. 6v.
80. The shrine of Guadalupe in Spain was the most important in the peninsula in the sixteenth century. William O. Christian, Jr., *Local Religion in Sixteenth Century Spain*, (Princeton, N.J.: Princeton Univ. Press, 1981), 121, 155-57. Upon their return from the New World, Spanish sailors and soldiers regularly made pilgrimages there. Juan Escalante de Mendoza, *Itinerario*, MS no. 3104, Biblioteca Nacional,

Madrid. Two who did so were Cortés and Alvarado. See *Capellanías, lámparas, y bienhechores de Guadalupe*, MS in the library, Real Monasterio de Guadalupe, Spain, fol. 20. Among the earliest written references to the shrine in Mexico are Bernal Díaz del Castillo, *Historia verdadera*, edition of Alonso Remón (Madrid: Emprenta del Reyno, [1632]), fol. 141v. Huntington Library rare book 45888. Díaz wrote at about the time of Cabrillo's voyage or a few years later, calling attention to the "many wonderful miracles" performed there. Donald Demarest and Coley Taylor have cited wills from 1539 to show that the devotion to the Mexican shrine was widespread by that date. See *The Dark Virgin* (Freeport, Maine: Coley Taylor, Inc., 1956), 224.

81. A. G. I., *Patronato* 20, no. 5, ramo 13, fol. 6v-7.

82. A. G. I., *Patronato* 20, no. 5, ramo 13, fol. 7.

83. A. G. I., *Patronato* 20, no. 5, ramo 13, fol. 7. One of the main complaints of the armada crewmen was that the Indians from Mexico were no help as interpreters in California. Herrera, *Historia general*, 4:fol. 115.

84. A. G. I., *Patronato* 20, no. 5, ramo 13, fol. 4v.

85. A. G. I., *Patronato* 20, no. 5, ramo 13, fol. 7. The manuscript says the men promised to make the pilgrimage *"desnudos en carne,"* but the phrase may have meant something like the phrase "en camisa," used by Columbus and his crew. See Martín Fernández de Navarrete, *Colección de los viajes y descubrimientos que hicieron por mar los Españoles*, 2nd edition (Madrid: Imprenta Nacional, 1858), 1:297. The usage is not clear. On one voyage to the Philippines a few years later the men went "unos desnudos otros en camisa," which leaves little doubt about how they were dressed. A. G. I., *Filipinas* 291, ramo 1 no. 5., letter from Guido de Lavezaris, Andrés Cabezelas, and Andrés de Mirandaola to the king, 26 July 1567.

86. A. G. I., *Patronato* 20, no. 5, ramo 13, fol. 7-7v.

87. A. G. I., *Justicia* 286, fol. 316.

88. A. G. I., *Justicia* 287, fol. 35v.

89. A. G. I., *Justicia* 263, fol. 25v-26.

90. Remesal, *Historia general*, 272-73.

Bibliography
Archival Collections

All archival materials have been described at length in the notes and the more important ones have been analyzed in Chapter 8, to which interested readers should refer for information on a particular source.

Algemeen Rijksarchief. The Hague, Netherlands.
Thomas Cavendish chart. VEL.733.683 340.
American Philosophical Society, Philadelphia, PA.
Guatemalan manuscript collection. Microfilm.
Archivo de Protocolos. Seville, Spain.
Oficio 3, libro 2, año 1514, fol. 452.
Oficio 4, libro 3, año 1511, fol. 1984.
Oficio 15, libro 2, año 1551, fol. 1814.
Archivo General de Centro America. Guatemala City, Guatemala.
MS. signatura A1.29, legajo 4672, expediente 401312.
MS. signatura A3.2, legajo 1539, expediente 22569.
Archivo General de Indias. Seville, Spain.
Guatemala, legajos 41, 128.
Mapas y Planos, legajos Mexico 6, Mexico 518, Indiferente General 1528.
Justicia, legajos 259-266, 280, 286, 290, 295, 296.
Patronato, legajos 20, 21, 68, 87, 182.
Archivo General de la Nación. Mexico City.
Mercedes, vol. 2.
Biblioteca de Francisco Zabalburu. Madrid, Spain.
"Relación de Fray Andrés de Ardaneta [sic]."
MS 1464.
Biblioteca del Palacio Real. Madrid, Spain.
Alonso de Santa Cruz. "Islario General."
Biblioteca Nacional. Madrid, Spain.

Relación Anónima. (Villalobos expedition.) MS Res. 18.
Juan Escalante de Mendoza. "Ytenerario de navegacion de los mares y tierras ociden-
tales." MS 3104
Bibliothèque Nationale. Paris, France.
  Andreas Homem. "Universa ac navigabilis totius terrarum orbis descriptio." Res.
  Ge.CC. 2719.
British Library. London, England.
  "Libro segundo que trata del fundamenta y principio de la armada que llebó
  Ruy López de Villalobos." Add. 9944.
  Diego Gutiérrez. "Americae sive quartae orbis partis nova et exactisima descrip-
  tio." Map *69810.(18.).
Gilcrease Institute of American History and Art. Tulsa, OK.
  Spanish Manuscript Collection.
Honnold Library. Claremont Colleges. Pomona, CA.
  Henry Raup Wagner Collection.
Huntington Library. San Marino, CA.
  Agnese portolan atlas. HM 10.
  Agnese portolan atlas. HM 25.
  Agnese portolan atlas. HM 27.
  "Derrotero gen[l] del Mar del Sur desde las Californias hasta los estrechos de
  Magellanes y San Vicente." HM 918.
  Gonzalo Fernández de Oviedo y Valdés. "Natural y general historia." HM 177.
Museo Naval. Madrid, Spain.
  "Primera Demostración hecha el año de 1545 de las dos costas ciñen el seno
  de California." VIII-A-75. 176/5720.
Newberry Library. Chicago, Illinois.
  Agnese portolan atlas. Ayer MS. Map 12.
  Agnese portolan atlas. Ayer MS. Map 13.
Real Biblioteca San Lorenzo de El Escorial. Spain.
  Relaciones historicas. Signatura V.II.4, no. LVI, fol. 167-70, 383-407, 413-56.
Real Monasterio de Guadalupe. Spain.
  "Capellanías, lámparas, y bienhechores de Guadalupe."
University of Pennsylvania
  Manuscrito Cakchiquel. Brinton Collection.

Printed Sources

Aiton, Arthur S. *Antonio de Mendoza, First Viceroy of New Spain.* Durham, NC:
  Duke University Press, 1927.
Albuquerque, D. R. Luis Mendoca. "An Aspect of the Political Application of
  the Tordesillas Treaty." *Cabrillo and His Era.* Sixth Annual Cabrillo Festival
  Historic Seminar (September 1978): 1-7.
Angleria, Petrus Martyris. *De Orbe Novo Petri Martyris ab Angleria.* Alcalá: Míchael
  de Equia, 1530. Huntington Library rare book 11392.
Annis, Verle L. *La Arquitectura de la Antigua Guatemala, 1543-1773.* Bilingual Edi-

tion. Guatemala: University of San Carlos, 1968.

Bancroft, Hubert Howe. *History of Central America.* 3. vols. San Francisco: The History Co., 1886-87.

Barbón, José A. *Bernal Díaz del Castillo.* Buenos Aires: Centro Editor América Latina, 1968.

Beagles, Bernice. "Record of What Happened in Guatemala." *Western Explorer: Journal of the Cabrillo Historical Association* 5 (September 1967): 20-23.

Bean, Lowell John and Harry W. Lawton, "Some Explanations for the Rise of Cultural Complexity in Native California with Comments on Proto-Agriculture and Agriculture." *Native Californians: A Theoretical Retrospective.* Edited by Lowell John Bean and Thomas C. Blackburn. Socorro, NM: Ballena Press, 1976.

Benítez, Fernando. *The Century after Cortés.* Trans. by Joan MacLean. Chicago: University of Chicago Press, 1965.

Bent, Thomas. "The Way of Making Pitch, Tarr, Rosin and Turpentine near Marseilles." Royal Society of London *Philosophical Transactions* 20 (August 1698): 291. Huntington Library rare book 98681.

Bolton, Herbert E. ed. *Fray Juan Crespi, Missionary Explorer on the Pacific Coast, 1769-1774.* Berkeley: Univ. of California Press, 1927.

Bolton, Herbert E. *Spanish Exploration in the Southwest, 1542-1706.* New York: Charles Scribner's Sons, 1916.

Borah, Woodrow. *Early Colonial Trade and Navigation Between Mexico and Peru.* Ibero-Americana, vol. 38. Berkeley: University of California Press, 1954.

Borhegyi, Stephen F. de. "Estudio arqueologico en la falda norte del Volcán de Agua." *Anthropología e Historia de Guatemala* 2 (Enero 1950): 3-4, 14-20.

Boswell, John E. "*Expositio* and *Oblatio*: The Abandonment of Children and the Ancient and Medieval Family." *American Historical Review* 89 (February 1984): 10-33.

Boyd-Bowman, Peter. *Indice geobiográfico de cuarenta mil pobladores Españoles de America en el siglo XVI.* Vol. 1. *1493-1519.* Bogotá: Instituto Caro y Cuervo, 1964.

Boyd-Bowman, Peter. *Patterns of Spanish Immigration to the New World (1493-1580).* Buffalo: State University of New York, Special Studies, 1973.

Brissault, Herma trans. *The Devastation of the Indies: A Brief Account.* New York: Seabury Press, 1974.

Brown, Alan K. The Aboriginal Population of the Santa Barbara Channel." *University of California Archaeological Survey Reports* no. 69 (January 1967): 99 pages.

Burrus, Ernest J. *Kino and the Cartography of Northwestern New Spain.* Tucson: Arizona Pioneers Historical Society, 1965.

Calcagno, Francisco. *Diccionario biográfico Cubano.* New York: Imprenta de N. Ponce de León, 1878.

California, Senate Concurrent Resolution No. 15. *Statutes of 1935,* 2409.

California, Senate Concurrent Resolution No. 44. *Statutes of 1935,* 2693-94.

California, Senate *Journal,* 51st sess., 21 January 1935, 142.

Cámara Municipal de Montalegre, unanimous resolution of 2 September 1978, addressed to the City Council of San Diego, California.

Juan Rodríguez Cabrillo

Caraci, Giuseppe. "Map of the Pacific Ocean by G. Tatton." *Tabulae geographicae vetustiores in Italia adservatae*. 2 vols. Florence: Otto Lange, 1926.1:12-15.

Carbia, Rómulo D. *La Crónica oficial de las Indias Occidentales: Estudio histórico y crítico acerca de la historiografía mayor de Hispano-America en los siglos XVI a XVIII*. Biblioteca Humanidades, Universidad de La Plata, vol. 14. La Plata: Universidad de La Plata, 1921.

Cárdenas de la Peña, Enrique. *Urdaneta y "El Tornaviaje"*. Mexico: Secretaría de Marina, 1965.

Carreño, Alberto María. "Don Fray Juan de Zumárraga Pioneer of European Culture in America." *The Americas* 4 (July 1949): 56-71.

Carrera Stampa, Manuel. "The Evolution of Weights and Measures in New Spain." *Hispanic American Historical Review* 29 (February 1949): 2-24.

Cartas de Indias. Madrid: Imprenta de Manuel G. Hernández, 1877.

Chamberlain, Robert S. *Castilian Backgrounds of the Repartimiento-Encomienda*. Carnegie Institution of Washington Publication No. 509. Contributions to American Anthropology and History No. 25. Washington: Carnegie Institution of Washington, 1939.

Chamberlain, Robert S. *The Conquest and Colonization of Honduras, 1502-1550*. Carnegie Institution of Washington Publication No. 58. Washington, D.C.: Carnegie Institution, 1953.

Chamier, Carlos Alfredo. *De como el periodismo en América se origino en Guatemala en 1541*. Mexico, Costa-Amic, [1968].

Christian, William O., Jr. *Local Religion in Sixteenth Century Spain*. Princeton, NJ: Princeton Univ. Press, 1981.

Cohen, Daniel M. "Names of the Hakes." *Marine Fisheries Review* 42 (January 1980): 2-3.

Conseil géneral des pêches pour la Méditerranée. *Catalogue des poissons ayant une importance comercial en Méditerranée*. Rome: Food and Agricultural Organization of the United Nations, 1960.

Cortés, Hernán. *Cartas de relacíon*. Intro. by Manuel Alcalá, Sepan Cuantos Num. 7. 5th ed. Mexico: Editorial Porrúa, 1970.

Cortés, Hernán. *Carta de relaciõ enbiada a su S. majestad del ẽperador nro senor por el capitã general de la nueva spaña: llamado fernãdo cortes*. Sevilla: Jacobo Cromberger Aleman, 1522. Huntington Library rare book 108651.

Cortesão, Armando. "Antonio Pereira and His Map of Circa 1545." *The Geographical Review* 29 (April 1939): 205-25.

Cortesão, Armando and Avelino Teixeira Da Mota. *Portugaliae Monumenta Cartographica*. 5 vols. Lisbon: n.n., 1960.

Cuevas, P. Mariano. *Cartas y otros documentos de Hernan Cortés*. Seville: Imprenta de F. Díaz, 1915.

Cuevas, P. Mariano. *Monje y marino: la vida y los tiempos de Fray Andrés de Urdaneta*. Mexico: Editorial Galatea, 1943.

Cutter, Donald C. "Sources of the Name 'California'." *Arizona and the West* 3 (Autumn 1961): 233-44.

Davidson, George. "The Discovery of San Francisco Bay." Geographical Society of the Pacific, *Transactions and Proceedings* ser. 2, vol. 4 (1907):000

Davidson, George C. "Voyages of Discovery and Exploration." In U.S. Coast and Geodetic Survey *Annual Report for 1886*. Appendix Number 7. Washington: G. P. O., 1887. 155-253.

Demarest, Donald and Coley Taylor. *The Dark Virgin*. Freeport, Maine: Coley Taylor, Inc., 1956.

Díaz del Castillo, Bernal, *Historia verdadera de la conquista de la Nueva España*. Edited by Alonso Remón. Madrid: Emprenta del Reyno, 1632. Huntington Library rare book 45888.

Díaz del Castillo, Bernal. *Historia verdadera de la conquista de la Nueva España*. Intro. and notes by Joaquín Ramírez Cabañas. 10th ed. Mexico: Editorial Porrúa, 1974.

do Campo, Florian. *Los Quatro libros primeros de la cronica general de España*. Zamora: Juan Picardo, 1543. Huntington Library rare book 139792.

Documentos Americanos del Archivo de Protocolos de Sevilla, siglo XVI. Madrid: Tipografía de Archivos, 1935.

Dorantes Carranza, Baltasar. *Sumaria relación de las cosas de la Nueva España*. Ed. by José Mariano Agreda y Sánchez. Mexico: Imprenta del Museo Nacional, 1902. Huntington Library rare book 269940.

Enciclopedia universal ilustrada Europeo-Americana. Barcelona: Hijos de J. Espasa, 1905-1930. 10:218-19.

Enciclopedia Universal Ilustrada, Europeo-Americano. Madrid: Espasa-Calpe, 1921. 44:333-35.

Encyclopedia Britannica 23 (1895): 57-59.

Estrada Monroy, Augustín. *Datos para la historia de la iglesia en Guatemala*. Biblioteca "Goathemala," vol. 26. Guatemala: Sociedad de Geografía e Historia de Guatemala, 1973.

Evans, Richard Stuart. "Translation from the Spanish of the Account by the Pilot Ferrel of the Voyage of Cabrillo along the West Coast of North America in 1542." In *Report of the United States Geographical Surveys West of the One Hundredth Meridian*. Vol. 7, *Archaeology*. Washington: G.P.O., 1879.

France, Bibliothèque Nationale. *Catalogue des cartes nautiques nes velin conservés au Département des Cartes et Plans*. Paris: Bibliothèque Nationale, 1963.

Fuentes, Patricia de, trans. and ed. *The Conquistadors: First-person Accounts of the Conquest of Mexico*. New York: Orion Press, 1963.

Fuentes y Guzmán, Francisco Antonio de. *Recordación Florida: discurso historial y demonstración natural, material, militar, y politica del Reyno de Guatemala*. Biblioteca "Goathemala," vols. 6, 7, 8. Guatemala: Tipografía Nacional, 1933.

Gage, Thomas. *Travels in the New World*. Ed. and intro. by J. Eric S. Thompson. Norman: University of Oklahoma Press, 1958.

Gall, Francis. *"Conquista de El Salvador y fundación del primigenio San Salvador, 1524."* *Antropolgía e Historia de Guatemala* 18 (January 1966): 27-29

García, Genaro. *Historia verdadera de la conquista de la Nueva España*. Mexico: Secretaría de Fomento, 1904.

García, Genaro, ed. *The True History of the Conquest of New Spain*. Trans. by Alfred

Percival Maudslay. Hakluyt Society Works. ser. 2, vol. 40. London: Hakluyt Society, 1916.

Gardiner, C. Harvey. *Naval Power in the Conquest of Mexico*. Austin: University of Texas Press, 1956.

Gastaldi, Giacomo de. *Cosmographia universalis et exactissima iuxta postremam neotericorum traditionem*. Venice: n.n., 1562.?

Gastaldi, Giacomo de. *La universale descrittione del mondo*. Venice: Matthio Pagano, 1561.

Gómara, Francisco López de. *Cortés: The Life of the Conqueror by his Secretary, Francisco López de Gómara*. Trans. Lesley Byrd Simpson. Berkeley: University of California Press, 1964.

Gómara, Francisco López de. *Historia general*. Medina del Campo: Guillermo de Millis, 1553.

Gómara, Francisco López de. *Primera y Segunda parte de la historia general de las Indias cõ todo el descubrimiento y cosas notables que han acaescido dende que se ganaron hasta el año de 1551. Con la conquista de Mexico y de la Nueva España*. Medina del Campo: Guillermo de Millis, 1553.

Goulart, da Costa Euclides. *Portugal Descubridor: Apontamentos respeitantes á descoberta de California*. Lisbon: Tipografia de Manutenção Militar, 1928.

Gonçalves, da Costa, João *Montalegre e terras de Barroso, notas historicas sobre Montalegre freguesias do concelho e região de Barroso*. Braga, Portugal: Edição de Cámara Municipal de Montalegre, 1968.

Grant, Campbell. "Eastern Coastal Chumash," *Handbook of North American Indians*. Edited by William C. Sturtevant. Vol. VIII, *California*. Edited by Robert F. Heizer. Washington: Smithsonian Institution, 1978: 505-19, 524-34.

Guerra y Sánchez, Ramiro. *Historia de Cuba*. Havana: Sociedad Editorial Cuba Contemporanea, 1921.

Hallenbeck, Cleve. *Álvar Núñez Cabeza de Vaca: The Journey and Route of the First European to Cross the Continent of North America, 1534-1536*. Glendale, CA: Arthur H. Clark Co., 1940.

Hammond, George P. and Agapito Rey. *Narratives of the Coronado Expedition, 1540-1542*. Albuquerque: University of New Mexico Press, 1940.

Harner, Michael. "The Emergence of Aztec Sacrifice." *Natural History* 86 (April 1977): 46-51.

Heizer, Robert F. "A Probable Relic of Juan Rodríguez Cabrillo." *The Masterkey* 47 (April-June 1973): 62-67.

Heizer, Robert F. *California's Oldest Historical Relic?* Berkeley: University of California, Robert W. Lowie Museum of Anthropology, 1974.

Henshaw, H.W. "Introductory Notes" to the translation by Richard Stuart Evans. "Translation from the Spanish of the Account by the Pilot Ferrel of the Voyage of Cabrillo along the West Coast of North America in 1542." In *Report of United States Geographical Surveys West of the One Hundredth Meridian*. Vol. 7. *Archaeology*. Washington: G. P. O., 1879: 293-98.

Herrera, Antonio de. *Historia general de los hechos de los Castellanos*. Intro. and notes by Antonio Ballesteros-Beretta. 12 vols. Madrid: [Tipografía Archivos],

1934-1953.

Herrera, Antonio de. *Historia general de los hechos de los Castellanos en las islas y Tierra Firme del mar océano.* 4 vols. Madrid: Juan de la Cuesta, 1615. Wagner Collection, Honnold Library, Pomona, CA.

Herrera y Tordesillas, Antonio de. *Descripción de las Indias Ocidentales.* 4 vols. Madrid: Nicolás Rodríguez Franco, 1730. Huntington Library rare book 48448.

Holmes, Maurice G. *From New Spain by Sea to the Californias.* Vol. 9 of the Spain in the West series. Glendale, CA: Arthur H. Clark Co., 1963.

Howell, John Thomas. *Marin Flora: Manual of the Flowering Plants and Ferns of Marin County, California.* 2nd ed. Berkeley: University of California Press, 1970.

Humboldt, Alexander von. *Ensayo politco sobre el reino de la Nueva España.* Edición crítica por Vito Alessio Robles. 5 vols. Mexico: D. F. Robredo, 1941.

Icaza, Francisco A. de. *Diccionario autobiográfico de conquistadores y pobladores de Nueva España.* 2 vols. Madrid: Imprenta de "El Adelantado de Segovia," 1923.

Icazbalceta, Joaquín García. *Bibliografía Mexicana del siglo XVI.* Mexico: Libreria de Andrade y Morales, 1886.

Icazbalceta, Joaquín García. *Colección de documentos para la historia de Mexico.* Mexico: Antigua Libreria, 1866.

Iglesia, Ramón. "Introduction to the Study of Bernal Díaz and His True History." *Columbus, Cortés, and Other Essays.* Trans. and ed. Lesley Byrd Simpson. Berkeley: University of California Press, 1964: 64-77.

Jensen, Joan M. "Notes from a Western Explorer." *The Western Explorer: Journal of the Cabrillo Historical Association* 4 (March 1967):1-5.

Jones, Philip Mills. "Archaeological Investigations on Santa Rosa Island." *University of California Anthropological Records* 17 (1956).

Keen, A. Myra and James H. McLean. *Sea Shells of Tropical West America: Marine Mollusks from Baja California to Peru.* 2nd ed. Stanford, CA: Stanford University Press, 1971.

Kelly, Celsus. *La Australia del Espiritu Santo.* 2 vols., Hakluyt Society Works, ser 2, vol. 126-27. Cambridge: Cambridge University Press, 1966.

Kelsey, Harry. "The California Armada of Juan Rodríguez Cabrillo." *Southern California Quarterly* 41 (Winter 1979):313-36.

King, Arden R. *Coban and the Vera Paz: History and Cultural Process in Northern Guatemala.* New Orleans: Tulane University Press, 1974.

King, Chester and Thomas Blackburn. "The Names and Locations of Historic Chumash Villages. *Journal of California Anthropology* 2 (Winter 1975): 171-79.

Kroeber, A. L. *Handbook of the Indians of California.* Bureau of American Ethnology Bulletin 78. Washington: Smithsonian Institution, 1925.

Kubler, George. *Mexican Architecture of the Sixteenth Century.* 2 vols. New Haven: Yale University Press, 1948.

Laet, Joannes. *Novis orbis seu descriptionis Indiae occidentalis.* Leyden: Ludovicus Elgevirus, 1633. Huntington Library rare book 139796.

Lagoa, Visconde de. *João Rodrigues Cabrilho, achegas para a sua biografia.* Lisbon: Agencia Geral do Ultramar, 1958.

Lamb, Ursula. "Science by Litigation: A Cosmographic Feud." *Terra Incognita,* the *Annals of the Society for the History of Discoveries* 1 (1969): 40-57.

Landstrom, Bjorn. *The Ship: An Illustrated History.* Garden City, NY: Doubleday & Co., 1961.

Las Casas, Bartolomé de. *Brevíssima relación de la destruyción de las Indias.* Seville: Sebastian Trugillo, 1522. Huntington Library rare book 1552.

Las Casas, Bartolomé de. *Historia de las Indias.* Ed. by Agustín Millares Carlo. Intro. by Lewis Hanke. Mexico: Fondo de Cultura Economica, 1951.

Las Siete Partidas. Trans. and notes by Samuel Parsons Scott. Chicago and New York: American Bar Association, 1931.

Le Boeuf, Burney J. "Report of an Expedition to the Gulf of California, Mexico, on Scripps Institution of Oceanography R/V *Ellen B. Scripps*, 12 June to 8 July 1984." Department of Biology, University of California, Santa Cruz. Mimeograph.

Lewis, Henry T. *Patterns of Indian Burning in California: Ecology and Ethnohistory.* Ballena Press Anthropological Papers, no. 1. Ramona, CA: Ballena Press, 1973.

Libro viejo de la fundación de Guatemala y papeles relativos a D. Pedro de Alvarado, prologue by Jorge García Granados. Biblioteca "Goathemala," vol. 12. Guatemala: Sociedad de Geographía e Historia de Guatemala, 1934.

Livermore, Harold L., ed. *Royal Commentaries of the Incas and General History of Peru.* 2 vols. Austin: University of Texas Press, 1966.

Lockhart, James and Enrique Otte, trans. and eds. *Letters and People of the Spanish Indies, Sixteenth Century.* Cambridge Latin American Studies. Vol. 22. Cambridge: Cambridge University Press, 1976.

López de Gómara, Francisco. *La historia general de las Indias.* Intro. and notes by Joaquín and Ramírez Cabañas. 2 vols. Mexico: Editorial Pedro Robredo, 1943.

Lorenzana, Francisco Antonio. *Historia de Nueva España escrita por su esclarecido conquistador Hernán Cortés.* Mexico: Imprenta del Superior Gobierno, 1770.

Los Angeles Evening Express, 26 September 1894, 3.

Lutz, Christopher H. "Santiago de Guatemala, 1541-1773: The Socio-Demographic History of a Spanish American Colonial City." Unpublished Ph.D. dissertation. 2 vols. University of Wisconsin, 1976.

MacNutt, Francis A. *Fernando Cortés: His Five Letters of Relation to the Emperor, Charles V.* 2 vols. New York: G.P. Putnam's Sons, 1908; reprint Glorieta, New Mexico, Rio Grande Press, 1977.

Markman, Sidney David. *Colonial Architecture of Antigua Guatemala.* Memoirs of the American Philosophical Society. Vol. 64. Philadelphia: American Philosophical Society, 1966.

Mathes, W. Michael. *The Capture of the Santa Ana, Cabo San Lucas, November, 1587.* Los Angeles: Dawson's Book Shop, 1969.

Mathes, W. Michael. "The Discoverer of Alta California: João Rodrigues Cabrilho or Juan Rodríguez Cabrillo." *Journal of San Diego History* 19 (Summer 1973): 1-8.

McLeod, Murdo J. *Spanish Central America: A Socioeconomic History, 1520-1720.* Berkeley and Los Angeles: University of California Press, 1973.

Mead, Giles W. and Daniel M. Cohen, "Comments on Common Names of Fishes." *Copeia* 30 (No. 4, 1960): 378-80.

Menéndez Pidal, Ramon. "Los incunables Americanos." *Colección de incunables Americanos siglo XVI.* Vol. 1. Madrid: Ediciones Cultura Hispánica, 1944.

Merriam, C. Hart. "Village Names in Twelve California Mission Records." Edited by Robert F. Heizer. University of California Archaeological Survey Reports, No. 74 (July 1968):

Miguélez, Manuel Fraile. *Catálogo de los códices españoles de la Biblioteca del Escorial.* Madrid: Imprenta Helénica, 1917.

Minsheu, John. *Dictionaire, in Spanish and English, First Published into the English Tongue by Ric. Percivale.* London: Edm. Bollifant, 1599. Huntington Library rare book 62921-22.

Mitchell, Mairin. *Friar Andrés de Urdaneta, O. S. A.* London: Macdonald & Evans, 1964.

Moratto, Michael J., Thomas F. King, and Wallace B. Woolfenden. "Archaeology and California's Climate." *Journal of California Anthropology* 5 (Winter 1978): 147-61.

Moriarty, James R. and Keistman, Mary, trans. and eds. "Cabrillo's Log, 1542-43, a Voyage of Discovery: A Summary by Juan Páez. *The Western Explorer* 17 (September 1968): 5-42.

Morison, Samuel Eliot. *The European Discovery of America.* Vol. 2. *The Southern Voyages, A. D. 1492-1616.* New York: Oxford University Press, 1974.

Morris, J. Bayard, trans. and ed. *Hernando Cortés: Five Letters, 1519-1526.* London: George Routledge & Sons, Ltd., 1928.

Mota, A Teixeira, da. "The Teaching of Navigation in Spain and Portugal in the Time of Cabrilho." *Cabrillo and His Era.* Sixth Annual Cabrillo Festival Historic Seminar (September 1978): 9-18.

Muro, Luis. *La expedición Legazpi-Urdaneta a las Filipinas (1557-1564).* 2nd ed. revised. Mexico: Secretaría de Educación Pública, 1975.

Nader, Helen. *The Mendoza Family in the Spanish Renaissance, 1350-1550.* New Brunswick, NJ: Rutgers University Press, 1979.

Navarrete, Martín Fernández de, Miguel Salvá, and Pedro Sainz de Baranda, *Colección de documentos inéditos, relativos al descubrimiento, conquista y organización de las antiguas posesiones españolas de América y Oceanía.* 42 vols. Madrid: Imprenta de José María Pérez, 1870.

Navarrete, Martín Fernández. *Colección de los viages y descubrimientos que hicieron por mar los españoles.* 5 vols. Madrid: Imprenta Nacional, 1837.

Navarrete, Martín Fernández de. *Colección de los viajes y descubrimientos que hicieron por mar los Españoles.* 2nd edition. 4 vols. Madrid: Imprenta Nacional, 1858.

Ortiz de Montellano, Bernard R. "Aztec Cannibalism: An Ecological Necessity?" *Science* 200 (May 1978): 611-17.

Otte, Enrique. "Mercaderes burgaleses en los inicios del comercio con México." *Historia Mexicana* 18 (July-September 1968): 109-44. 18 (October-December 1968): 258-85.

Oviedo y Valdés, Gonzalo Fernández de. *Historia general y natural de las Indias, islas, y Tierra-Firme del Mar Océano.* 4 vols. Madrid: Imprenta de la Real Academia de la Historia, 1853.

Oviedo y Valdés, Gonzalo Fernández de. *Primera Parte de la general y natural historia de las Indias.* Seville: Imprenta de Juan Cromberger, 1535.

Oviedo y Valdés, Gonzalo Fernández. *Sumario de la natural historia de las Indias.* Ed. José Miranda. Mexico: Fondo de Cultura Economica, 1950.

Pagden, A. R., trans. and ed. *Hernan Cortés: Letters from Mexico.* New York: Grossman Publishers, 1971.

Palacio, Diego García de. *Instrucción náutica para navegar.* Mexico: Casa de Pedro Ocharte, 1587.

Paso y Troncoso, Francisco del. *Espistolario de Nueva España, 1505-1818.* Series 2. *Biblioteca Histórica Mexicana de Obras Inéditas.* 16 vols. Mexico: Antigua Librería Robredo de José Porrúa e Hijos, 1940.

Pérez Bustamante, Ciriaco. *Don Antonio de Mendoza, Primer virrey de la Nueva España (1535-1550).* Vol. 3 of *Anales de la Universidad de Santiago.* Santiago: Tipografía de "El Eco Franciscano," 1928.

Pérez Cabrera, José M. "The Circumnavigation of Cuba by Ocampo: When Did It Take Place?" *Hispanic American Historical Review* 18 (February 1938): 101-108.

Pérez Pastor, Cristóbal. *Bibliografía Madrileña, ó descripción de las obras impressas en Madrid.* Madrid: Tipografía de la "Revista de Archivos, Bibliotecas y Museos," 1907.

Perry, Mary Elizabeth. *Crime and Society in Early Modern Seville.* Hanover, NH: University Press of New England, 1980.

Phillips, Carla Rahn. "Spanish Ships and Shipbuilding during the Renaissance." *Boat and Shipbuilding in San Diego.* San Diego: Cabrillo Historical Association, 1983. 1-24.

Portillo y Díaz de Solano, Alvaro del. *Descubrimientos y exploraciones en las costas de California, 1532-1650.* 2nd ed. Madrid: Ediciones Rialp, 1982.

Pourade, Richard E. *The History of San Diego: The Explorers.* San Diego, CA: The Union Tribune Publ. Co., 1960.

Pulido Rubio, José. *El piloto mayor de la [Casa de] Contratación de Sevilla: Pilotos mayores del siglo XVI (datos biográficos).* Biblioteca Colonial Americana, Centro Oficial de Estudios Americanistas. Vol. 10. Seville: Tipografía Zarzuela, 1925.

Rainero, Román. "Observations sur l'activité cartographique de Giacomo Gastaldi (Venice, XVe siècle)." Paper read at VIII Congres International Sur L'Histoire de la Cartographie, Berlin, 17-20, September 1979. Typescript. Rijksarchief map room, The Hague.

Recinos, Adrián and Delia Goetz. *The Annals of the Cakchiquels.* Norman: University of Oklahoma Press, 1953.

Recinos, Adrián. *Pedro de Alvarado, Conquistador de Mexico y Guatemala.* Mexico: Fondo de Cultura Económica, 1952.

Rees, Abraham. *The Cyclopedia or Universal Dictionary of Arts, Sciences and Literature.* London: Longman, Hurat, Rees, Orme, & Brown, 1819. Vol. 27, "Pitch," and vol. 25, "Tar."

Reina, Rubén E. University of Pennsylvania, Hispanic-Latin American Research Project. Typed extracts and transcripts.

Remesal, Antonio de. *Historia general de las Indias Occidentales y particular de la gobernación de Chiapa y Guatemala*. Edited by Carmelo Sáenz de Santa María. Biblioteca de Autores Españoles. Vols. 175 and 189. Madrid: Ediciones Atlas, 1964.

Reyes M., José Luis. *Anales de la Sociedad de Geografía é Historia de Guatemala* 23 (March-June 1948): 92-97.

Reyes M., José Luis "Relación del espantable terremoto," *Anales de la Sociedad de Geografia e Historia de Guatemala*, 23 (March-June 1948): 92-97.

Rodríguez Becerra, Salvador. *Encomienda y conquista: los inicios de la colonizción en Guatemala*. Publicaciones del Seminario de Antropología Americana. Vol. 14. Seville: Universidad de Sevilla, 1977.

Rodríguez, Juan. *Relación del espantable terremoto que agora nuevamente ha acontecido en las Yndias en una ciudad llamada Guatimala*. 2nd ed. Madrid: n.n., 1543. Facsimile reprint in *Colección de incunables Americanos siglo XVI*. Vol. 1. Madrid: Ediciones Cultura Hispanica, 1944.

Rogers, Woodes. *A Cruising Voyage Round the World, First to the South-Seas, thence to the East-Indies and Home-wards*. London: A. Bell and B. Lintot, 1712.

Rubio, Fernando. "Las noticias referentes a America, contenidas el manuscrito V-II-4 de la Biblioteca de el Escorial." *Revista de Indias* 11 (January-June 1951): 111-21.

Rubio Mañé, J. Ignacio. "La expedición de Miguel López de Legazpi a Filipinas." *Boletín del Archivo General de la Nación*, ser. 2, vol. 5, nos. 3-4 (1964), 429-798.

Sáenz de Santa María, Carmelo. *Introduccíon crítica a la "Historia verdadera" de Bernal Díaz del Castillo*. Madrid: Instituto Gonzalo Fernández de Oviedo, 1967.

Saint-Lu, André. *La Vera Paz: Espirit Evangélique et Colonisation*. Paris: Centre de Recherches Hispaniques, 1968.

Salas, Alberto María. *Las Armas de la Conquista*. Buenos Aires: Emecé Editores, 1950.

Sánchez, Manuel Rubio. *Historia del puerto de la Santísima Trinidad de Sonsonate ó Acajutla*. San Salvador: Editorial Universitaria, 1977.

Sanchíz Ochoa, Pilar. *Los hidalgos de Guatemala: realidad y apariencia en un sistema de valores*. Vol. 13 of *Publicaciones del Seminario de Antropología Americana*. Seville: Universidad de Sevilla, 1976.

Santa Cruz, Alonso de. *Crónica del Emperador Carlos V.* 5 vols. Madrid: Imprenta del Patronato de Huérfanos de Intendencia e Intervención Militares, 1923.

Santa Cruz, Alonso de. *Libro de las longitudines*. Ed. and intro. Antonio Blázquez and Delgado Aguilera. Vol. 5 of Biblioteca Colonial Americana, Centro de Estudios Americanistas de Sevilla. Sevilla: Tipografia Zarzuela, 1921.

Scheina, Robert Lewis. "Mass Labor: The Key to Spanish Maritime Construction in the Americas during the Sixteenth Century." *The Mariner's Mirror* 58 (May 1972): 195-202.

Sherman, William L. "A Conqueror's Wealth: Notes on the Estate of Don Pedro de Alvarado." *The Americas* 26 (July 1969): 199-213.

Sherman, William L. *Forced Native Labor in Sixteenth Century Central America*. Lincoln: University of Nebraska Press, 1979.

Silva, J. Francisco V. "Itinerario Marítimo de California al Río de la Plata." Segundo

Congreso de Historia y Geografía Hispano-Americanas, Sevilla, 1921. *Actas y Memorias*. Madrid: Establecímiento Tipográfico de Jaime Rates, 1921.

Simpson, Lesley Byrd. *Cortés: The Life of the Conqueror by his Secretary, Francisco López de Gómara*. Los Angeles: University of California Press, 1964.

Smith, Buckingham. *Colección de varios documentos para la historia de la Florida y tierras adyacentes*. London: Casa de Trubner & Co., 1857.

Spain, Ministerio de Trabajo y Previsión. *Selección de las Leyes de Indias*. Madrid: Imprenta Artistica. 1929.

Spain, Museo Naval. *Colección de documentos y manuscritos compilados por Fernández de Navarrete*. Neudeln, Liechtenstein: Kraus-Thompson Organization, 1971.

Spate, O. H. K. *The Spanish Lake*. Vol. 1 of *The Pacific since Magellan*. 2 vols. Minneapolis: University of Minnesota Press, 1979.

Soares, Celestino. *California and the Portuguese*. Lisbon: SPN Books, 1939.

Squier, E. G. *Collection of Rare and Original Documents and Relations concerning the Discovery and Conquest of America*. New York, Charles B. Norton, 1860.

Stanislawski, Don. "Early Spanish Town Planning in the New World." *Geographical Review* 37 (January 1947): 94-105.

Szecsy, Janos de. *Santiago de los Caballeros de Goathemala en Almolonga: investigaciones del año 1950*. Trans. from the original English by Yolanda de Oreamuno. Guatemala: Editorial del Ministerio de Educación Publica, 1953.

Taylor, Alexander Smith. *Discovery of California and Northwest America: The First Voyage to the Coast of California, Made in the Years 1542 and 1543 by Juan Rodríguez Cabrillo and His Pilot Bartolomé Ferrelo*. San Francisco: Le Count and Strong, 1853. Huntington Library rare book 455.

Taylor, Alexander Smith. *The First Voyage to the Coasts of California: Made in the Years 1542 and 1543. By Juan Rodriguez Cabrillo and His Pilot Bartolome Ferrelo*. San Francisco: Le Count & Strong, 1853.

Thompson, Donald A. and Nonie McKibbin. *Gulf of California Fishwatchers Guide*. Tucson: Golden Puffer Press, 1976.

Torre, Tomás de la. *Desde Salamanca, España, hasta Ciudad Real, Chiapas, diario de viaje, 1544-45*. Intro. and notes by Franz Blom. Mexico: Editora Central, [1945].

True, David O. "Cabot Explorations in North America." *Imago Mundi* 13 (1956): 11-25.

Turner, Ralph V. "The *Miles Literatus* in Twelfth- and Thirteenth-Century England: How Rare a Phenomenon?" *American Historical Review* 83 (October 1978): 928-45.

Uncilla y Arroita-Jáuregui, Fermín de. *Urdaneta y la conquista de Filipinas*. San Sebastián: Imprenta de la Provinica, 1907.

U.S., Department of the Interior, National Park Service. *Cabrillo National Monument, California*. Leaflet. Washington: G. P. O., 1974.

U.S. Department of the Navy. *Sailing Directions for the West Coast of Mexico and Central America*. Hydrographic Office Publication No. 26. 9th edition. Washington: G.P.O., 1951.

Van Bemmelen, Willem. *De Isogonen en de XVI^{de} en XVIII^{de} Eeuw*. Utrecht: J. Van Douten, 1893.

van der Straet, Jan. *America Retectio*. Shearman Collection, Los Angeles County Museum of Natural History; also in the Huntington Library, rare book 322072.

Varela, Consuelo. Ed., intro., and notes. *El viage de Don Ruy López de Villalobos a las Islas del Poniente, 1542-1548*. Milan: Instituto Editoriale Cisalpino-LaGoliardica, 1983.

Vega, El Inca Garcilaso de la. *Historia general del Peru*. Cordova: Viuda de Andrés Barrera, 1617. Huntington Library rare book 183418.

Velasco, Juan López de. *Geografía y descripción universal de las Indias recopilada por el cosmógrafo-cronista Juan López de Velasco desde el año de 1571 al de 1574*. Ed. by Justo Zaragoza. Madrid: Establecimiento Tipográfico de Fortanet, 1894.

Vigil, Ralph H. "A Reappraisal of the Expedition of Pánfilo de Narváez to Mexico in 1520." Copy of undated, unpublished MS received from the author in January, 1979.

Vigneras, Louis-Andre. *The Discovery of South America and the Andalusian Voyage*. Chicago: Published for the Newberry Library by the University of Chicago Press, 1976.

Vila Vilar, Enriqueta. *Gran Enciclopedia Rialp*. Madrid: Ediciones Rialp, 1973. 6:580.

Villacorte C., J. Antonio, ed., *Libro viejo de la fundación de Guatemala y papeles relativos a D. Pedro de Alvarado*. Vol. 12 of the Biblioteca "Goathemala" de la Sociedad de Geografía e Historia. Guatemala: Tipografía Nacional, 1934.

von Langsdorff, G.H. *Voyages and Travels in Various Parts of the World during the years 1803, 1804, 1805, 1806 and 1807*. 2 vols. London: Henry Colburn, 1814.

Wagner, Henry R. *The Cartography of the Northwest Coast of America to the Year 1800*. 2 vols. Berkeley: University of California Press, 1937.

Wagner, Henry R. "Francisco Ulloa Returned." *California Historical Society Quarterly* 19 (September 1940): 240-44.

Wagner, Henry R. *Juan Rodriguez Cabrillo, Discoverer of the Coast of California*. San Francisco: California Historical Society, 1941.

Wagner, Henry R. *The Life and Writings of Bartolomé de las Casas*. In collaboration with Helen Rand Parish. Albuquerque: University of New Mexico Press, 1967.

Wagner, Henry R. "A Map of Cabrillo's Discoveries." *California Historical Society Quarterly* 11 (March 1932): 44-46.

Wagner, Henry R. *Nueva bibliografía Mexicana del siglo XVI*. Mexico: Editorial Polis, 1940.

Wagner, Henry. "A Map of Sancho Gutierrez of 1551." *Imago Mundi* 8 (1951): 47-49.

Wagner, Henry R. "The Names of the Channel Islands." Historical Society of Southern California, *Annual Publication* 15 (1933): 16-18.

Wagner, Henry R. *Spanish Voyages to the Northwest Coast of America in the Sixteenth Century*. San Francisco: California Historical Society, 1929.

Weider, Frederik Caspar. *Monumenta Cartographica: Reproductions of Unique and Rare Maps, Plans, and Views in the Actual Size of the Originals, Accompanied by Cartographical Monographs*. 5 vols. in 1. The Hague: Martinus Nijhoff, 1925-1933.

Wright, Irene A. *The Early History of Cuba, 1492-1586*. New York: Macmillan Co., 1916.

Ximénez, Francisco. *Historia de la provincia de San Vicente de Chiapa y Guatemala* de la orden de predicadores. Biblioteca "Goathemala," vols. 1-3. Guatemala: Sociedad de Geografía e Historia, 1929.

Index

Glossary

The listings below are not general dictionary definitions. They simply reflect contemporary usage as found in the sixteenth century documents and books quoted in this work.

Adelantado: governor of a frontier province

Alcalde mayor: official having civil and judicial power in a district or municipality

Alguacil: constable

Alguacil mayor: chief constable

Almiranta: ship under orders of the second-in-command of a fleet

Almirante: second-in-command of a fleet

Arcabuz: arquebus; a firearm operated by a matchlock and trigger

Asiento: contract

Audiencia: judicial and governing body of a region

Auto: legal proceedings

Ayuntamiento: town council; cabildo

Ballesta: crossbow

Ballestero: crossbowman

Bandera: banner

Barlovento: windward

Barrio: district of a municipality

Batea: large wooden bowl with projecting handles

Batel: ship's boat, about a third the size of a bergantín

Bergantín: a small boat propelled by

oars or sails; a launch

Caballería: land assigned to a cavalryman, 600 paces wide and 1,000 paces long; about 105 acres

Cabildo: city council or ayuntamiento

Calidad: social rank

Cacique: Indian chief

Canoa: canoe

Capitana: flagship

Casa de Contratación: House of Trade in Seville, governing commerce with the Indies

Casa poblada: household of a hidalgo

Castellano: gold worth about 450 maravedís

Cazón: shark

Cédula: decree

Chronista: chronicler

Ciudad: city

Conquistador: soldier who took part in the Conquest

Consejo: council

Coronel: military commander

Coronista: chronicler

Cosmógrafo mayor: official cartographer and geographer in the Casa de Contratación

Cubierta: deck

Despensero: ship's steward

Encomendero: holder of an encomienda

Encomienda: a group of Indians assigned to serve or pay tribute to an encomendero

Escribano: lawyer or notary

Expediente: group of papers on a single subject drawn together in a special file

Fiscal: public prosecutor

Fogón: fireplace

Fragata: small boat propelled by oars or sails

Fusta: small boat propelled by oars or sails

Galeota: small galley
Galera: galley
Gallego: native of the Spanish pro-
vince of Galicia
Gobernador: governor
Hidalguía: nobility
Hidalgo: noble
Indio: American aborigine
Jarcia: ship's rigging
Justicia mayor: chief magistrate of a
region
Legajo: bundle of documents
Legua: league; about 2.5 miles
Lenguada: flatfish
Limpieza de sangre: purity of blood
(no Jewish, Moorish, or Indian
ancestry)
Maestre: officer in command of a ship
Maestre de campo: commanding
officer
Manta: blanket
Maravedí: basic unit of coinage, worth
about two cents in present values
Mar del Sur: South Sea; Pacific
Ocean
Marinero: seaman
Mar Océano: Atlantic Ocean
Mastil: topmast
Nao: ship
Navío: ship
Padrón general or padrón real: official
set of charts in the Casa de
Contratación
Patronato real: royal patronage and
rights in ecclesiastical matters
Peón: foot soldier
Peonía: land assigned to a foot soldier,
half the size of a cabellería
Peso de oro de minas: an uncoined
gold unit with a value approx-
imating that of the castellano
Piloto: navigator and chief sailing of-
ficer of a ship
Piloto mayor: chief pilot of an ar-

mada; chief pilot in the Casa de
Contratación
Plan: lowest deck of a ship
Pleito: lawsuit
Poblador: settler
Poniente: the west
Principal: member of the hereditary
Indian nobility
Probanza: presentation of evidence
Procurador: solicitor
Pueblo: town; Indian village
Puente: half deck; sterncastle
Quintal: hundred weight
Ramo: section of an archive
Ranchería: small settlement
Real: gold coin worth 34 maravedís
Regidor: member of a cabildo
Registro: license
Repartimiento: system of forced Indian
labor
Residencia: routine investigation of an
official's conduct following his term
of office
Señor: lord
Solar: urban house lot
Tameme: Indian porter
Teniente de gobernador: governor's
appointed representative
Tonel, Tonelada: units of weight used
in estimating the carrying capacity
of a ship; each has a value of
somewhat more than a ton
Traza: grid pattern used in town
planning
Valle: valley
Vara de justicia: ceremonial staff or
verge used as a symbol of office
Vecino: citizen; resident landowner of
a municipality
Villa: small town
Visita: investigation of the government of a region or of an official's
conduct during his term of office,
usually implying suspicion of

  wrongdoing
Visitador: inspector; judge
Xiquipil: measure of cacao; about
  8,000 beans

About the Author

Harry Kelsey is the former chief curator of history at the Natural History Museum of Los Angeles County. He is also the author of *The Doctrina and Confesionario of Juan Cortés*, *Frontier Capitalist: The Life of John Evans*, and *Sir Frances Drake: the Queen's Pirate*.

Juan Rodríguez Cabrillo by Harry Kelsey

"This is the first balanced study of Rodríguez Cabrillo, and readers familiar with the explorer will be pleased to learn of his extensive background as a mariner, soldier and entrepreneur. . . . Those who know nothing of him but are interested in the early history of the New World, particularly of California, will be fascinated by this energetic personality in the age of 'wooden ships and iron men.' Kelsey's book is scholarly and readable, well illustrated and nicely printed—a quality work. It is a major contribution to Spanish Californiana and a 'must' for all libraries and collections in the field."
—The Californians

"Biography? This is a biography! The author . . . has written what will stand as the definitive biography of Cabrillo for many years."
—The Journal of San Diego History

"Harry Kelsey's *Cabrillo* is engaging, well-illustrated, imaginatively researched, and intelligently written with an eye for context as well as for vivid and concrete detail." *—Southern California Quarterly*

"At last a distinguished biography of California's first authenticated European visitor is now available to students and scholars. . . . Kelsey has resurrected Cabrillo from fancy and myth and made him a truly recognized hero.

This is an impressive and scholarly biography and is an important contribution to California, western, and colonial Spanish-American history. It is gratifying that the first full-length portrayal of Juan Rodríguez Cabrillo is so well done. It should stand the test of time as the definitive work on the subject."
—Utah Historical Quarterly

"This book is a fine demonstration of what modern historical research can do, how it is done, and how to present it. Among the problems confronting the author were the lack of documentation on the birth date and place of his hero, variations of the name, and numerous uncertainties of times and circumstances. Facts had to be extracted from contradictory evidence and from judgments about the intent and result of actions, their effect on other people, and the general course of events."
—The Journal of American History

Western History Titles
from the Huntington Library Press

Voyage to California Written at Sea, 1852:
The Journal of Lucy Kendall Herrick
edited by Amy R. Russell, Marcia R. Good, and Mary G. Lindgren and
with an introduction by Andrew Rolle
$24.95

The Butterfield Overland Mail
by Waterman L. Ormsby,
edited by Lyle H. Wright and Josephine M. Bynum
$12.95

The Boom of the Eighties in Southern California
by Glenn S. Dumke
$24.95

The Cattle on a Thousand Hills: Southern California, 1850–1880
by Robert Glass Cleland
cloth, $24.95, paper, $12.95

Ho for Calfornia! Women's Overland Diaries from the Huntington Library
edited and annotated by Sandra L. Myres
$14.95

A Victorian Gentlewoman in the Far West:
The Reminiscences of Mary Hallock Foote
edited and with an introduction by Rodman W. Paul
$14.95

For a complete catalog, see our web site:
http://huntington.org/HLPress/HEHPubs.html